"Based on his in-depth knowledge of Asia and the retail industry, firsthand experience in the NGO sector, and his research on China's treaty ports, Patrick articulates ASW's business history, corporate management practice, and Chinese business philosophy in a balanced manner. It is indeed a book recommended for students and graduates pursuing their careers in the business world, and for the general public interested in the modern history of Hong Kong and China. It will also be interesting for those investing in the retail sector to learn how Watsons might take its next quantum leap in the decade of the 2020s."

Andrew Chi Fai Chan, PhD, SBS, JP
President, Greater Bay Area Business School
Emeritus Professor in Marketing, The Chinese University of Hong Kong

"The book describes the thrilling saga of the transformative journey towards global leadership of A S Watson in the last 180 years. Patrick, with his multifaceted and granular writing style, provides us with one of the most meaningful and practical leadership books I have read in the last few decades. The real-life business examples offer a great management toolbox for companies which want to "*Built to Last*". A must read for leaders and corporations which want to sustain their competitive advantage across centuries."

Pierre Guyot
Chairman, Limflow SA
Former CEO, Molnlycke Healthcare AB

"Patrick Chiu has always been a role model when the fusion of business acumen, superb analytics, and cultural understanding came into play. This book is truly his masterpiece of using the experience and the empirical data spanning more than a century of an iconic company to draw the proper conclusions and show the right elements for an enrichment of the toolbox every manager should not only be familiar with, but be ready to use in our fast moving business environment. This book is one of the rare examples of where the fun to read is perfectly combined with the learning to be had — to cope with the always very unique challenges around the topic of M&A."

Andreas Joehle
Equity Partner, Ufenau Capital Partners AG
Former Global CEO, The HARTMANN Group

"Patrick's book on AS Watson's journey to sustain and to be a responsible employer is a timely one in the COVID-19 pandemic period. Watson's 180-year business history and the adoption of *Wangdao* and best practice management in the past four decades could serve as a model for those entrepreneurs who have an eye for the global market."

Huang Junli, PhD
Executive Director and Associate Professor, Institute of Entrepreneurs
Peking University

"Forbes and AS Watson are leading global media and retail companies with over a century of corporate heritage. Patrick has vividly elucidated the composition of Watson's DNA, retained with its core competencies harnessed since the early 1840s. In addition, Watson's aggressive overseas investments and mergers and acquisitions in Europe and the United Kingdom after the Asian financial crisis in the late 1990s enabled it to become one of the most outstanding health and beauty retailers globally."

T.C. Yam
Founder & Chairman of Integrated Capital
Board Member of Forbes Media LLC

"Patrick's articulation of AS Watson's corporate social responsibility is a model of its kind since the late 19th century. A classic example was John Humphrey's scholarship to sponsor students to study medicine at the Hong Kong College of Medicine for Chinese, with beneficiaries including Dr Sun Yat-sen, my late great grand uncle, who later became the first provisional president of the Republic of China in 1912."

Chung To
Founder and Chairman, Chi Heng Foundation

"After arriving in Hong King in 1979, I was part of the ASW leadership team in the early stages of the expansion, apart from opening over 100 stores in Hong Kong, we opened in Taiwan and Singapore in 1987 and then Beijing and Macau in 1989, the first retailer to be opened in both Taiwan and Mainland China.

It is quite remarkable how Watsons has now expanded over the following 30 years to be the worldwide force it now is with over 16,000 stores worldwide."

Rodney Miles
Founding Chairman, Strawberrynet.com
Director, Hong Kong Retail Association

"*Transformation from Colonial Chemist to Global Health and Beauty Retailer: A.S. Watson* is a must read whether you are a student of Pharmacy, Retail, Asian History, or indeed the Globalisation of business. As someone who has competed against Watsons for some 30 years, I feel that Patrick Chiu gives an in-depth and fascinating account of the development of the Health and Beauty giant and the characters behind its success. Particularly notable are the transformational deals in Europe and China and the digitalisation of the business. What makes this text stand apart is a comprehensive review of the business theory applied to the development and success of A.S. Watson."

Gordon Farquhar
Former Director, Dairy Farm Health & Beauty
Former CEO, Mannings North Asia
Former Managing Director, Boots International

Transformation from

Colonial Chemist to Global Health and Beauty Retailer

A S Watson

Transformation from
Colonial Chemist to Global Health and Beauty Retailer
A S Watson

PATRICK CHIU

World Scientific

NEW JERSEY • LONDON • SINGAPORE • BEIJING • SHANGHAI • HONG KONG • TAIPEI • CHENNAI • TOKYO

Published by

World Scientific Publishing Co. Pte. Ltd.
5 Toh Tuck Link, Singapore 596224
USA office: 27 Warren Street, Suite 401-402, Hackensack, NJ 07601
UK office: 57 Shelton Street, Covent Garden, London WC2H 9HE

Library of Congress Cataloging-in-Publication Data
Names: Chiu, Patrick, author.
Title: Transformation from colonial chemist to global health and beauty retailer : A S Watson / Patrick Chiu.
Description: New Jersey : World Scientific, [2022] | Includes bibliographical references and index.
Identifiers: LCCN 2021060401 | ISBN 9789811251528 (hardcover) | ISBN 9789811251535 (ebook for institutions) | ISBN 9789811251542 (ebook for individuals)
Subjects: LCSH: A. S. Watson (Firm)--History. | Drugstores--China--Hong Kong--History. | Chain stores--China--Hong Kong--History.
Classification: LCC HD9672.C54 A38 2022 | DDC 338.7/6151095125--dc23/eng/20220210
LC record available at https://lccn.loc.gov/2021060401

British Library Cataloguing-in-Publication Data
A catalogue record for this book is available from the British Library.

Upper image of the front cover: The *Hongkew Medical Hall*, a branch of the *British Dispensary*, operated by McTavish & Lehmann in Shanghai. @1909 (Courtesy of Raymond Forward)
Lower Image of the front cover: Watson's The Chemist, Ximen Branch, Taipei. @2022 (Courtesy of Phoebe Shih)

For any available supplementary material, please visit
https://www.worldscientific.com/worldscibooks/10.1142/12703#t=suppl

Desk Editors: Soundararajan Raghuraman/Lixi Dong

Typeset by Stallion Press
Email: enquiries@stallionpress.com

To my loving wife, Helen

About the Author

Patrick Chiu (Manchu name Irgen Gioro) was born in Guangzhou and grew up in Hong Kong. He traces his origins back to the Bordered Yellow Tribe inhabited near Kirin, Manchuria (now Changchun, Jilin province, Northeast China). He graduated with a BSc. pharmacy degree at De Montfort University, Leicester, an MBA at the University of Hull, and attended the Global Management Programme at IMD, Lausanne. His career spans across business, charity, and health and beauty retail sectors.

Prior to his full-time engagement as an author in 2019, Patrick was the chief executive of Chi Heng Foundation, a Hong Kong-based global charity organisation with branches in Canada, China and Singapore serving AIDS orphans and the underprivileged children. Before that, Patrick had a long business career with increasing responsibilities as business director, president, and managing director of leading Hong Kong, European, and US-based companies including BD, Dade Behring (now Siemens), Molnlycke Health Care, Morningside Advisory, and Nature's Bounty (now The Bountiful Company) responsible for the Asia Pacific/Greater China region.

Patrick's first book, *A History of Western Pharmacy in Colonial Hong Kong*, was ranked as a Top 10 seller in the Autumn 2017 Commercial Press Book Fair in Beijing. He is a regular contributor to Master-Insight, an economic and political e-news media for the Greater China audience, and *Pharmaceutical Historian*, the official Journal of the International Society for the History of Pharmacy, since 2016.

He is married and lives in Hong Kong.

Foreword by Ian Francis Wade

Having spent almost 40 years as a resident of Hong Kong and 25 years of that time with A.S. Watson (ASW), I never dreamed that one day I would be sitting down to acknowledge the efforts of Patrick Chiu. But here I am, commending him for diligently and professionally putting together the entire history of ASW. The task of assembling almost 200 years of detailed information enriched with dramatic highs and lows of business and politics is a major achievement. It is well woven and well worded.

During the gestation period of assembling the content of his book, Patrick and I met on many occasions to review progress. While the two major chains of CVS in the US and Walgreens Boots Alliance in the US/UK have interesting histories, they originated in much more mature environments, with customers having greater affluence. Apart from Japan, the rest of Asia did not have a major middle class in the 20th century until the late 1980s and 1990s.

Indeed, I personally remember this social process unfolding. For example, one September evening in 1981, I got a call from Bill Griffith of M.S.L., London asking me if I would be interested in a position in Hong Kong. I asked him if he could explain exactly where it was. After a period of negotiation, I decided to make the trip to Hong Kong in late autumn. Landing in 22 degrees having left Yorkshire in heavy snow, the logic of change did strike me.

During the few days of meetings with John Richardson and his team, the difference in environment and company culture was very evident. But the job itself was pretty much the same. My thought process was to accept the position of group managing director and try a 2-year stint. In the end, it did not quite work out like that. Far from it.

On March 15, 1982, I left the Excelsior Hotel to walk across Victoria Park to Watsons Estate in North Point, the site of the Watsons Water Factory built in 1912. My colleagues were welcoming. Settling in was an easy process. The long list of tiny businesses was ungainly to manage. I immediately set about focusing on those that would be core for the future. Some management changes were going to be necessary to stimulate focus and a proper pace of progress.

In the early 1980s, I pushed ahead with store growth to support Hutchison Whampoa Limited's need for cash flow. In the dark days of 1983, Watsons was able to maximise cash flow for the group. It was also able to support local charities, including the Community Chest. Although the Hong Kong dollar lost ground, it was eventually fixed at 7.8 to the US dollar — as it still stands today.

Those early years showed that volume growth would be difficult in our home market. My thoughts were to watch Taiwan, Singapore, and the Mainland for the emergence of a worthwhile middle class. These were all places where we had done well during the past 150 years or so. While continuing to move at pace in Hong Kong, the second half of the 1980s saw us landing in all 3 places with innovative stories behind each entry.

Taiwan was under martial law when I arrived and the ruling Kuomingtang (KMT) party was the only J.V. partner. In 1987, government policies changed, so we did not need a partner. Because of the generosity of Li Ka-Shing in the Mainland, I got a warm welcome everywhere. My J.V. partner in Shanghai was headed by Han Zheng — who is now a Vice Premier, and a member of the Standing Committee of the Communist Party of China Central Committee Political Bureau. The 1990s saw us add Thailand and the Philippines to the stable, both with joint ventures. Then, the fateful year of 1997 saw Asian economies experience sharp difficulties after July 2's market collapse. To make matters more delicate, all of ASW's retail eggs were in the Asian basket. It also became obvious to me that food retailing had growing competition in the Mainland from the US, Europe, and local players with profitability eroding. I therefore took the decision to put our major investment into health and beauty.

With Mr. Li's agreement, I decided to look at Europe for acquisitions. I also began to realise that using banks for finding suitable companies was far too expensive. So all negotiations were done by my team and myself. Mr. Li agreed to a ceiling of 1.5 billion Euros. So off we went. An obvious target was the Dutch-owned Kruidvat Group whose owners were potential sellers. With a purchase price of around 1.5 Billion Euros, Mr. Li decided we should use a well-known investment bank. They estimated a price of not less than 1.8 billion Euros. After several dinners with the owners, we settled on 1.285 Billion Euros. Interestingly, all the proceeds from the sale of Kruidvat Group were given by the De Rijcke family to charity.

After numerous other investments (which included the procuring of 40% of Dirk Rossman's company in Germany and Central Europe), we became the largest health and beauty company in Europe in terms of store numbers.

By this time, we had discount and middle market health and beauty stores, but few upmarket fragrance and cosmetic stores. Marionnaud was the major chain in France and Europe with 1,300 stores in this category. It was eventually acquired and became a challenging proposition. Meanwhile, Mr. Li got the Commandeur de la Légion d'Honneur from the French President for his business and charity moxie. All I got was headaches. However, the retail scene had been set for ASW and the transformation of a group of minute stores into a major player in Asia and Europe had been achieved. But it sure did take a while.

Manufacturing: This category was new to me when I arrived in 1982: the mixture of beverages, ice cream, and pharmaceuticals was unusual. In fact, it was a circumstance of history, and a long one at that. Shortly after my arrival, the pharmaceutical factory in Kwai Chung burnt down, so with history thought to be unrepeatable, two categories remained.

Ice Cream: We attempted to bolster our Mountain Cream ice cream business by buying the Shanghai Yimin No.1 Food Factory, which was a huge town where all the employees lived. The world of ice cream was shaping up to be a duel between Unilever and Nestle. In this light, I took the opportunity to sell the Hong Kong and China brands to Unilever for a cool US$95 million. Much like our ice cream, the deal was sweet.

Beverages: Moving from ice to its liquid form — ASW has an incredible history of over almost two centuries of selling water. Of course, water margins were well worth sipping when I joined Watsons. And I fell in love with the brand Watson's Water. In fact, I featured it to promote the health of Hong Kong's young athletes aged 5–18 years. The brand was the major sponsor of the Macau Grand Prix for over 20 years, too. Even today, models of Watson's Water cars are still being created! The other major sponsorship was tennis. We were the promoter of international tennis in Hong Kong for many years, attracting the world's best players.

Having realised the appeal of the large office and kitchen carboy, I decided to visit Europe again with this product. The strategy was to buy many small companies in multiple countries, and eventually selling it to Nestle for 582 million Euros. It was the only global play for Watsons I had going on then.

Priceline/Booking: In the early 2000s, I got an unusual call from Goldman Sachs New York asking if Mr. Li would have an interest in buying Priceline based in Norwalk, CT on the east coast of the US. Priceline was an early player in the internet travel business. I met its chairman and the head of CITI Bank. Some directors were doubtful, but Mr. Li supported the acquisition. The original model was based on discounted air fares. Lamentably, when American Airlines vetoed this, we had to find a new platform to move forward.

Having shown the American management where Europe was, we came up with the idea of discounting hotel rooms. Priceline became the largest internet travel company in the world with a share price to amaze. Due to the prudence of Hutchison, we sold early, but what an experience.

Mr. Li Ka-Shing: Speaking of that richly endowed experience, after 25 years of satisfying times with Hutchison (of which I served with 3 different CEOs), I am mostly indebted to Mr Li Ka-Shing. He always stepped in to give support on all major decisions. His financial achievements are legendary, his management skills and timing were what set him apart. He is, in fact, quite unique in Hong Kong. Much has been written and said of him. Nonetheless, I am proud to have been his employee. I have always found him humble, and never authoritative.

The Journey: ASW was an amazing journey for me. I was lucky to be supported by a great team of people who worked hard around many parts of the world. Lastly, Hong Kong has been kind to me. And if ASW helped to put it on the map commercially along with Mr. Li's other international ventures, that is satisfaction enough. Reading parts of that long saga in the pages here is also deeply rewarding.

Ian Francis Wade BBS, Commendatore
Vice Patron, Hong Kong Community Chest
Member, Advisory Board, Hong Kong Red Cross
Board Member, Hong Kong Youth Arts Foundation
Senior Director, Priceline.Com (now Booking.Com, 2002–2006)
Managing Director, AS Watson Group of Companies (1982–2006)

Foreword by Dr. Andrew C.F. Chan

Hong Kong's colonial history from 1842 to 1997 is rife with enthralling and intriguing stories. One of these storied specimens is none other than that of A.S. Watson. The 180-year business history of A.S. Watson traces its origins to the legendary Royal Navy's landing in Sheung Wan, Hong Kong Island, in 1841. The Hong Kong Dispensary, the predecessor of A.S. Watson, was established by two British ship surgeons. They had a virtual monopoly selling and supplying Western medicines for three-quarters of a century. During that period, the laws of the colony only allowed pharmacies to be run by British or foreign pharmacists (then called "chemists"). These "legally licensed" chemists sold narcotic drugs, including opium substitutes. It was not until 1908 that they permitted the first locally trained Chinese to become a qualified chemist.

How times have changed. Today, there are four major companies in Hong Kong whose history dates back to the 19th century; namely CK Hutchison, Jardine Matheson, Swire, and Wharf. These companies continue to play a significant role in retail service sectors and are among the largest employers today. CK Hutchison and Wharf are now owned by the Hong Kong Chinese families of Mr. Li Ka-Shing and the late Sir YK Pao since 1978 and 1985, respectively. Over the past 70 years, entrepreneurs in the fields of culture, industry, commerce, and technology in the Greater China region have practised *Wangdao*, a Confucian school of business philosophy. This has seen them actively participate in philanthropy and contribute generously to provide education for the underprivileged. Such individuals include the late Sir Run Run Shaw of Shaw Brothers, Mr. Li Ka-Shing of Cheung Kong Holdings, Liu Chuanzhi of Lenovo, Stan Shih of Acer, and many others.

Over the past two decades, I have interviewed many business leaders in two important business education programmes, "Dialogue with the CEO" and "New Thinking of Management".[1] Successful Hong Kong business leaders share the common philosophy of, "being good and virtuous, being noble and benevolent". These Confucian *Wangdao* values extend to "serving the community", "caring for the country", "looking out to the world", and "committing to environmental protection".

Mr. Li Ka-Shing is a world-renowned Chinese entrepreneur, building his fortunes from scratch during World War II to making his first pot of gold in the 1950s. After Li's Cheung Kong Holdings Ltd. became the majority shareholder of Hutchison Whampoa Limited (HWL) in 1979, Mr. Li Ka-Shing successfully integrated *Wangdao* into the training and discipline of his senior managers' best practice management. Li also encouraged the leaders of HWL's subsidiaries in every country and region to vigorously promote corporate social responsibility.

For example, Ian Wade, a veteran in the UK's retail sector, joined Hutchison Whampoa as the group managing director in 1982. He was one of the few visionary retailers that co-founded the Hong Kong Retail Management Association in 1983, representing the trade sector and raising the status and professionalism of retailing through awards, education, and training. In a quarter of a century association with ASW, Wade transformed a struggling retail and manufacturing business to one of the global Top 3 retailers in the health and beauty sector. Indeed, he has left a legacy in Asia and Europe's retail industry.

These are Hong Kong legends of medicine and retail business. Thankfully, the author of this book, Patrick Chiu, has captured many of them here. More than 3 years ago, I met Patrick when he was the chief executive of Chi Heng Foundation.[2] He practised the long lessons he learnt in his earlier career in global consumer and health care companies in the Asia-Pacific region. He also applied practical management skills at Chi Heng Foundation to optimise resources and enhance productivity to increase outcomes for all beneficiaries, as well as providing educational and psychological support to the AIDS orphans and "left-behind children".[3]

Patrick is a prolific writer and business history columnist. He has published many original research papers and several books on cosmetics, medicine, and pharmacy's modern history in Asia and China.

This time, Patrick raises the bar once again on this topic. In Part 1 of this book, Patrick vividly describes Watson's journey of globalisation over the past 180 years. He details how Watsons survived waves of social unrest, civil wars, global financial turmoil, political crisis, and pandemics that confronted Hong Kong, China, and the world. Perhaps one of the most exciting developments in this history transpired between 1999 and 2005, when ASW achieved quantum leaps and consolidated its position as a leading global drug store chain under Wade's leadership.

In Part 2 of this book, Patrick articulates my "*Left-and-Right Thinking Circles*" theory behind Wade's branding strategy. He further draws upon Wade's other "Prosperity Strategies" in parallel with the "4+2 Formula" advocated by Nitin Nohria *et al*. Over the past 15 years, the global market has undergone tremendous changes in China, Asia, and Europe. And with it, ASW has undertaken a pragmatic growth approach to dodge the headwinds of the subprime mortgage crisis, the Eurozone crisis, China–US decoupling, Brexit, and the recent COVID-19 pandemic.

Based on his in-depth knowledge of Asia and the retail industry, first-hand experience in the NGO sector, and his research on China's treaty ports, Patrick articulates ASW's business history, corporate management practice, and Chinese business philosophy in a balanced manner. It is indeed a book recommended for students and graduates pursuing their careers in the business world, and for the general public interested in the modern history of Hong Kong and China. It will also be interesting for those investing in the retail sector to learn how Watsons might take its next quantum leap in the decade of the 2020s.

Andrew Chi Fai Chan, PhD, SBS, JP
President, Greater Bay Area Business School
Emeritus Professor in Marketing, The Chinese University of Hong Kong
Head, Shaw College, The Chinese University of Hong Kong (2010–2020)
Director, EMBA Programme, The Chinese University of Hong Kong (2002–2020)

Endnotes

[1]Both programmes are co-organised by The Executive Master of Business Administration Course of the Chinese University of Hong Kong and the Radio Television Hong Kong every Sunday since 2003.
[2]Chi Heng Foundation is a tax-exempt charity organisation with branches in Canada, China, and Singapore serving AIDS orphans and underprivileged children in China. http://www.chihengfoundation.com/.
[3]"Left-behind children", also known as "stay-at-home-children", are children who remain in the rural villages while their parents leave to work in tier one and two cities and only return once a year during the annual lunar new year holiday.

Book Reviews

Jeanne H. Y. Fu, PhD, Professor, Head of Department of Management and, Head of Honours Academy, The Hang Seng University of Hong Kong.

A.S. Watson is an international retailing giant in the industry with roots dating back two centuries ago. Its rich history of organisational development and change lends diverse analytical angles for business scholars and historians to understand how a family conglomerate transformed itself into a highly diversified international empire of personal health care and cosmetic products. Garnering the business facts and figures in a meticulous manner, the author has crafted a book of perceptivity and profundity. It carefully blends stories of different legendary figures and business leaders in his thorough review and dissection of the globalisation of Watsons. The thorough research and professional interpretations covered in the book connect the ties between the selection of capable firm leaders and their constant navigations of both the internal and external environments of the firm. This book represents not just a sound narrative of the company development, but also a sophisticated business analysis through an objective and independent professional lens. Speaking overall, this book captures major developmental milestones of ASW that will be of interest to a wide range of readership: from economic historians to strategic management scholars.

Andrew T. Chan, PhD, Associate Professor, Associate Head of Department of Management, The City University of Hong Kong.

As a first of its kind book-length treatment of the business history of the global brand A.S. Watson, its strength is the author's keen management insights and the description of compelling business scenarios of the company over its expansion. Patrick Chiu is persuasive yet objective, bringing his over 30 years' rich experience in the fast-moving consumer goods and retail industries. Patrick's pharmacist and health care background lends further credibility to his analysis of the ASW case. The book illuminates humanist concerns for Hong Kong's history. Moreover, the author is passionate to elicit evidence about traditions, business acumen, foresight, and resilience; especially about how these qualities have been played out along the trajectories of the Watsons Group over the course of its gloried 180 years of operations in Asia and in the world. This work is highly recommended for general readers and specialists alike; namely readers of general history, the history of business in Hong Kong and China, as well as students and researchers of Asia-Pacific commerce and international business.

Preface

A.S. Watson ("ASW") celebrated its 180th anniversary in 2021 amidst the COVID-19 pandemic. Before the pandemic, the global number 3 retailer in health and beauty was also increasingly encountering fierce competition from international speciality stores such as Holland and Barrett, Sephora, and its direct competitors, CVS and Walgreen Boots Alliance. In the past 5 years, the "*New Retail*" trend has rapidly replaced physical retailing as the mainstream business model in China.[1] It is expanding fast beyond its borders, and this phenomenon is highly likely to become the biggest challenge to ASW in the years ahead.

ASW, its health and beauty retail arm commonly known as "Watsons" in Asia, traces its humble beginnings back to a matshed colonial apothecary shop called the Hong Kong Dispensary (the "Dispensary") when it was set up back in 1841. Drs. Alexander Anderson and Peter Young, the Dispensary founders, could not have fathomed that a little retail chemist outlet would return to its British roots after 160 years abroad in 2000 as a globalised enterprise. Likewise, the residents of Katowice, Silesia, could not have imagined that the part-owner of their Drogerie Rossmann would become a retailer called A.S. Watson, named after Alexander Skirving Watson (1837–1864) who was born there 185 years ago. Indeed, Watsons was not anywhere in the equation for a long period of time. It is now though.

Back at the turn of the 20th century, ASW was the largest supplier of narcotic substitutes for opium smokers in the Far East. It had over 100 owned or co-branded drug stores in China and the Philippines. What a long strange trip it has been since those blurry beginnings. Its modern operators look back at those days a bit in shock and awe. One of its guiding helmsman of contemporary times certainly does — Ian Wade.

Before joining ASW as the Group Managing Director in March 1982, Ian Wade was the youngest executive director of the Asda Supermarket Group in the UK. During his quarter of a century of service at the firm from 1982 to 2006, Wade oversaw the turnaround of a rapidly deteriorating business comprising a fragmented portfolio. This included over twenty money-losing retail shops, restaurants, and aerated water manufacturing facilities that had been developed over a period of 140 years.

It was an interesting coincidence that Wade joined ASW in 1982, the same year when I happened to begin work at ASW's import and pharmaceutical division. Yet, the two of us never crossed paths in those years. Fast forward nearly 40 years, I formally met Wade in an interview for my second book, *A History of Hong Kong Pharmacy and Pharmaceutical Market,* in January 2019. Our initial two-hour interview session evolved into engaging biweekly meetings for 20 weeks for this current book, *Transformation of Colonial Chemist to Global Health and Beauty Retailer: A S Watson*, published in honour of its 181st Anniversary.

This book unearths ASW's origins and brings up the story to the challenging times we find ourselves in today. In Part 1, Chapters 1–9 detail the history of the earlier years of ASW in order to establish key perspectives for the globalisation of its retail business from 1982–2006. For this enlivening modern history, Wade shared his recollections about the global expansion of the ASW Group and its ParkNShop Supermarket's 1984 entry into the Mainland. Readers will learn that Watson's The Chemist (WTC) entered Taiwan and Singapore in 1987 and 1988. A decade later, ASW returned to its distant British roots by launching the Powwow brand of home and office delivery water business in London in 1999.

Moving from this dynamic part of the Watsons' journey, Part 2 consists of Chapters 10–14, delving deeply into Wade's business model and best practice management strategies. This is riveting business strategy to understand. It details the actions of his leadership team, which took Watsons from being an Asian regional multinational retail player onto the global stage with tangible firepower — becoming number 3 in the world's health and beauty sector.

In my year-long research and interviews with other former business executives and associates of ASW and Hutchison (HWL), it became clear that success was not merely about luck and timing. Wade was inspired by Li Ka-Shing, HWL's former chairman, to develop ASW as a truly "East

Meets West" business entity. The elements of Confucian *Wangdao* or best practice management, the branding strategy, and the *Good to Great* and "4+2 Formula" were incorporated into everyday operations. Wade was a driver of global expansion, and his work resulted in leaps and bounds in the growth of ASW. Indeed, a quantum leap acquisition of the Kruidvat group in 2002 was the highlight of his business career. On the other hand, his successor, Dominic Lai, is a builder focusing on systems and processes with continuous improvement in profitability. This was executed amidst steep depreciations of the British pound and Euro currency in the 2010s. Lai recovered lost ground largely by launching the long-overdue "DARE" strategy in 2016.

The biggest challenge in the compilation of ASW's financial data has always been the dissection of information and frequently changing reporting formats in the consolidated HWL corporate annual and interim reports. In the early years, profitability was recorded as net profit after tax, later as operating income or EBIT, and more recently as Earnings Before Interest, Taxes, Depreciation, and Amortisation or EBITDA. A separation of the health and beauty business sub-division from the rest of the Retail and Manufacturing Division has been reported since 2012. A clearer and more consistent presentation of ASW's financial performance eventually arrived in HWL's 2014 annual report when Temasek, a Singapore sovereign wealth fund, became a substantial indirect shareholder of ASW in March 2014 (Chapter 14).

The turbulent years of 2020 and 2021 were critical for all retailers and ASW was no exception. The COVID-19 pandemic, formally announced by the World Health Organisation on March 12, 2020, has reshaped consumer behaviour. In fact, ASW saw a tenfold increase in online year-on-year sales. As vaccines rollout gains pace and hopefully COVID-19 cases keep dissipating further in Hong Kong, China, Asia, and the world, a question looms for ASW. Is it ready to deepen its New Retail strategy and further enlarge its global footprint in the hitherto uncharted large emerging markets such as Brazil and India, following on its steps in China and Russia? In this era of globalisation on its 181-year anniversary, it would seem that it has all the lessons from its long life to help it do so.

Endnotes

[1]"New Retail" has become a buzz term in recent times when IMD professors Dr. Winter Nie and Mark Greeven published their 4-year research work on the latest development in the fusion of social media and e-commerce.

Acknowledgements

As a researcher and author in business history and modern management, I have learnt from academics, business executives, entrepreneurs, historians, and journalists who have excelled in their respective fields. My interactions with distinguished researchers in the academic world of business administration and the imperial history of medicine and pharmacy have enriched and motivated me to write a non-corporate sponsored business history and management book on one of Hong Kong and Asia's oldest chemists — A.S. Watson.

When I was the Chief Executive of Chi Heng Foundation, I was profoundly inspired by Dr Andrew C.F. Chan, the then Dean of Shaw College (2010–2020) and Director of EMBA Course of the Chinese University of Hong Kong (2003–2010), on Confucian values and Chinese philanthropy. I am also deeply grateful to Ian Wade, who has made Hong Kong his home, for his support in the authoring of this book by sharing his consumer insights and many years of in-depth retailing experience.

It is my great honour to have both Ian Wade and Dr. Andrew C.F. Chan write forewords for this book, too. I would also like to thank Dr Jeanne Fu of the Hang Seng University of Hong Kong, and Dr Andrew T. Chan of the City University of Hong Kong; they have kindly reviewed and provided invaluable advice to the first drafts of this work.

I am indebted to my academic, business and journalist friends; namely Stuart Anderson, Dave Besseling, Ning Chang, Chris Cottrell, Gordon Faquar, Pierre Guyot, Junli Huang, Andreas Joehle, Rodney Miles, Chung To, "Big Red - Jim Wetrich", Rodney Miles, Stuart Wolfendale and T.C. Yam, who have provided invaluable advice to me in writing this book.

Some have also generously praised at the back cover and the beginning pages of the book.

Finally, I thank Dr KK Phua, Chairman and Editor-in-Chief, and Ms Angela Lixi Dong, Assistant Director, of World Scientific Publishing Co. Pte. Ltd. for giving me the opportunity to publish this book.

Contents

Part 1

From Colonial Chemist to Global Health and Beauty Retailer

Junks, *Inner Harbour, Macau*, Dr Thomas Boswell Watson, @1850, pen and ink.

Source: Courtesy of Bonhams UK.

Chapter 1

1841–1896: The Birth of A.S. Watson

Initial Public Offering and Opium Substitutes

The Birth of the Hong Kong Dispensary

The origins of ASW's rich glory dated back to its quiet beginning as a simple eye surgery outlet known as the Canton Ophthalmic Clinic. It was established by Dr James H. Braford and others in the Thirteenth Factories to provide free eye surgery for poor locals in 1828.[1,2] By 1832, the clinic had evolved, becoming the Canton Dispensary. As history would have it, this was the first retail chemist & druggist to install a soda fountain in the whole of China.[3]

Among the newcomers to China were Drs Alexander Anderson and Peter Young. Both were naval surgeons attached to the British Military and the merchant navy in the late 1830s. They also simultaneously served as volunteers at the Canton Dispensary. Soon after, Captain Charles Elliott, Plenipotentiary and Chief Superintendent of British Trade in China declared Hong Kong's occupation on January 26, 1841. It attracted international attention, with more British nationals keen to join the colony. Anderson and Young relocated from Canton to Hong Kong, and jointly set up a matshed apothecary at Possession Point, Hong Kong Island. After a couple of years of practising as apothecaries at Possession Point, the Anderson and Young Partners officially opened the Hong Kong Dispensary (the Dispensary) at the Morgan's Bazaar in Admiralty in the City of Victoria on January 1, 1843.

Table 1. List of Hong Kong Chemists & Druggists in 1848.

Chemists & Druggists	Location	Manager/Proprietor
Hong Kong Dispensary	Queen's Road	Dr James Hume Young
Victoria Dispensary	Pottinger Street	Messrs. Thomas Hunter and George K. Barton
Medical Hall	Queen's Road	Alexander S. Taylor
Messrs. Stockers & Co.'s Dispensary	Queen's Road	Charles Stocker
Farriers	Queen's Road East	George Frazer
Messrs. Castles & Co.	Stanley Street	Not Known

Source: Hong Kong Almanack 1848.

Two years later, the foundation stone of the Dispensary was firmly laid at 16 Queen's Road, Central. Today, it is the New World Tower. It commemorated its permanent presence in the Crown Colony of Hong Kong.[4,5] The Dispensary was among a handful of chemists who supplied western medicine and consumer goods to the merchant navy and sailors passing through Victoria in 1848[6] (Table 1). In 1856, Dr Preston of the Dispensary appointed Dr J. Llewellyn, a surgeon, to move to Shanghai to operate a branch of the Dispensary at 1 Nanking Road. It is now the Swatch Art Peace Hotel. It was becoming a tale of two cities in its own right.

The Watson Family and the Revitalization of the Dispensary

These operations, though, were mere seedlings. It would take a Watson to make them fertile. The original Watson family traces their origins back to Scottish landowners. Alexander Scott and Thomas Boswell were ranked the first and third among the six children of James Watson[7,8] (Figure 1).

In May of 1834, when Alexander Scott was just 25 years old, he went to work as an engineer in the foundry and factory owned by the Bank of Poland in the province of Silesia. When Scott eventually settled down to start his own family, he immediately arranged for his fiancée, Agnes Keidslie, to go to Warsaw. They married there on July 19, 1834. Their seven children, including the third son, Alexander Skirving, were all born in Dabrowa, Silesia.

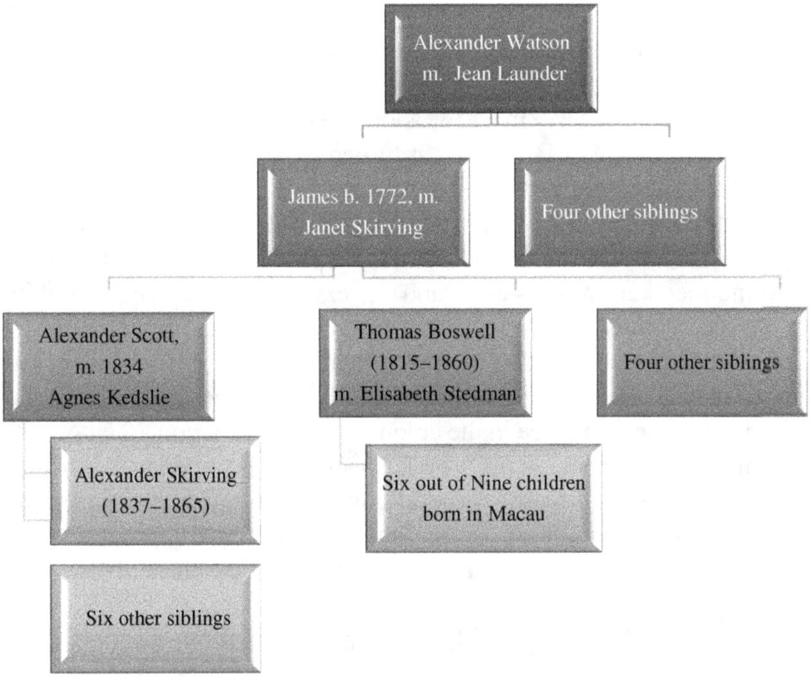

Figure 1. Family Tree of A.S. Watson. Information about Alexander Scott Watson.

Source: *Jeremy Watson's Family Stories*, The Watsons of the UK and South Africa.

Another one of James Watson's offspring would go on to great expectations too. His son would become the esteemed Dr Thomas Boswell Watson (aka T.B. Watson, 1815–1860). Upon graduation from the Faculty of Medicine of the University of Edinburgh in Scotland, T.B. Watson journeyed on an adventure to the Far East in 1845. He eventually acquired Dr Alexander Anderson's clinic in Macau, with his wife Elizabeth joining him the following year. In 1848, T.B. Watson, who was also a keen amateur artist (Figure 1), wrote to his sister in Scotland about life in Macau, remarking:

> *In addition to the Portuguese, we count ourselves, only four families and one or two Americans and French.*[9]

After 12 years in Macau, T.B. Watson sold his clinical practice and joined the Dispensary across the mouth of the Pearl River in Hong Kong as the senior partner in 1856, but his health deteriorated in the following year. He contacted his brother Alexander Scott in Silesia and invited his third son, Alexander Skirving, then aged 22, to come to Hong Kong to take over the Dispensary. In 1858, soon after Alexander Skirving settled down in Hong Kong, T.B. Watson returned to Scotland after 15 years in the Far East, including three in Hong Kong.

With Alexander Skirving's good sales skills and hard work, the Dispensary increased the business in the supply of medicines and necessities to the merchant navy, sailors and the expatriate community. Within a year, he successfully transformed the Dispensary from a medical clinic into a fully-fledged retail chemist. In those days, almost all Hong Kong laws were local adaptations of the original English Acts to ensure the same governance system was in place in the colonies.[10] Peculiar among them was the licensing of opium as medicine. The Dispensary was only one of a handful of chemists authorized by the colonial government to dispense and supply opium to those with medical needs. Others were licensed opium dens that served habitual users and were taxed heavily. The first piece of legislation governing the sales of opium was titled "An Ordinance for Licensing and Regulating the Sale of Prepared Opium" in 1858. It allowed for:

> *Preparing and selling prepared opium bona fide for medicinal purposes by a medical practitioner, chemist or druggist having a European or American diploma.*[11]

However, with a small population of 100,000 local Chinese in 1860, sales of medicinal opium to patients were insignificant. That would change two decades later.

Alexander Skirving faced his first challenge when the Dispensary was burnt to the ground on October 19, 1859. He quickly resurrected the business and operated temporarily in other premises until a custom-built chemist shop with an extensive drug compounding area was completed a year later. In a sea journey which could last weeks if not months, sailors who felt ill or became injured on board required immediate pain relief. The Dispensary was the leading chemist supplying laudanum and other narcotic substitutes initially to these transiting freighters in the 1850s. It soon became the largest wholesaler by manufacturing the Watson's brand of laudanum as a household medicine.

On the Mainland, Dr J. Llewellyn, who had been appointed to go to Shanghai to run the Dispensary in early 1856 at No.1 Nanjing Road, decided to move to Ningbo and sold the Dispensary business to E.C. Kirby in 1860. A year later, Kirby decided to part ways and changed the trade name to 'Laou Teh Kee Dispensary'. ASW acted promptly and appointed SW Cleave to continue the Dispensary's Shanghai branch at No. 16 Nanjing Road, a stone's throw away from the original shop. In the meantime, Alexander Skirving was actively expanding the Dispensary's product portfolio, including importing proprietary medicines such as Holloway Ointments and Pills, and photographic supplies from Bolton & Barnitt, a chemist in London, England. Alexander Skirving also placed advertisements in local Chinese language newspapers to reach out to local consumers and business customers. After celebrating the 25th anniversary of the Dispensary in 1865, Alexander Skirving returned to England the following year. But his return home would not last long. He died in Brompton, Middlesex on November 29, 1866, at the young age of 28.

The First Pot of Gold and Initial Public Offering

In the wake of Alexander Skirving's early demise, a man called Mr Bell took over the business in 1866. His full name is lost to history, but he hired John David Humphreys (JDH) as a bookkeeper the following year (see Chapter 10). Just two years later, Bell retired and transferred the shares and management of the Dispensary to Arthur Hunt and JDH. Whatever they did with this legacy was well received. The Dispensary was awarded the designation of Appointed Chemist to the Hong Kong Governor and the Duke of Edinburgh, in commemoration of the visit of His Royal Highness to the Colony, by the then colonial Governor, Sir Richard Graves MacDonnell, for its service to the expatriate community in 1869.[12,13]

By word of mouth, the reputation of the Dispensary serving as the colonial Government's preferred chemist spread quickly to Shanghai, Singapore, Tokyo, and throughout the Far East.

While the going was good, Hunt decided to retire and sold his shares to JDH in 1874. This made JDH the sole owner or 'Taipan'. In Cantonese, the word taipan denoted a powerful foreign business executive or entrepreneur during Hong Kong's colonial heyday. This gravitas was not lost on JDH, and he used it wisely to navigate it in handling the company's move in the Mainland's mass market.

In Europe, sales of opium substitutes became increasingly significant in the 1890s due to the availability of codeine and other synthetic narcotic analgesics, in particular the discovery of heroin in 1897. In this part of the world, JDH reckoned that it would not be sustainable to rely on imports of opium substitutes and family medicines — because the appetite for it was voracious. Being a smart entrepreneur, he was working towards a Watson's brand to resolve this issue (Chapter 10).

In her article *Opium in Victorian Britain*, Ellen Castelow observed:

> *Opium and other narcotic drugs played an important part in Victorian life. Shocking though it might be to us in the 21st century, in Victorian times it was possible to walk into a chemist and buy, without prescription, laudanum, cocaine and even arsenic.*
>
> *The most popular preparation was laudanum, an alcoholic herbal mixture containing 10% opium. Called the 'aspirin of the nineteenth century,' laudanum was a popular painkiller and relaxant, recommended for all sorts of ailments including coughs, rheumatism, 'women's troubles' and also, perhaps most disturbingly, as a soporific for babies and young children. And as twenty or twenty-five drops of laudanum could be bought for just a penny, it was also affordable.*
>
> *The 1868 Pharmacy Act attempted to control the sale and supply of opium-based preparations by ensuring that they could only be sold by registered chemists. However this was largely ineffective, as there was no limit on the amount the chemist could sell to the public.*[14]

The first milestone in the Dispensary's corporate history occurred when it went for an Initial Public Offering (IPO), becoming A.S. Watson & Company, Limited (aka ASW), a registered limited liability company in Hong Kong on January 16, 1886. This move begs an important question; what was JDH's real motivation for accepting a dilution of his shareholding in ASW when the business enjoyed an exceedingly high annual profit for its hotly sought-after opium substitutes?

One motive was that the expatriate population of Hong Kong had trebled from 3,000 in 1860 to 10,000 in 1880. There was a chronic shortage of quality homes for westerners who had made Hong Kong their permanent residence. JDH eyed the property market as being ripe for superb investment opportunities in the coming decades. He was also keen to invest in gold mining in Australia which he reluctantly left for Hong Kong in 1867 due to lack of financing after spending two years there. JDH realized a substantial gain close to four lakhs HK$400,000 after 13 years by disposing of a considerable part of his shareholding in ASW.[15]

The incentive for investors to acquire the majority shareholding in ASW was the cash flow generated by the highly profitable opium substitutes manufactured by ASW for sales in the Mainland, Taiwan (aka Formosa) and Southeast Asia. After the IPO, JDH remained on as the single largest shareholder, retaining his position as the general manager of ASW.

The registration of ASW as the 15th limited liability company with the Companies Registry in Hong Kong on January 16, 1886 brought an infusion of fresh capital from investors. JDH invested part of this money to import more equipment from Europe to enlarge the production capacity of opium substitutes for the Mainland and export markets. The raised capital was used to relocate the Shanghai branch of the Dispensary to larger premises on the Bund. It also paid for the installation of soda water manufacturing plants in both Shanghai and Manila. Meanwhile, JDH was grooming his eldest son, Henry ('Humphreys', 1867–1943), to take over as the next taipan.

Young master Humphreys attended boarding school in the South Seas, Portsmouth, the United Kingdom, subsequently completing his pharmacist diploma in 1888 at the School of Pharmacy run by the Pharmaceutical Society of Great Britain (PSGB). He was just 21.[16] While enrolled at PSGB in London, Humphreys acquired knowledge of the formulation and manufacturing techniques of family medicines. Upon returning to Hong Kong in early 1889, Humphreys joined the family business as the pharmacist and manager of ASW. His first assignment was to implement a branding strategy. Humphreys achieved this within the first six months, notably the following:

- registering the trademarks of wines, spirits and soft drinks (items 1–47), opium substitutes (items 60–67 and 74–75), infant food (item 56) and toiletries (items 48–49, 57–73, and 78) (Figure 2);
- reformulating Watson's Anthelmintic Bonbons (rebranded as "Worm Cakes" in the 1930s) with a longer shelf-life for the hot and humid months in the southern provinces of the Mainland and the Philippines (items 50–55).

After visiting branches in Peking, Canton, Hankow (now a district of Wuhan) and Shanghai in 1890, Humphreys suggested that his father and

THE HONGKONG GOVERNMENT GAZETTE, 11TH MAY, 1889. 427

GOVERNMENT NOTIFICATION.—No. 228.

Notice is hereby given that Messrs. A. S. WATSON & Co., LIMITED, of Victoria, Hongkong, have complied with the requirements of Ordinances 16 of 1873, and 8 of 1886, for the registration in this Colony of their Marks as applied to Wines, Spirits, Liquors, Medicines, Perfumes, Erated Waters, and other articles of a Dispensing Chemist and Druggist, as more particularly set forth in the following Schedule and that the same have been duly registered, viz.:—

SCHEDULE.

1. Watson's Vin de Quinquina.
2. Do. Prickly Heat Lotion.
3. Hongkong Tai Yeuk Fong Hair Wash (English and Spanish.)
4. Watson's Chiretta Bitters.
5. Do. Tonic Bitters.
6. Watson's Finest Selected Old Scotch Malt Whiskey (Mellow Brand) "Glenorchy."
7. Watson's Finest Selected Old Scotch Malt Whiskey "Aberlour Glenlivet."
8. Old Irish Whiskey (*A* quality.)
9. John Jameson's Fine Old Irish Whiskey (*B* quality.)
10. Very fine Old Irish Whiskey (*C* quality.)
11. Watson's H.K.D. Blend of the Finest Scotch Malt Whiskies (*D* quality.)
12. Watson's very Old Liqueur Scotch Whiskey (*E* quality.)
13. Finest Old Jamaica Rum.
14. Superior very old Cognac Brandy (*B* quality.)
15. Very old Liqueur Cognac Brandy (*C* quality.)
16. Hennessy's Finest very old Liqueur Cognac Brandy 1872 Vintage (*D* quality.)
17. Sherry Pale Dry (Light Dinner Wine (*A* quality.)
18. Sherry Superior Pale Dry (good) Dinner Wine (*B* quality.)
19. Sherry Natural Manzanilla (superior quality) (*C* quality.)
20. Sherry superior Old Pale Dry (*C C* quality.)
21. Sherry very superior Old Pale Dry (*D* quality).
22. Sherry extra superior Old Pale Dry (*E* quality) very finest quality old bottled.
23. Genuine Breakfast Claret (*A* quality.)
24. St. Estephe (*B*-quality).
25. St. Julien (*C* quality.)
26. La Rose (*D* quality.)
27. Thorne's Blend Old Scotch Whiskey.
28. John Jameson's Old Irish Whiskey.
29. Fine Old Irish Whiskey.
30. Hennessy's Old Pale Brandy.
31. Finest Old Jamaica Rum.
32. Finest Old Genuine Bourbon Whiskey.
33. Finest Old Tom Gin.
34. Pale Dry Creaming Champagne (Brand G. R. S. & Co., Epernay.)
35. Pot Brand with Name, Address and Trade Mark printed on.
36. Watson's Phosphoric Champagne.
37. Lithia Water.
38. Effervescent Gingerade.
39. Sarsaparilla Water.
40. Sparkling Raspberryade.
41. Seltzer Water.
42. Ginger Ale.
43. Tonic Water.
44. Soda Water.
45. Lemonade.
46. Pure Supercarbonated Potash Water.
47. Watson's Mineral Tonic Water.
48. (Chinese) White Face Powder No. 140.
49. („) Rouge Powder No. 128.
50. Watson's Anthelmicetic Bon-Bons or Worm Tablets No. 132 (Label printed in English and Chinese) ......$1 size.
51. Do. do. 50 cts. „
52. Do. do. 25 „ „
53. Do. do. 10 „ „
54. Worm Bon-Bons (Chinese.)
55. Watson's Anthelmicetic Bon-Bons or Worm Tablets.
56. Watson's Infant's Food (Chinese.)
57. Envelope for Ching Fun (Chinese.)
58. Watson's Florida Water (Chinese) 30 cts. size.
59. Do. (Do.) 10 „
60. Opium Smoker's Cure Pills No. 201 (Chinese) $1 size.
61. Do. Do. 50 cts. „
62. Do. Do. 25 „ „
63. Do. Do. 10 „ „
64. Opium Smoker's Cure Lozenges No. 202 (Chinese)......$1 size.
65. Do. Do. 50 cts. „
66. Do. Do. 25 „ „
67. Do. Do. 10 „ „
68. Red Face Powder No. 203 (Chinese.)
69. Hand-bill for Red Face Powder No. 203 (Chi.)
70. Do. Pink Colour do.
71. Do. Blue do. do.
72. Do. Wh. Face Powder No. 140 (Chi.)
73. Do. Rouge Powder No. 128 (Chi.)
74. Do. Opium Smoker's Cure Pills No. 201 (Chinese.)
75. Do. Opium Smoker's Cure Lozenges No. 202 (Chinese.)
76. Do. Bon-Bons No. 132 (Chinese) large size.
77. Do. Bon-Bons No. 132 (Chinese) small size.
78. Watson's Oriental Tooth Powder.

&c., &c., &c.

By Command,

FREDERICK STEWART,
Colonial Secretary.

Colonial Secretary's Office, Hongkong, 7th May, 1889.

Figure 2. Trade Mark Registration of A.S. Watson & Co. Ltd. in 1889.

Source: Hong Kong Government Gazette.

the ASW shareholders invest an additional HK$200,000 capital to generate consumer demand and improve supply chain management through a number of measures:

- supporting intensive media advertising and promotion of opium substitutes, imported and own proprietary medicines, including Watson's Anthelmintic Bonbons;
- extending credit to expand ASW's retail network and increase opium substitutes stock-up;
- producing high-quality products, such as opium substitutes, soda water and family medicine.

Opium Substitutes — The "Rising Star", Fizz *et al.*

Today, discussing opium sales in a business-like way might seem to show indifference to the moral scourge this was on Chinese society. Yet comprehending its structure carries historical insight. After the Second Opium War (1858–1860), legalized importation of opium was ratified by China at the Convention of Peking in 1860, which was later recognized as a great humiliation. Sadly, annual demand for opium shot through the roof to over 13,000 metric tons — half of which was imported mostly from India in 1880.[17,18]

Based on estimations, 40,000–60,000, or roughly 25–37% of Hong Kong's Chinese population, had become opium smokers after 1860 and this remained so until the close of the 19th century. The opium pipe was a status symbol of the wealthy smokers in the late Qing period[19,20] (Figure 3).

However, JDH did not engage in the direct opium trade like his peers Elias Sasson (1820–1880), Hormusjee Naorojee Mody (1838–1911) or the firm of Jardine & Matheson. As a retail chemist, he was pursuing the "Blue Ocean Strategy" as a first mover in launching opium substitutes imported from the UK to replace opium smoking in Hong Kong.

He launched this with a media campaign in 1882 that targeted the mass market instead of a privileged few (Figure 4). JDH saw Shanghai's unique location at the mouth of the Yangtze River evolving as the nationwide logistic centre succeeding Hong Kong. He entrusted John Davey as the Shanghai Dispensary Manager and James Jones as the assistant in 1882 to prepare for the roll-out of opium substitutes. In Hong Kong, one of these opium substitutes saw serious spikes in profits — morphine.

Figure 3. Cloisonné Opium Pipe, @ 19th Century. Engraved on the pipe-bow are the two five-talon dragons, representing the imperial status of the Qing dynasty.

Source: Courtesy of Hong Kong Police Museum.

Eleven years later, in early 1893, ASW's retail and wholesale business showed another jump in the sales of morphine to the public. This trend had accelerated after followers of American medical missionary, Dr John Glasgow Kerr of the Canton Hospital, introduced morphine injections as an "anti-addiction remedy" for "coolies". Indeed, the derogatory moniker coolies was a Hindi word used in India and exported to some British colonies that referred to unskilled labourers or porters engaged in heavy lifting work. The coolies found that they could save more than 80% on highs by injecting morphine under the skin. This was much cheaper than purchasing residual opium scraps collected from used opium pipes.[21,22]

All western chemists, including ASW, had long queues outside their dispensaries each morning for morphine supplies.

The impact on business at the time was such that *Hau Fook Hong*, the official 'Opium Farmer' representing the licensed opium dens, requested the then Colonial Treasurer to address the loss of opium revenues on May 24, 1893 due to the serious competition from morphine injections.[23,24] Because of this, the 1893 Morphine Ordinance was promptly promulgated on September 23, prohibiting unauthorized use of morphine injections

英國屈臣氏戒洋煙精粉發售

戒烟精粉功用說　戒煙精粉者乃本局獨得秘法不惜工本務期剋制洋煙之癮無碍吸煙之人令其自然戒斷永無後患與別家所售戒煙諸藥迥不相同歷蒙　中國列位大學士督憲撫憲各大人獎譽早已京省馳名矣惟近日妒忌爲佈散謠言似謂服此戒煙雖斷癮而難保無虞等語則大負本局立心與　中國除害之意况且服此不獨斷癮兼可令人健飯身體日壯請看以下春君緝熙辨惑論與抄繹中外西報自當了然幸勿爲浮言所阻致誤有志戒烟者之大機會也於本局實爲厚望焉　每包銀七毫

Figure 4. Advertisement of Opium Substitutes in Hong Kong. Launch of Locally Formulated Opium Substitutes in Hong Kong by A.S. Watson of Great Britain.

Source: *Circulation Daily*, November 27, 1882.

without medical supervision or a prescription issued by a medical practitioner (Figure 5). ASW, however, continued the export of opium substitutes to the Mainland, Formosa and Southeast Asia as a leading exporter well into the first part of the 20th century.

When ASW installed ultra-modern distillation equipment in 1876, other local pharmacies such as Dakin Dispensary, Koeffer Dispensary and a couple of local businesses soon followed suit. Torpedo-shaped bottles were filled with six soda water flavours by semi-automated machinery. Due to its range of flavoured soda water, its retail network and its experienced team of salesmen and delivery fleet, ASW captured all retail outlets

No. 13 of 1893.

An Ordinance enacted by the Governor of Hongkong, with the advice and consent of the Legislative Council thereof, for the suppression of the pernicious practice of injecting preparations of Morphine by unqualified persons.

(LS) WILLIAM ROBINSON,
Governor.

[23rd September, 1893.]

WHEREAS it is desirable to forbid, in this Colony, the practice of injecting Morphine except in cases where such treatment has been prescribed by some duly qualified medical practitioner, and to make provision for effectually suppressing such practice. Preamble.

Be it enacted by the Governor of Hongkong, with the advice and consent of the Legislative Council thereof, as follows:—

1. This Ordinance may be cited as *The Morphine Ordinance, 1893.* Short title.

2. For the purposes of this Ordinance— Interpretation.

Morphine shall include Morphia and all salts of Morphine and any solution thereof that can be used as an injection, but not preparations for ordinary internal use containing Morphine as an ingredient but not suitable for purposes of injection.

Duly qualified Medical Practitioner shall mean a practitioner registered under "The Medical Registration Ordinances 1884 to 1893."

Chemist or Druggist shall mean chemist or druggist holding an European or American certificate of qualification.

3. Any person, who shall administer by injection any Morphine to any other person, except in cases where the same has been prescribed by some duly qualified medical practitioner, shall, on conviction before a Magistrate, be liable in each case to a fine not exceeding fifty dollars or to imprisonment with or without hard labour not exceeding two months. Administration of morphine forbidden in certain cases.

The onus of proving the exception shall lie on the person so administering the Morphine. Onus of proof.

4. Any person, who shall, except in cases where Morphine has been prescribed by some duly qualified medical practitioner, furnish Morphine to any person, except to a duly qualified medical practitioner or to a chemist or druggist shall, on conviction before a Magistrate, be liable to a fine not exceeding fifty dollars, or to imprisonment with or without hard labour not exceeding two months. Furnishing morphine.

Figure 5. Morphine Ordinance 1893.

Source: Hong Kong Government Gazette.

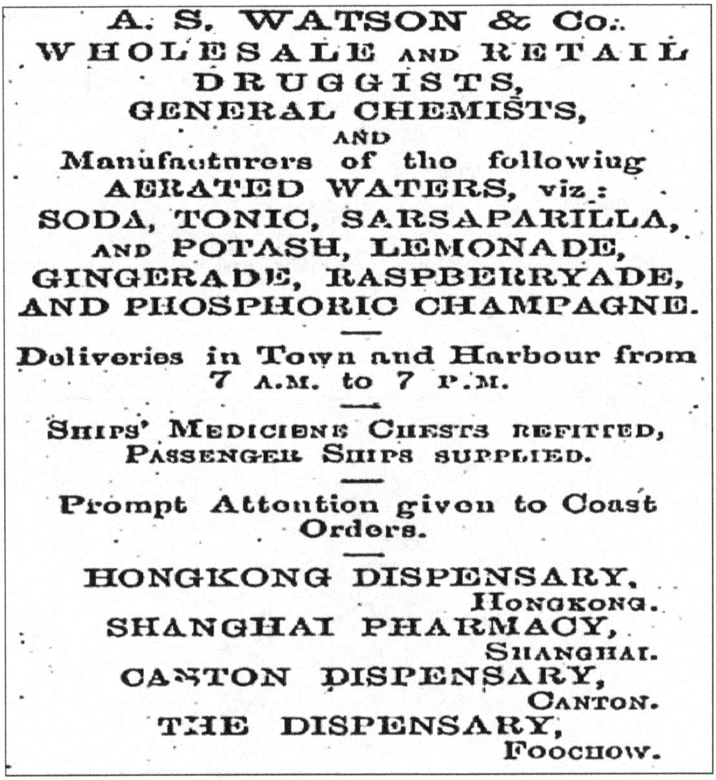

Figure 6. ASW's Advertisement of Locally Produced Soft Drink.

Source: The Hong Kong Telegraph, October 12, 1881.

and upmarket hotels and restaurants in Hong Kong. It soon became the natural leader of the beverage market with advertisements placed in local newspapers (Figure 6). In the following decade, ASW extended its soda water manufacturing capability to Manila in 1884 and Shanghai in 1886 (Table 2). It also was the first to sell alcoholic and beverage drinks in ceramic jars, serving corporate and private banquets and parties in Hong Kong (Figures 7 and 8).

The ASW brand of beverages and soda water produced in the Philippines in 1884 became the 'talk of the town':

> *The plant, which has a manufacturing capacity of 15,000 bottles of waters daily, embraces everything that knowledge and experience can*

Table 2. ASW's Soda Water Plants in Hong Kong, the Mainland and the Philippines.

Year	Location	Remarks
1832	Canton	Soda fountain installed at Canton Dispensary, Shameen (Shamian) Island.
1876	Central, Hong Kong	Located at 1–3 Stanley Street, Central. First Soda water plant in Asia, six flavours of beverages including soda water produced. Local competitors including Dakin Dispensary, Koeffer Dispensary, etc. soon followed suit.
1884	Manila, the Philippines	Branch founded in 1883 with factory in place in 1884.
1886	Shanghai	Located at 321 Chiangshi (Jiangxi) Road.

Source: A History of Hong Kong Pharmacy & Pharmaceutical Market.

Figure 7. Ceramic Jar of Ginger Ale @ 1870.

Source: Courtesy of Shanghai Museum of Medicine.

> *suggest for the enhancement of process and result; ... together with the unsurpassed excellence of their productions, substantiate the leading position which the firm occupy in this branch of activity in the Orient. Their delicious beverages are sent to all parts of the Philippines, and when an order is given for any of the hotels or bars in Manila for a lemonade, ginger ale, soda, or other non-intoxicating drink, "Watson's" is sure to be bought.*[25]

Figure 8. Torpedo-Shaped Watson's Soda Water Bottle @ 1876.

Source: Courtesy of Shanghai Museum of Medicine.

In addition to opium and fizzy water, Watson's herbal bonbons also won them encomiums from the last quarter of the 19th century onwards.

In 1849, American pharmacist Charles Pfizer and his cousin, Charles Erhardt, a candy maker from Germany, established Charles Pfizer and Company in Brooklyn, New York City. They produced a herbal bonbon containing santonin, a therapeutic but toxic anti-intestinal parasitic drug sourced from Central Asia.[26]

As it went, ASW initially imported the branded santonin bonbons from the United Kingdom. For effective eradication of intestinal parasites among the migrant labourers and children in Hong Kong, Humphreys was keen to develop the anti-intestinal parasitic drug at a lower cost and benefit more customers — bringing in greater volumes and profits. He was personally involved in sourcing the active ingredients, designing the packaging materials, inserts, the production and the fine fettle details of sales and distribution were also under his purview.

Humphreys applied his knowledge of pharmacognosy (the study of medicinal plants) by improving santonin's therapeutic effectiveness. The contents of santonin extracted from wormseeds vary considerably in the different species and hybrids of the wormseed flower heads and in varying seasons of the year. He improved the manufacturing process further and followed the specifications of santonin laid down in the latest edition of the 'British Pharmacopoeia' to stringently ensure the consistency in

Figure 9. Multi-Coloured Pagoda-Shaped Watson's Worm Cakes (Bonbons).

Source: Imitation Graphics.

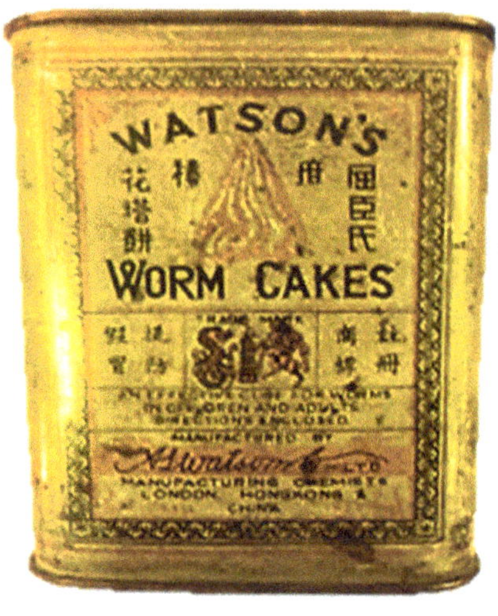

Figure 10. Watson's Worm Cake Metal Box @ 1930s.

Source: Courtesy of Shanghai Museum of Medicine.

quality of each batch of the multi-coloured pagoda-shaped bonbons. The bonbons were packed in metal boxes, with the front side containing the product description in English and the three other sides with full Chinese details (Figures 9 and 10).

This colourful product launched in the late 1880s was a resounding success and soon became the most popular family medicine made by ASW. The planning exercise for this product also became the standard operating procedure for new products at ASW for many years to come.

Watson's brand of santonin dewormer was sold for close to a century until the santonin supply was interrupted due to heavy snow in Siberia in 1972. ASW changed the active herbal ingredient of santonin to the synthetic drug piperazine. The production of the new formula continued until 1986 when the pharmaceutical plant was burnt down and the manufacturing of herbal and generic medicines ceased permanently.[27]

Endnotes

[1]The Thirteen Factories or "Hongs" were Western trading houses from Europe and the United States allowed to set up an office and warehouse by the Manchu government of China in the late 18th century in the designated area of Shameen, Canton. Each of the "Thirteen Hongs" conducted their import and export business via their respective Chinese agents or "Co-Hongs" who also served as the guarantors of their foreign principals should a trade dispute arisen.

[2]Lazich, Michael C., Seeking Souls through the Eyes of the Blind: The Birth of the Medical Missionary Society in Nineteenth-Century China, Hardiman David (Ed.), *Healing Bodies, Saving Souls: Medical Missions in Asia and Africa*, Rodopi, New York, 2006: 63.

[3]Our History, A.S. Watson Group Corporate Website. https://www.aswatson.com/our-history/.

[4]Waters, Dan, Hong Kong Hongs with Long Histories and British Connections, Royal Asiatic Society Hong Kong Branch, Hong Kong, 1990, 30(3): 238–240. http://hkjo.lib.hku.hk/archive/files/8deeba7475f950a5f3938fc24f687bbe.pdf.

[5]The Hong Kong Almanack, 1948, D. Noronha, Hong Kong: 37. https://lib.hku.hk/files/hkspc/pathfinders/HK%20Directories.pdf.

[6]The City of Victoria was the first official name of Hong Kong in 1842 when it became a crown colony after the Treaty of Nanking was signed by the governments of China and the United Kingdom.

[7]Jeremy Watson's Family Stories. http://www.spanglefish.com/JeremysWatsonWellsMillerandCrawfordfamilystories/index.asp?pageid=693818.

[8]The Watsons of the UK and South Africa, Information about Alexander Scott Watson. https://www.genealogy.com/ftm/w/a/t/Jeremy-H-Watson/WEBSITE-0001/UHP-0067.html.
[9]Waters, Dan, Hong Kong Hongs (Note 4): p. 239.
[10]Chiu, Patrick, The First Hundred Years of Western Pharmacy in Colonial Hong Kong, *Pharmaceutical Historian, London*, 43(3): 44. https://publikationsserver.tu-braunschweig.de/receive/dbbs_mods_00065401.
[11]An Ordinance for Licensing and Regulating the Sale of Prepared Opium, Anno Vigesimo Primo Victoriae Regine, No. 2 of 1958, Hong Kong Government Gazette. Saturday, March 20, 1858. https://lib.hku.hk/hkgro/view/g1858/724632.pdf.
[12]*Ibid.* (Note 3).
[13]The term "chemist" has been used in the UK since the 17th century and became widely recognized as a person to sell, dispense and compound poisons in the mid-19th century.
[14]Castelow, Ellen, Opium in Victorian Britain, Historic UK. https://www.historic-uk.com/HistoryUK/HistoryofBritain/Opium-in-Victorian-Britain/.
[15]In 1863 the Hong Kong Government declared the silver dollar — then a kind of international currency — to be the legal tender for Hong Kong, and in 1866 began issuing a Hong Kong version of the silver dollar until 1935, when, the Hong Kong dollar would be taken off the silver standard and linked to the pound sterling at the rate of HK$16 to the pound. Since October 15, 1983 the Link between the Hong Kong dollar and the US dollar was at the fixed rate of HK $7.80 to one US dollar.
[16]Chiu, Patrick, Henry Humphreys (1867–1943): A Visionary in Retail Pharmacy in Colonial Hong Kong, *Pharmaceutical Historian, London*, September 2018, 48(3): 78. https://www.ingentaconnect.com/content/bshp/ph/2018/00000048/00000003;jsessionid=bgutpejaencjm.x-ic-live-01.
[17]The 13,000 metric tons of opium were made up of 6,500 metric tons of local production and 6,500 metric tons imported from India, of which 4,553 metric tons were official imports with levy paid and the rest were smuggled via Hong Kong into the mainland, in 1880.
[18]The Drug Situation Prior to the Establishment of an International Drug Control System, a Century of International Drug Control, 18–27. https://www.unodc.org/documents/data-and-analysis/Studies/100_Years_of_Drug_Control.pdf.
[19]The Qing dynasty was the last imperial dynasty of China, and it was founded by the Manchurian rulers in Beijing in 1644 and was overthrown by the Han ethnic majority Republican revolutionaries in 1911.
[20]Munn, Christopher, The Hong Kong Opium Revenue, 1845–1885, Brook, T. and Wakabayashi, B. (Eds.), *Opium Regimes, China, Britain and Japan*, 1839–1952, Californian University Press, Oakland: 110. https://www.academia.edu/33514205/Brook_-_Opium_Regimes.

[21]In the second season of 1893, an average of 1,000 people were taking two shots a day. This alternative of morphine injection to opium smoking without supervision quickly caused many casualties with overdosing and infection when sharing of needles to save costs by drug users. In addition, morphine drug usage also adversely affected the legal sales and profits of licensed opium dens. Even if the costs of buying morphine powder, distilled water, syringes and needles from local western pharmacies were added up, it was still much cheaper than smoking low quality opium residue collected from used opium smoking pipes.
[22]Dikkoter, D., Laamann, L., and Zhou, X. (2005). Narcotic Culture: *A History of Drugs in China*, Hong Kong University Press, Hong Kong: 177.
[23]The term "opium farmer" referred to a master franchise holder of opium supply for a given period granted by the Colonial Government of Hong Kong as the franchisor in the 19th century. The master franchise holder operated as an agent who supplied the prepared opium to the licensed opium dens, and was not a de facto farmer who cultivated opium by profession.
[24]Letter of Hau Fook Hong, Representative of Opium Farmers, Hong Kong, May 24, 1883, GA1983: 970. http://sunzi.lib.hku.hk/hkgro/view/g1893/647977.pdf.
[25]A.S. Watson Co. & Ltd., *Commercial Manila, Sea Ports of the Far East, Illustrated: Historical and Descriptive, Commercial and Industrial Facts, Figures, and Resources, Allister Macmillan, London*, 1907: 227. https://babel.hathitrust.org/cgi/pt?id=hvd.32044081992034&view=1up&seq=9.
[26]Santonin is an active substance obtained from Aremisia species originated from Siberia and Turkistan. It became a standard drug and listed in the British Pharmacopoeia in the late 19th century.
[27]Personal interview of Chan Chung Fu, former pharmacist manager, A.S Watson Pharmaceutical Manufacturing Division. November 3, 2018.

Chapter 2

1897–1941: The End of the Qing Empire

Turbulent Sailing in Republican Times

Taipan Humphreys' First Two Decades

After Humphreys succeeded his late father as the new Taipan and Chairman of the Board of Directors of ASW in 1896, he launched the first edition of the Watson Pocket Calendar in 1897 to commemorate the beginning of a new era (Figures 1 and 2). ASW's business continued to grow with more retail chemists opening and an increasing number of Chinese traditional medicine remedies available to the Mainland's mass market. In Victoria, ASW celebrated its Diamond Anniversary with over 100 retail drug stores in the Mainland and the Philippines in 1901. Of course, these were tumultuous times.

ASW's Peking (now Beijing) branch was burnt down at the height of the tragic "Boxer Rebellion" in the summer of 1901. This caused serious disruption to its retail and wholesale businesses in North China. With the Mainland business recovering to normality by 1904, Humphreys continued implementing ASW's brand-building strategy with another round of fundraising with its capital increased to $900,000.[1] By 1908, ASW had opened its flagship store in the prestigious Alexandra Building in the Colony, which was crowned as the only modern retail pharmacy in Asia (Figure 3). The building was the "talk of the town" from the Straits Settlements to Shanghai. ASW's imposing presence received extensive coverage:

Figure 1. Replica of 1897 A.S. Watson Pocket Calendar, Front Cover.

Source: Courtesy of Ian Wade.

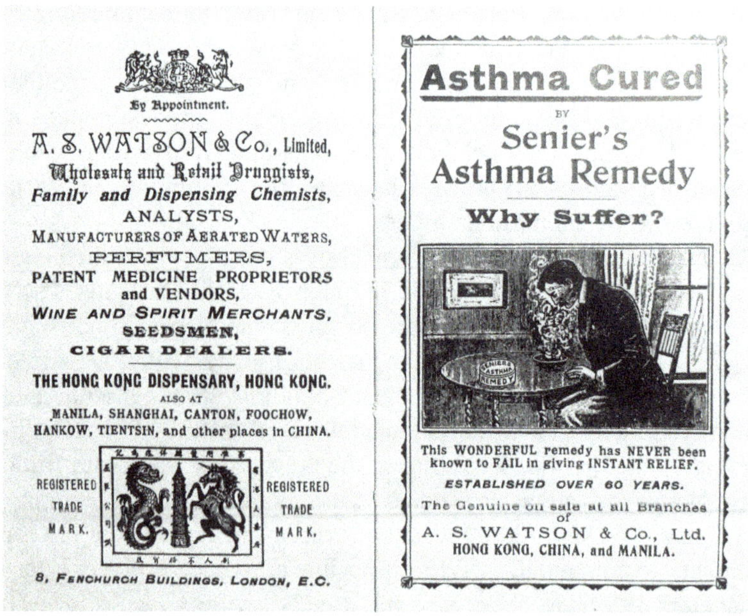

Figure 2. Replica of 1897 A.S. Watson Pocket Calendar, Inside Figures 1 and 2.

Source: Courtesy of Ian Wade.

The ground and first floors of that magnificent and imposing block known as Alexandra Buildings are occupied by the Hong Kong Dispensary, otherwise the well-known firm of AS Watson & Co. Ltd., Chemists, Druggists, Soda water manufacturers, etc. Travellers passing through Hong Kong should pay a visit to the Hong Kong Dispensary where they may obtain every requisite for their voyage, including toilet articles, medicines, perfumery, tobacco, cigars and wines of the very finest quality, at prices that will compare favourably with those selling at home or at any place along the route.[2]

In the following year, ASW acquired the Hongkew Medical Hall and Donald Mennie continued as the manager[3] (Figures 3 and 4). During this time, the Shanghai market had become increasingly competitive with local entrepreneur-owned retail chemists lowering their prices to gain volume share of the opium substitute business.

The expatriate-owned ones could not compete on prices due to higher costs and standards. This resulted in many closures or mergers with other retail pharmacies. At the same time, European, Japanese and Chinese companies supplied newer and more potent opium substitutes, caffeine, cocaine, and heroin pills, all cumulatively flooding the Mainland Chinese market.

A downturn in business began in the years leading up to the (aka "World War I") in 1914. Natural disasters followed by the collapse of the rubber futures on the Shanghai Stock Market in 1910 brought economic panic. Many retail pharmacies and wholesalers suffered cash flow problems and ASW had to write off significant credits it had extended. The Manchurian Plaque of 1910–1911 and the eventual Republican revolution on October 1, 1911 shook the market even further, resulting in a drastic depreciation of 50% of Chinese silver currency. Humphreys presented a grim picture in the annual results for 1911 at the 27th Annual General Meeting held on June 1, 1912:

The first thing that will probably strike you on looking at the accounts is the very heavy capital loss occasioned by the closing of our Manila and Mactavish & Lehmann branches, especially the former. The Manila loss, though regrettable, was in our opinion, inevitable, and in cutting it, we feel confident that we not only acted in the best interests of the shareholders, but were fortunate under the circumstances in being able to sell both the drug business and the soda water business as going concerns.

Figure 3. Alexandra Building, Central, Hong Kong @ 1920s.

Source: Courtesy of Shanghai Museum of Medicine.

The first half of 1911 showed a trading loss for the Manila branch, but after the sale in May last, the Manila account showed a profit which was represented by interest on the mortgages of the drug business and soda water factory respectively and surplus rentals accruing from the Escola lease. With this object in view all outlying branches will be closed as soon as suitable opportunities occur. The nature and scope of a small pharmacy nowadays are such as to require rigid economy and unremitting toil on the part of those engaged in it to make both ends meet.

Figure 4. The Hongkew Medical Hall, a Branch of the British Dispensary Operated by McTavish & Lehmann in Shanghai. @1909.

Source: Courtesy of Raymond Forward.

> *These conditions rarely obtain in such a business unless worked by the owner. What shareholders overlook is this – that the General Managers are, and have been for many years, largest shareholders of the stock. They own or control at the present moment one-sixth of the shares of the Company, so the interests of the General Managers are practically identical with the interests of AS Watson & Co. And it would be criminal policy for them to go against the interests of AS Watson & Co.*[4]

It was indeed a painful lesson to all — Humphreys in particular. He had, after all, taken over the chairmanship of ASW from his late father just 14 years prior, with vigour and expectations. Rapid expansion during the period of 1897–1911 led to a quantum leap in revenues but excessive liabilities. However, with ASW's virtual monopoly of opium substitutes in

Figure 5. ASW's Purpose-Built North Point Plant @1912. The plant produced purified water for soda water, liquid oral medicines, family medicines together with a dormitory for the British expatriate management.

Source: Courtesy of John Munn/Gwulo.com.

the Southeast Asia market showing no sign of abating, creditors and shareholders had not lost faith in Humphreys to turn around the business.

As a belt tightening exercise to improve cash flow to cut losses in the Mainland, Humphreys implemented a strict financial policy from 1912 to 1917 by closing or selling off all retail and manufacturing chemists in the Mainland and the Philippines with the exception of the retail chemist business and soda water plants in Canton and Hong Kong[5] (Figure 5). From then on, ASW built up its reserves to weather any storm or prolonged bad weather.

World War I Years

At the beginning of the First World War (1914–1918), Hong Kong's economy was not seriously affected. Humphreys gave a detailed report of the company's 1915 annual results at the 75th anniversary of ASW and its 31st AGM held on June 9, 1916, with the following excerpts:

> *During my 28 years in charge of Watson's business, its performance has been almost as volatile as all other businesses. From time to time, we need to deal with fundamental changes, but it does not hinder the overall progress and expansion. Some of the losing branches have long been closed, and now our business is bigger than ever; more importantly, our financial situation has never been better.*[6]

1917 was indeed a challenging year in the domestic market, albeit with some relief in Shanghai with Mennie becoming the owner- manager of ASW's North China operations by acquiring the right to use the ASW brand. Humphreys reported in the 33rd AGM held on May 6, 1918:

> *Since the outbreak of war, eight staff have gone to the Front from Hongkong and China alone. Two of these, viz., Lieut. McLeod and Capt. Evers have made the great sacrifice; the Latter being killed by a sniper's bullet while gallantly leading his Company into action. No more men can be obtained, and if there is any further drain on our manpower, one or more of our establishments will have to be closed. In addition, to the above, three men from the London Agency have joined up, of whom one has been killed. The accounts before you, though showing results well above average, are not so good as those for 1916. Between September and December, 1917, supplies were scanty and loss of business ensued in consequence.*
>
> *Again, the fire in April last year (in Hong Kong) further assisted to deplete our stocks (which you will observe in the balance sheet are $162,908.81 less than the year previous) and in addition, dislocated for a time a considerable portion of the business and also restricted sales. Turning to the year under review, the Shanghai Pharmacy branch has been sold, and the loss on same has been provided for in the profit and loss account. The sale was made in accordance with a decision long since determined upon and approved by the Consulting Committee, to concentrate in Hong Kong and Canton, where we have need of all our capital and can employ it more remuneratively.*
>
> *Stocks have been coming better of late, though not as well as we should like, and we are particularly short of our best sellers, due to Government restrictions at Home (UK). For instance, one important article was denied a permit on the ground that it contained sugar. We offered by telegram to supply the sugar from Hongkong; we were months afterwards informed that it was not so much a question of sugar as tonnage.*[7]

The management buy-out of ASW's Shanghai business and brand licensing by Donald Mennie in 1917 was a long overdue action. Mennie's entrepreneurship and local connections kept the ASW brand intact in both the retail and soft drink sectors until decades later with the Japanese take-over of the Shanghai International Settlements in 1942. With WWI ending on November 11, 1918, the supply of raw materials and finished products resumed. ASW's 1919 business performance was outstanding. Humphreys's report at ASW's 35th AGM held on March 6, 1920 shows this rebound:

> *A comparison of same with those of previous years cannot fail to be gratifying to shareholders. On no previous occasion have trading profits reached such a high level, and only once have the net profits now shown been exceeded. That was in 1900, when trading profits were supplemented by no less a sum than $82,173, in respect of property sales.*[8]

Due to the chronic shortage of pharmacists during and after WWI, ASW had to close the Victoria Dispensary in Hong Kong. In the years running from 1912 to 1919, Humphreys operated the ASW business under extreme difficulties with unprecedented challenges in the Mainland, Europe, and the local market. But he was able to keep the Hong Kong retail chemist business and the soda water plant and had learnt the hard way since his late father had passed the baton to him in 1896.

Head-On Blows One after Another, 1922–1933

After 3 years of smooth sailing from the end of WWI, Humphreys faced a series of events that hindered ASW's growth until his retirement in 1933. His successor Douglas Clark continued with ASW's strategy and had 8 consecutive years of development before the Japanese occupation in December 1941. The most significant loss was the opium substitute business which ASW had enjoyed as a leader for over 40 years from the 1880s to 1920. It started to face initial competition from European and Japanese traders, but by the 1920s the Mainland producers became the leading players.

In Hong Kong, the crushing Dangerous Drugs Ordinance and Regulations passed by the Legislative Council in October 1923 effectively shut off the retail sales of narcotic drugs by ASW's retail

Figure 6. The Canton Dispensary Operated by ASW at No. 4, Third Avenue, Shameen ("Sandy Surface", now Shamian), Canton. Completed in the mid-1920s with an adjacent warehouse for the storage of beverages, the Canton Dispensary was located in a tree-lined paved road in Shameen Island, of the Anglo-French concession.

Source: Author's Image Bank.

chemists.[9,10] The Communist-inspired labour strikes of 1925–1926 delayed the opening of its Canton soda water plant and adversely impacted its retail business on Shameen in Canton (Figure 6). The subsequent Great Depression of 1928–1931 and the eventual Japanese occupation in December 1941 all cumulatively weakened the impetus of ASW and brought it to the ground.

The Labour Strikes of 1922–1926

Going into the 1920s, labour unrest in Hong Kong was simmering. Wages were far and persistently below the legal limit for several years after WWI. The first organised labour strike by local seamen was inspired by the Communist movement in the Mainland and commenced in Hong Kong on January 12, 1922. During that Chinese New Year, more than 30,000 workers were involved, with shipments and deliveries disrupted for 2 months.

The labour strike did not finally end until the British shipowners agreed to increase wages for their workers by 24–30%, which happened on March 5, 1922. A second, cross-boundary Canton–Hong Kong labour strike occurred on June 23, 1925 and lasted for 16 months. A violent demonstration in Shameen, Canton triggered this strike, and the Anglo-French Settlement in Canton saw 200 casualties, including 50 deaths due to gunfire by British, French, and Portuguese forces on June 23, 1925.[11]

On March 20, 1926, Chiang Kai-shek, the then de facto military chief of the Republican government, quashed a coup staged by the communists.[12] At the 41st annual general meeting of ASW held on March 27, 1926, Humphreys, who chaired it, reported the performance of 1925 as follows:

> *I regret that I have to come before you with a report that compares unfavourably with those you have been accustomed to receive several years past. No blame can be attached to the management or heads of departments for this. You are fully aware of the adverse conditions that have prevailed during part of the period under review, and taking same into consideration, I do not think the accounts can be considered unsatisfactory.*[13]

During this period, ASW's businesses were hard hit like many sizeable manufacturers and traders of the day.

The Great Depression of 1929–1933

Towards the end of 1926, Hong Kong's economy began to pick up. But the smoother ride did not last long. Hong Kong once again faced the worst global economic crisis of the 20th century between 1929 and 1937. The economic slowdown began on October 29, 1929 when an unprecedented crash of the Wall Street stock market swept across the world, leading to the Great Depression. This had a serious impact on both developed and developing countries in Asia, notably Malaysia and Indonesia. The latter were mainly driven by palm oil, latex, and mineral commodities exports to Europe and the United States. They bore the brunt of the pain in Southeast Asia.

Beginning in 1930, the employment of Chinese migrant workers in tin mines and rubber plantations in Malaysia and Indonesia was terminated. These workers were repatriated to the Mainland due to dwindling export business. Hong Kong, as an entrepot for such commodities, was again hit hard with transshipments fewer and further between. Port activities in which a large number of coolies were employed virtually came to a halt.

By 1931, ASW's retail chemist business in Hong Kong had fallen sharply. As the market leader in opium substitutes, proprietary medicines, and soda water in Hong Kong and Southeast Asia, its business was substantially affected. Before he departed for retirement in Canada, Humphreys held the 48th annual general meeting of ASW on March 21, 1933 (see Chapter 10). Excerpts of his comments in the last report to the shareholders give insight.

> *I regret that I now come before you with an account that, compared with the previous year's report, must be considered disappointing; I feel this especially, as this is the last occasion that I shall preside at the annual meeting of the Company. Profits have generally responded to our activities, but unfortunately, the prevailing world-wide business and financial depression has, of course, adversely affected the Company's business, especially in its more profitable departments.*
>
> *This factor is responsible in a great measure for the poor results shown. In regard to this Company's business, this will be more readily understood when the fact is appreciated, that on account of the lack of business during the past year or so, hundreds of thousands of Chinese who had for years been a source of considerable revenue and profit to the Company have been expatriated from Indochina, Straits Settlements, FMS and the Dutch Indies.*[14]

Pre-Japanese Occupation Period, 1933–1941

As the Great Depression started to tail-out in 1933, ASW regained lost ground with the steady growth of its soda water and OTC herbal bonbons in the Hong Kong and Canton markets. Competition intensified with more locals and returnee chemists entering the market. Also, local businessmen

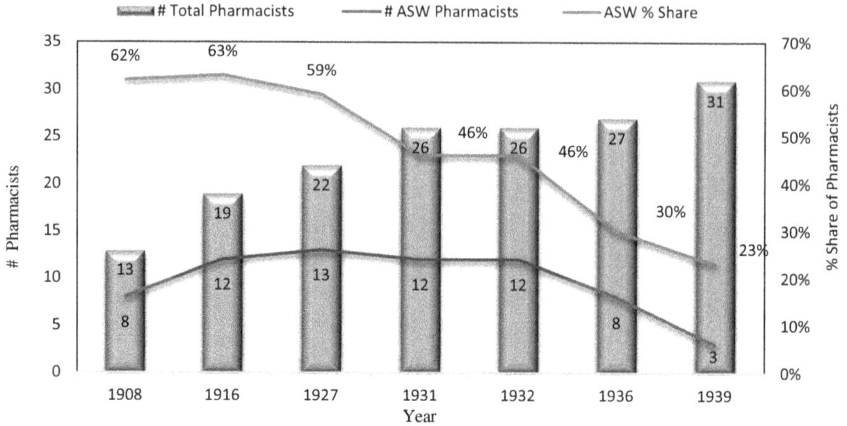

Figure 7. ASW's Share of Pharmacists in Hong Kong.

Source: Hong Kong Government Gazette.

were investing more in the Western pharmacy business. To contain costs, ASW's British expatriate pharmacists dropped from 12 in 1931 to three in 1939. This was just adequate to manage two retail chemists and soda water and family medicine production facilities (Figure 7). At ASW's 54th AGM held on March 28, 1939, chairman of the board D.E. Clark reported 1938's performance:

> *It will be observed from the Accounts now before you that Profit on the year's working amounts to $318,627.95 which is considerably higher than figures submitted to you on similar occasions in recent years. This gratifying result is attributable to the marked improvement shown by all Hong Kong Departments both as regards trading and profit. The subsequent depreciation of the National currency as against the Hong Kong dollar made further profitable trading (in Canton) impossible. The Canton Dispensary, our Shameen Retail Department, was closed down in May last.*[15]

Of course, Japan had started the war in China at the Marco Polo Bridge in Peking on July 7, 1937, 2 years before. This soon moved southward with Shanghai's occupation in November the same year, and then Canton in December 1938. As a result of the war, Hong Kong's population swelled from 1 million in 1937 to 1.8 million in 1940 (Figure 8). The

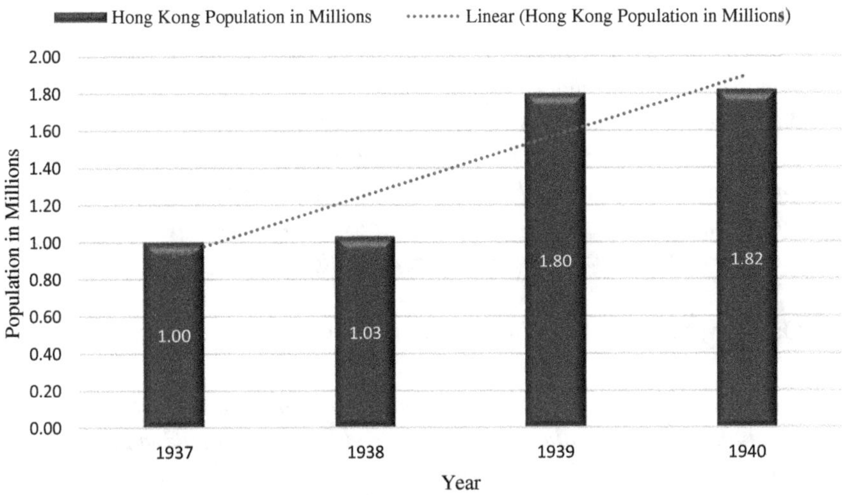

Figure 8. 1937–1940 Hong Kong Population Growth.

Source: Hong Kong Blue Book.

large influx of refugees included the wealthy, small-time traders, skilled workers and labourers fleeing the southern provinces of China into Hong Kong, and as history would show such demographic change had made a social and economic impact on this small British colony.

The influx of refugees had led to a much revitalised retail trade, busy opium dens, great demand in goods and services, and jumps in revenue for 3 years in a row for both ASW and the colonial government. At the height of the Second Sino-Japanese War (1937–1945), the Japanese army was rallying troops in Canton, 82 miles from Hong Kong. ASW decided not to celebrate the Company's first centenary. Mr D.E. Clark, who had been the chairman since 1933, presided at the 55th AGM of ASW held on April 3, 1941:

> *This year, marking the 100th anniversary of the founding of the business, it gives me added pleasure to be in a position to present to shareholders so favourable a Report — it is in fact the best of our record. Like all other concerns our Company has on this occasion experienced fluctuations of fortune and I can well recollect — about thirty years ago (1911)*

when the Company was undergoing one of its difficult periods — certain anonymous correspondences appeared in the local Press written, presumably, by a Shareholder, to the effect that the Company was moribound and, consequently, should be wound up.

Replying to this, the Chairman at that time, Mr Humphreys – not only convincingly refuted this contention, but additionally indicated that our business, far from being moribound as asserted, had on the other hand never been in a stronger financial position.[16]

On the future of ASW, Clarke had the following remarks:

It is nevertheless a source of pride and satisfaction to the Management to be able to state, without fear or contradiction, that the Company at the present time enjoy a far sounder standing than ever before. it is impossible for one to venture more than a guess, particularly in view of existing circumstances; I shall not, therefore, attempt anything of this nature, but I can rightly state that we enter our second century of operations full of confidence concerning the years ahead.[17]

Clarke was perhaps over-enthusiastic on the future of ASW in light of the imminent war activities with Japan, which eventually resulted in a 3-year and 8-month occupation of Hong Kong. Or perhaps he purposely sounded upbeat to alleviate nervous shareholders who would otherwise withdraw their financial support of ASW at this critical moment.

Watson's Brand of Soda Water and Coca Cola

The selection of location for the soda water plant was a critical factor as it had to be close to its market. An efficient logistics system in the recycling of used glass bottles had to be in place.[18] Since establishing a large-scale distilled water plant in the new North Point factory in 1912, the production volume of beverage, soda water, and pharmaceuticals doubled and there was extra capacity to fill.

When the WWI ended in 1917, ASW's soda water business flourished again. The company began shipping its supplies to customers in Kwangtung (now Guangdong) province in the late 1910s. With rapidly increasing demand, ASW's board planned to set up a new soda water plant in the suburb of Canton, which was scheduled to open in 1924. Due to local labour strikes initiated by the communist elements in the Nationalist government, ASW's soda water plant delayed its opening for a few years and it came into operation in 1928. Despite the fierce local competition, ASW remained the soda water leader in Canton as consumers trusted its brand and quality.

In Shanghai, ASW launched the Chocolate Soda in the early 1920s, which aroused discussion among the young and trendy who became loyal consumers of ASW's beverages (Figure 9).

With its advanced bottling equipment and logistic system in Hong Kong and Shanghai, ASW was appointed as the bottler of *Coca Cola* in these two markets in 1927.

For this, an intensive marketing campaign was launched with China's leading actress, *Ruan Lingyu*, who famously posed with her left hand holding a glass of the beverage in a *cheers* sign. The advertisement also carried a *Coca Cola* display sign with a red background which symbolised good fortune, joy, and luck (Figure 10).

Figure 9. Early 1920 Watson's Chocolate Soda in the Shanghai Market.

Source: Author's Image Bank.

Figure 10. 1927 Coca Cola Advertisement with Shanghaiese Actress — *Ruan Lingu*.

Source: Author's Image Bank.

It was an instant hit in Shanghai with the brand's Chinese name *Kekou Kele*, and *Pleasing to the Mouth, Pleasing to the Heart* as its advertising punch line. The brand colour was another bonus with white letters in red background representing festivities and fortune in Chinese culture. Sadly, ASW's bottling plants soon closed after the Japanese occupation in December 1941. ASW's plant in Hong Kong was abandoned, and the one in Shanghai owned by Meenie was confiscated and auctioned off to a local businessman.

Losing Out to the European, Japanese, and Mainland Drug Producers

After the Qing Empire's fall in 1911, ASW was initially competing with Japanese traders. They procured the import of morphine as opium replacement cures and sold it in local and Japanese owned dispensaries in the Mainland. Dikotter *et al.* described the drug scene as being initially driven by European and Japanese exporters. Later on, they lost out to the Mainland and Hong Kong underground drug producers who dominated the domestic market as active exporters:

> *After modest beginnings, heroin imports of European and Japanese origin reached Shanghai, Tianjin and Dalian at a monthly rate of five tonnes by the early 1920s, sufficient for thirteen million doses. Ten years later, the League of Nations narcotic report for 1936 concluded that 'morphine, heroin and morphine pills have become more common, especially along the coast and in the northern provinces, consisting a greater menace to the country. The clandestine manufacturing of heroin was encouraged by incorporating the 1925 League of Nations Convention into Chinese law in 1928. This made its importation increasingly hazardous, and dealers reacted by mass-producing heroin locally, producing a seemingly unlimited quantity for the market.*
>
> *The production of heroin in China before the 1935 Six-Year Opium Suppression Plan reached astounding proportions, making it over 20 per cent more economical than the cheapest product offered by European rivals: the global flow of narcotics to China went into reverse towards the West.*[19]

In Hong Kong, with prescriptions becoming mandatory by law for the dispensing of cocaine, heroin, and morphine in 1923, the underground narcotics market became even more vibrant, with low-waged "coolies" looking for cheap and easy-to-carry narcotics underpinning demand. Locally produced illicit heroin tablets were circulated in Hong Kong in 1927. By 1939, the government estimated that more than 100 million illegally manufactured heroin pills were produced and 3.7 million were seized. It was estimated that 5,557 opium addicts received their supply from legal sources, and seven times that, more than 40,000 opium addicts, bought from illegal sources.[20]

ASW in Shanghai

In the 20 years from 1842 to 1862, Shanghai stood out among the five treaty ports and became China's unrivalled trade centre in the

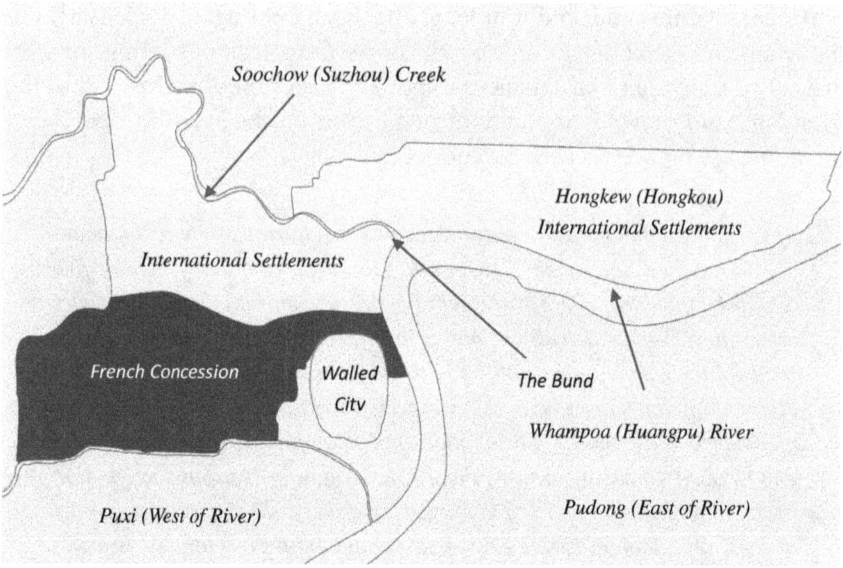

Figure 11. 1845–1863, The Shanghai International Settlements and the French Concession. Biege colour area: International Settlements (Merger of the British and US Concessions on September 26, 1863).

Source: Author's Image Bank.

mainland.[21] Shanghai's unique geographical location was easily accessible by inland and marine transportation. Other factors included free trade with minimal administrative or legal interference in the International Settlements[22] (Figure 11). The influx of many Indian, Jewish, and Western traders from 1860 to 1900 made Shanghai a global city like London, New York, or Paris. The International Settlements and the French Concession in Shanghai were managed like small British or French colonies with their own by-laws and regulations. The thriving economy also boosted Shanghai's population, which surpassed that of Hong Kong in 1905 (Figure 12).

ASW first entered Shanghai in 1850 and had made several attempts to scale up its business operations there over almost 60 years until its latest acquisition of the Hongkew Dispensary in 1909. Its investment was cut short due to the currency depreciation after the Republican revolution in

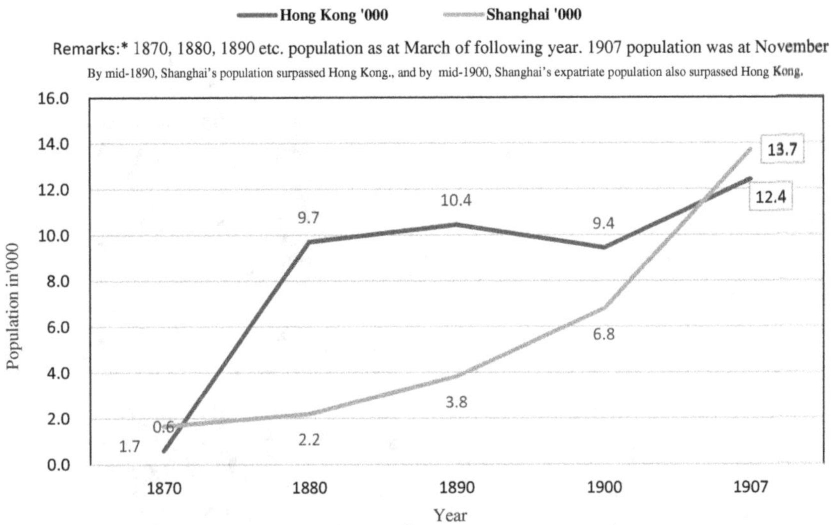

Figure 12. 1870–1907 Expatriate Population.

Source: Hong Kong Blue Book, Twentieth Century Impressions of Hong Kong, Shanghai, and Other Treaty Ports of China.

1911. The retail and wholesale drug market continued to thrive on the sale of opium substitutes with the majority of chemists being owned by local entrepreneurs.

Mennie's management buy-out of ASW's two pharmacies and a soda water plant in Shanghai in 1917 was at a great discount and the ASW Watson brand was licensed to him at an annual fee. The Japanese declared the "Pacific War" on the United States by bombing the Pearl Harbor naval base in Hawaii on December 7, 1941 and Shanghai fell immediately into the hands of the Japanese who also confiscated the businesses owned by British and US nationals in the International Settlements.[23,24] Mennie was a famed photographer of his time. Between 1914 and 1927 he published several books of his images by Kelly and Walsh including The Grandeur of the Gorges (1926), depicting scenes along the (Figure 13). He was interned at the Lunghua Civilain Assembly Centre with other foreign nationals and died there in 1944.

Figure 13. Red Boat — Life Boat in Yangtze River. The Grandeur of the Gorges 1926. Donald Mennie (1875–1944). Mennie was a British pharmacist who came to China in 1899 and worked at the Peking (Beijing) branch of the British Dispensary operated by Mactavish & Lehman & Co. Mennie was a renowned photographer, he made the captioned photograph above while on an expedition in the cruise of the Three Gorges in 1926.

Source: Courtesy Kelly and Walsh Hong Kong.

Endnotes

[1]In 1904, ASW raised its capital from $600,000 to $900,000 with additional shares equivalent to $300,000. The raised funding was to move its retail shop to the newly opened Alexandra Building (now Alexandra House), located at 18 Chater Road, Central, and purchased land to house a new plant with greater production capacity for soda water and pharmaceutical products.

[2]*Hong Kong, The World's Shop Window, Handbook to Hong Kong*, Kelly and Walsh, Hong Kong, 1908, pp. 106–112.

[3]The Hongkew Medical Hall, previously called the British Dispensary, was traded as Macavir and Lehmann.

[4]A.S. Watson and Co. Ltd., *Company Meeting*, Hong Kong Telegraph, Saturday, June 1, 1912:5. https://mmis.hkpl.gov.hk/old-hk-ollection.

[5]Henry Humphreys, (1867–1942): A Visionary in Retail Pharmacy in Colonial Hong Kong, *Pharmaceutical Historian, London*, 2018 (5): 77–81. https://www.ingentaconnect.com/contentone/bshp/ph/2018/00000048/00000003/art00003.

[6]A.S. Watson & Co. Ltd., *Company Meeting*, Hong Kong Daily Press, June 10, 191, p. 2. https://mmis.hkpl.gov.hk/old-hk-collection.

[7]A.S. Watson Co., Ltd., *Company Meeting*, Hong Kong Daily Press, May 6, 1918, p. 4. https://mmis.hkpl.gov.hk/old-hk-collection.

[8]A.S. Watson & Co. Ltd., *Company Meeting*, The Hong Kong Daily Press, March 8, 1920, p. 5. https://mmis.hkpl.gov.hk/old-hk-collection.

[9]The four narcotic drugs controlled by the 1923 Dangerous Drugs Ordinance and Regulation were morphine, cocaine, ecgonine, and diamorphine (commonly known as heroin).

[10]1923 Dangerous Drugs Ordinance. http://oelawhk.lib.hku.hk/items/show/1367.

[11]Carroll, John Mark, *A Concise History of Hong Kong*, Rowman & Littlefield, Lanham, 2007, p. 100.

[12]The many disruptive civilian strikes lost its backers. Six months later, on October 10, 1926, the 15th anniversary, of the Republic of China, the Canton Provincial Port Strike Committee announced the lifting of Hong Kong's blockade putting an instant end to the Labour Strike by the 140,000 strong-workers in Hong Kong.

[13]A.S. Watson & Co. Ltd., *Company Meeting*, The Hong Kong Daily Press, March 29, 1926, p. 3. https://mmis.hkpl.gov.hk/old-hk-collection.

[14]Messrs. A.S. Watson & Co. Ltd., *Disappointing Year Revealed at Annual Meeting*, Hong Kong.Hong Kong Daily News, March 22, 1933, p. 6. https://mmis.hkpl.gov.hk/old-hk-collection.

[15]Reports of the Proceedings of the 54th Ordinary Yearly Meeting of A.S. Watson & Co. Ltd., Hong Kong University Special Collection Library.

[16]Hundredth Anniversary of Founding of A.S. Watson and Company, Ltd., *Hong Kong Daily Express,* April 4, 1941, p. 8. https://mmis.hkpl.gov.hk/old-hk-collection.

[17]*Ibid.*, p. 8.

[18]Logistic costs would become prohibitive and shipping easily perishable glass bottles and recycling them for refilling purpose was a significant consideration that was the norm in the industry.

[19]Dikkoter, D. *et al.*, *Narcotic Culture* (Note 28): pp. 139–140.

[20]Laidler, K. A. J., Hodson, D., Traver, H., The Hong Kong Drug Market, A Report for UNICRI on the UNDCP Global Supply in Illicit Drug Markets: 4, 2000.

[21]The five treaty ports were Amoy (Xiamen), Canton (Guanmgzhou), Fuchow (Fuzhou), Shanghai, and Tiensin (Tianjin). Shanghai, at the mouth of Whampoa River, as the logistics centre for inland and outbound movement of goods.

[22]The Shanghai British Concession was formally established on November 20, 1846, the US Concession two years later in 1848 and the French Concession in 1849. To effectively implement the extra-territorial jurisdiction, the British and United States governments merged the two concessions into the Shanghai International Settlements on September 21, 1863.

[23]Shanghai was a thriving city except during a five-week military conflict between the Japanese and the Nationalist Army from January 28 to March 3, 1932. It remained as the most important business hub in Asia until Japan declared war against China in 1937.

[24]The International Settlements, administered by the Shanghai Municipal Council through a board of directors with representation of British and the US traders, was taken over by the puppet Reorganised National Government of the Republic of China in Nanjing under Japanese control soon after December 7, 1941.

Chapter 3

1942–1981: Japanese Occupation and Post WWII Era

Diversification and Privatisation

A Phoenix from Ashes

During the haunting period of 3 years and 8 months that saw Japan occupy Hong Kong between December 1941 and August 1945, there was a mass exodus as the population dropped from 1.8 million to 600,000. This was prompted by starvation, hyperinflation, on-going shortages, and constant fear of execution at the hands of the Japanese imperial forces. However, the roughly 10,000 expatriates who were not from the Axis countries of Germany, Italy, or Japan or neutral states were interned in one civilian and three prisoner-of-war camps. All Western retail chemists including ASW were closed. British pharmacists were locked up and Chinese pharmacists fled across to the Mainland[1] (Table 1).

With the scourge of WWII ended on September 1, 1945, three departments of ASW restarted their operations; namely Soda water, Drug Manufacturing, and Dispensing. From this reopening a new and colourful course for the company would be set across the middle to late 20th century. In these early post-war years, business commencement was made possible by the recovery of substantial stock quantities. These had been transferred to various premises by the Japanese military and the soda water plant and machinery and properties in North Point luckily escaped major damage.

Table 1. ASW Management Interned at the Stanley Camp.

#	Surname	Other Names	Date of Birth	Date of Death	Position
1	Clarke	Douglas, Edward	1882	NA	Chairman, JDH
2	Croucher	Noel Victor	1891	1980	Shareholder
3	Jupp	John Edmund	1902	1942	General Manager, JDH
4	Stephen	Alistair James	1912	NA	Pharmacist
5	Tarrant	John Arthur	1972	1956	Shareholder
6	Willoughby	George	1909	1945	Pharmacist

Source: Hong Kong Government Gazette, Gwulo.com.

Table 2. Reconstructed Statements of 1940/1941 and 1942/1945.

Financial Year	Headings	Key Items	Net Profit in HK$
1940/1941			658,735.53
1942/1945	Charges less Income (London Office)	London Agents	46,773.29
		Allowances as Compensation for losses	180,000
		Normal Depreciation	199,727.98
	Profit & Loss Appropriation Account (After deducting these from the credit balance brought forward from December 1941)		317,208.38
	War Losses Account (Loss of stocks and debts written off due to loss of sundry debtor records)		1,997,666.66

Source: ASW Minutes of Annual General Meetings, 1940/41 and 1942/45.

ASW's 1940/1941 and 1942/1945 financial statements were reconstructed after the war even though the Share Register was lost. However, the General Ledger dealing with the accounts over November 1940 and December 1941 was miraculously found intact. The interim chairman, Charles Bernard Brown, presented the financial statements at the 57th AGM held on December 30, 1946, with summaries shown in Table 2. With the war past and normality returning, the soda water business from 1947 to 1951 was booming again due to massive immigration from the Mainland to Hong Kong. Re-exports to the Mainland peaked at the height of the Korean War in 1951.[2] However, the total amount of trade from Hong Kong with the rest of the world declined from 1950 to 1955 due to the Korean War (June 25, 1950–July 27, 1953). A trade embargo on goods imported and exported from the Mainland was imposed by the United Nations during the war.

Corporate Leadership

Bernard Brown, a partner in the local trading company Linstead & David, was appointed by the shareholders to be the interim Chairman of ASW in the first year after the Japanese occupation ended. William Patterson, a long-serving ASW manager, acted as the director and secretary and rebooted the business immediately after the war. Clark resumed as ASW's board chairman until 1950 when he retired after 47 years in the Colony.[3] William Alfred Stewart succeeded his positions at JDH and ASW in 1951 and 1952 (Table 3). When ASW's profit flattened in 1951, the new board of directors requested the termination of a commission-based purchase agreement held by JDH since 1920 to save HK$400,000 p.a. or 20% of its NPAT.

William Patterson, a veteran of ASW for 33 years, was appointed as managing director in February 1952, but sadly died suddenly in July 1953. Before taipan Patterson's death, he had started to seek overseas opportunities in Malaya as the top priority. AS Watson & Co. (Malaya) Ltd. was formed with a local partner under a franchise agreement to manufacture and market soda water and medical specialities. Robert Sleap, his deputy, was appointed as the General Manager in 1953 to oversee growth.

However, ASW continued to struggle, and its profit slid. To contain costs and closely manage its soda water and pharmaceutical business, ASW moved its corporate office from Gloucester Building, Central to the soda water and pharmaceutical manufacturing factory in North Point in 1956. John Douglas Clague, nicked name Duggie by his peers, was the chairman of Hutchison International Ltd (HIT), which owned a stake in ASW. Duggie was elected by fellow board members to become the chairman of ASW in 1957, guiding its growth from then on (Figure 1). HIL became the majority shareholder of ASW in 1963 and Clague remained as the chairman of ASW until 1977, when he retired after 20 years of service.[4]

Table 3. 1940–1962 ASW Board of Directors.

Position	1940 (55th) April 4, 1941	1945 (57th) December 30, 1946	1946 (58th) June 6, 1947	1951 (63rd) Mar 16, 1951	1958 (70th) March 17, 1959
Chairman	Douglas E. Clark (JD Humphreys)	Charles B. Brown	Douglas E Clark (JD umphreys)	William A. Stewart (David, Boag & Co. Ltd.)	John D Clague (Chairman, Hutchison International)
Directors	Shouson Chow	Shouson Chow	Shouson Chow	Shouson Chow	Li Fook Wo
	William Paterson (Secretary, ASW)	William Paterson (Secretary, ASW)	William Paterson (Secretary, ASW)	William Paterson (Secretary, ASW)	R.A. Wadeson (Deacon)
	J. Scott-Harston	MH Turner (Deacon, Harston & Shenton)	MH Turner (Deacon, Harston & Shenton)	R. Johannessen	Donovan Benson (Mercantile Bank)
	ST Williamson (William & Co.)	ST Williamson (William & Co.)	ST Williamson (William & Co.)	R.A. Wadeson (Deacon)	R. Sleap (ASW)
				Li Tse Fong	DAF Mathers (Secretary, ASW)
				P.S. Cassidy (Chairman, John D. Hutchison)	

Source: ASW Minutes of Annual General Meetings.

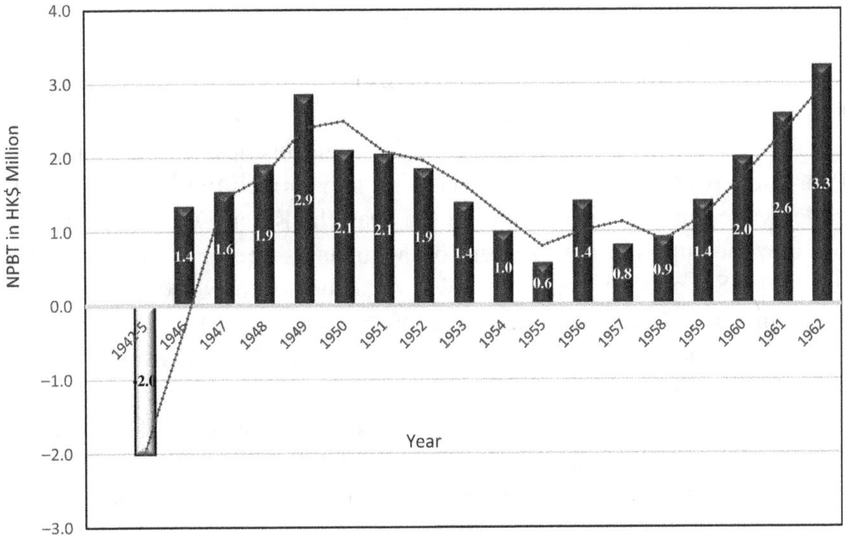

Figure 1. 1945–1962 ASW Net Profit Before Tax in HK$ Million.

Note: *1950–1953 profit decline was due to declining sales to export markets in Singapore and Malaysia.
**1956 peak was due to one-time stock-up prior to tariff increase of imported aerated water by South Korea in 1957.
***1959–1962 steep profit increase was due to booming of economy with textile agreement signed with the UK in 1959.
Source: ASW Minutes of Annual General Meetings.

The Global Oil Crisis and ASW's Diversification Risks

When HIT became the majority shareholder of ASW in 1963, Clague left ASW's management intact with Robert Sleap continuing on as the general manager until his retirement at the end of 1967. He was then briefly succeeded by Dennis Lyth as the managing director of ASW. Jock Mackie succeeded Lyth and David Wilson was appointed as the general manager of ASW in 1970 to grow its business portfolio.[5] Between 1973 and 1974, global oil prices more than tripled. This was triggered by production reduction imposed by the Organisation of Petroleum Exporting Countries (OPEC) in response to the Arab-Israeli War.

Hong Kong and Southeast Asia's export-led economies shrank as they were adversely impacted by Western markets' consumption power.

Meanwhile in 1976, David Wilson became the taipan until his retirement at the end of 1981 (see Chapter 4).

ASW's traditional soda water, retail pharmacy, drug manufacturing, and wine businesses grew nicely in 1971 and 1972 with a low teen number in NPAT. In 1972, ASW realigned its retail business by detaching the Pharmaceutical Division's retail chemists and formed the Retail Division under Malcolm Maddison. Later in the year, the Retail Division branched out into the supermarket segment by acquiring three retail outlets under the ParkNShop (PNS) brand. ASW's decision to enter the supermarket segment was in line with anticipated new consumer habits associated with greater freedom for women — spending habits shifting accordingly.

Working females in Western countries increasingly shopping in supermarkets had become the norm by the 1970s. The prospect of Hong Kong's middle-class families following the trend of their British counterparts would present tremendous opportunities to grow. However, the initially opened PNSs were small in size, lacking the product range and having high prices; the cost-conscious Hong Kong Chinese housewives were simply not ready for this novel retail concept. It would eventually take almost a decade for local consumers to shop for quality and moderately priced daily necessities at supermarkets.

In 1973, ASW also acquired Peter Pan Toy Shops. This was another high-end retail business that catered to middle-income consumers who would generally shop twice a year for toys — on their children's birthdays and Chinese New Year. ASW followed an ambitious expansion programme by entering into other business areas and Southeast Asian markets in 1973 (Table 4).

Hong Kong emerged from the long shadows of the global oil crisis much faster than other developing countries such as Singapore, South Korea, and Taiwan.[6] The recovery was partly due to Hong Kong Government trade officials seeing the urgency to conclude the timely Multifibre Agreement in 1974.[7] Although ASW's revenues showed substantial growth, its profitability remained in low single-digit figures for much of the swinging 1970s. This was largely due to a lack of critical mass with a fragmented business portfolio set to a high-cost structure made up of an entirely expatriate management team. By 1975, ASW's parent company HIL experienced severe financial difficulties due to the Indonesian mining industry's crash. The hefty purchase of mining equipment became a burden due to high interest rates, wide fluctuations in commodity pricing, and a sharp drop in foreign exchange currencies.

Table 4. The Watson's Growth Tree, 1964–1973.

Segment	International	Retail	Pharmaceutical	Investment	Property	Catering	Food & Beverage
Capital Employed	$2.2M	$13.9M	$7.5M	$39.6M	$37.1M	$6.4M	$13.4M
1973	Purchase of Maclaine Watson	Purchase of Peter Pan	Formation of Watson-Soul Pattinson	Sales of Subsidiaries	Purchase of Kwai Chung Site	Purchase of Copper Chimney	Aqua Aroma Ltd.
		Purchase of Kon Tiki	Purchase of South China Medical	Formation of Watson's The Wine Merchant	Purchase of Finland & Co.		Soft Drinks Department
							Vending Department
1972		Purchase of Park'N Shop	Formation of Staybond	Shui Hing Sold	Tsuen Wan Completed		
		Tawson Opened					
1971	Investment In Thailand			North Point Sold for Shares in HIL			
				"B" Block Completed			
1970		"In-Time" Shop Opened					
1969		HK Hotel Shop Opened			"B" Block Commenced		
		Peak Shop Opened					

(*Continued*)

Table 4. (*Continued*)

Segment	International	Retail	Pharmaceutical	Investment	Property	Catering	Food & Beverage
1967–1968	No Active Investment and Expansion Activities due to Social Unrest						
1966				20% Interest in Duty Free Sales Purchase of Subsidiary Companies	"A" and "C" Blocks Completed		
1965							
1964	Sale of AS Watson (Chemicals)	Hilton Shop Opened			North Point Commenced		

Source: ASW Annual Reports.

Moreover, the World Economic Survey of December 20, 1977 highlighted a widespread risk uncertainty and unease about prospects for the world economy in 1978 — with wary forecasts for a more extended period.[8] Bill Wyllie, a local Australian entrepreneur well known in corporate restructuring, was recruited by HSBC to succeed Clague in 1975. HIL acquired the rest of the shareholding of Hong Kong & Whampoa Dock Co. Ltd. (HKWD) in 1977 creating Hutchison Whampoa Ltd. (HWL). Allan Hutchsion of the HKWD became the chairman of the merged company. HSBC eventually bailed out HWL by taking a 22.4% shareholding position with an "equity swap" arrangement. HWL subsequently went public with a listing on the Hong Kong Stock Exchange in 1978.

In the June 1979 AGM, Allan Hutchison stepped down as chairman of HWL with Bill Wyllie, the then chief executive, succeeding as the new taipan of both HWL and ASW. John Richardson, who joined HIT as director of corporate planning in early 1976, became the Deputy Chief Executive of HWL in 1979. Paul Fox, a veteran retailer in the UK, was recruited by David Wilson, managing director of ASW, to come aboard as the retail director in 1978.

Fox himself recruited Rodney Miles, a general store manager at the largest Sainsbury's supermarket branch in London, to become the operations director of PNS in Hong Kong in 1979. Before Miles's arrival, PNS's business strategy was to grow as a supermarket chain with a Western food portfolio. When Miles joined, he was convinced that the future of PNS was to win over Chinese consumers instead of focusing on the small expatriate population. This was indeed a visionary move.

A Change of Dynasty and the Legendary Superman Li

In the late 1970s, ASW relaunched the brand of "Watson's The Chemist" (WTC), which had been used since the 1920s, with a new corporate logo to replace the century-old "Pagoda Tower flanked by the Dragon and Unicorn" corporate brand image. The new Watsons health and beauty store image was modelled after Boots the Chemists — a self-service, pharmacist-led health and beauty store in the UK.

Sales assistants were trained with better product knowledge to advise consumers on its range of health and beauty products. The first WTC flagship store opened in Melbourne Plaza, which was located in the "golden mile" area of Hong Kong's premium Central business district on Queen's Road Central in 1980.

HWL faced a turning point in September 1979 when HSBC sold its 90,000,000 ordinary shares of HWL (22.4%) to Cheung Kong Holding Limited ("CKH").[9,10] Li Ka-Shing (dubbed by the local press as Superman Li), chairman of CKH, became the single largest shareholder and was appointed as a non-executive board member of HWL in 1979. Li continued to increase HWL's shares in the open market totalling 31% in early 1980 and became the chairman at the end of the year succeeding Wyllie who became the deputy chairman.[11] The market believed the primary motive behind Li's acquisition of HWL was this strategic reason; the large land bank was previously used as a dockyard that one of its subsidiaries held in Hunghom, Kowloon. HWL soon began to develop this piece of idle property into the large private housing estate, Whampoa Gardens, in the mid-1980s.

In 1981, HWL decided to privatise the publicly quoted non-property related businesses of ASW, Anderson Asia and Hutchison-Boag, by acquiring the minority interests of all three companies at a consolidated sum of HK$560 million (see Chapter 11). There was one investment made by HIL that remained within its portfolio which Clague had been especially fond of, the Sheraton Hotel in Tsim Sha Tsui, Kowloon (Figure 2).

Figure 2. J.D. Clague (Centre) on the Roof-Top of Sheraton Hotel, Kowloon @ 1973.

Source: Courtesy of Racing Memories, Hong Kong Jockey Club.

Searching for the Path Forward

As a traditional retail and manufacturing company dabbling its toes in the service sector in the 1970s without success, HWL had undergone tremendous changes in its ownership and shareholding of ASW, particularly during the 1976–1980 period.

In 1976, ASW's sales and Profit After Minorities and Taxation (PAMT) were HK$255 M and HK$9 M, respectively. PAMT was 3.5% of sales in 1976, which was very low. Yet, sales and PAMT increased by 2.1 and 1.8 times to HK$539.5M and HK$16 M in 1980 with rapid expansion in its retail business to 52 outlets and 1,863 employees (Figures 3 and 4). Leasing and salary expenditures had however kept its profit contribution

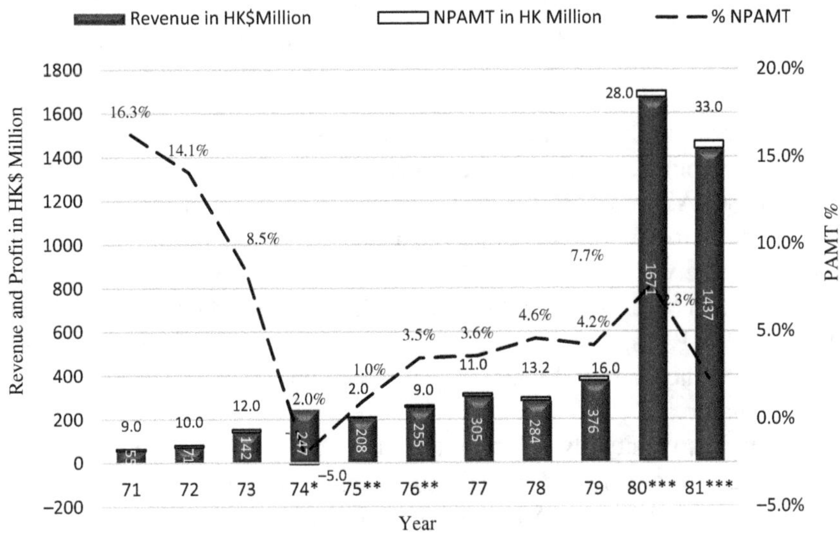

Figure 3. 1971–1981 ASW Revenue, Profit After Minorities and Taxation (Before Extraordinary Items).

Note: *Losses of HK$5 M or 2% of sales in 1974.
**Revenue drops in 1975 and 1978 were due to weak soft drink sales.
***Consolidated ASW and HIT accounts of retail and trading divisions in 1980 and 1982 included the income from the disposal of agency business in Singapore and Malaysia, and the sales of three properties in Hong Kong and Macau. The proceeds of this were to acquire the remaining 48% shareholding owned by minorities in 1980.
Source: ASW Annual Reports.

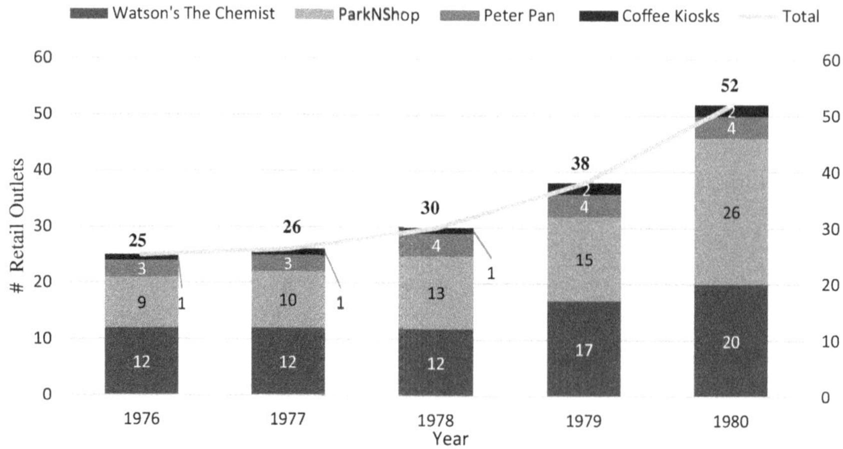

Figure 4. 1976–1980 ASW's Retail Outlets' Growth.

Source: ASW/HWL Annual Reports.

at a disappointingly low level of 3% of sales — a challenge faced by retailers in Hong Kong for decades to come.

In 1980, ASW reported HK$16 million or 57% of the consolidated profits of the Retail and Trading Division.[12] However, when the extraordinary income was generated with the disposal of its agency business in Singapore and Malaysia, and three properties were discounted in 1980 and 1981, ASW's P/L statement would be in the red.[13,14] The financial results also showed the trading division's lower operating profits due to its very business nature.

ASW was eventually privatised, with HWL acquiring the remaining 48% shares owned by individual investors. It became a wholly owned subsidiary of HWL in 1980, with Richardson's top priorities being to improve the cash flow and profitability of HWL. ASW's assets were its highly knowledgeable and experienced expatriate management. However, they would become a financial burden when the business did not achieve its critical mass.[15] In reviewing the composition of the workforce of ASW's subsidiary business, it became evident that the frontline staff's quality of service was a top priority since retention of customers and enlargement of the customer base was and remains a crucial success factor.

Generally speaking, the 40-year period of 1942–1981 was another "roller coaster" ride for ASW. Its emergence from the Japanese Occupation was a miracle, which saw a dramatic recovery up to 1949 when the Chinese Communist Party drove out the Nationalist government. The trade embargoes imposed against the newly founded Communist China government during and after the Korean War adversely affected Hong Kong's important China re-exports, and ASW was desperate to revive its business sustainability.

In 1953, ASW's board of directors approved the Malaysian master franchise agreement signed with local Kuala Lumpur investors. The business model for Southeast Asian countries, such as Burma and Thailand, mapped out minimum investments and maximum returns. Unfortunately, the soda water and pharmaceutical ventures never took off in that region as initially planned due to increasing social unrest as British colonial rule drew to an end. ASW faced a stagnant period from 1953 to 1957 when business steadily improved, led by rising exports of light industrial goods such as textiles and garments from Hong Kong to the Western countries.

Soda water was the core business of ASW. To optimise its capacity, ASW also acquired the license rights of Canada Dry® to manufacture and market its products in Hong Kong in 1965. ASW became one of the top three players along with Coca Cola® and Vitasoy® in the local bottled beverage market. In 1963, Clague's HIL became the majority owner of ASW with a 52% shareholding. ASW followed HIL's aggressive expansion strategy and grew from a handful of companies in the 1950s to over thirty companies by 1973.

Its business expansion into new areas (including catering, frozen foods, supermarkets, toy retailing, and property development) spanned across key Southeast Asia countries. However, such a diversified business became unsustainable when the global oil crisis suddenly arose in late 1973. Hit by the financial "tsunami", Clague's dreams became nightmares. It would take 8 years before HIL (subsequently merged with the Hongkong and Whampoa Dock Co. Ltd., and renamed as Hutchison Whampoa Ltd in 1978) and its subsidiary ASW emerged from the long struggle to stay afloat in 1981. The revival of ASW was made possible when Li came to its rescue with additional investments and new leadership appointments.

Endnotes

[1]Of whom 2,400 were British colonial administrators, businessmen and their family members interned in the civilian camp at Stanley, Hong Kong Island.

[2]A well-known fact that a few local shipping companies were involved in the transshipment of vast quantities of imported antibiotics, petrol, and other strategic items to the Mainland in the midst of trade embargo by the United Nations and the United States.

[3]Douglas Clark, another long-term veteran of ASW since 1933, who doubled-up as the chairman of JDH and the chairman of ASW, was interned by the Japanese military. He returned to Hong Kong after a period of relief and repatriation to the UK in 1946.

[4]John Douglas Claque (1917–1981) (known to his friends as "Duggie") was a legend in Hong Kong in the 1950s-1970s. He was born in Bulawayo, Rhodesia (now Zimbabwe), grew up in the Isle of Man, and came to Hong Kong as a Royal Artillery Officer with the Manx Regiment, in 1940. Clague was interned as a POW briefly and escaped to Huizhou, a city in Guangdong province and 57 miles northeast of Hong Kong, where he set up the British Army Group Advanced Headquarters (AHQs) in April 1942. AHQ was an extension of the Military Intelligence Unit 9 of the War Ministry of the British government. Its main function was to help the escape of British prisoners-of-war (POWs) from Japanese internment camps in China and also to collect intelligence in territories including Hong Kong under Japanese occupation.

[5]Jock Mackie, a Scottish national, who came to Hong Kong and joined Jardines Matheson's sports agency business in 1948. Mackie later acquired Robertson, Wilson & Company, with financial help from taipan Clague.

[6]The four were dubbed as Asia's "Four Little Dragons".

[7]The 20-year Multifibre Agreement was under the World Trade Organization which allocated garment quotas from 1974–1994.

[8]World Economic and Social Survey Archive: 1970–1979, Department of Economic and Social Affairs Economic Analysis, United Nations. https://www.un.org/development/desa/dpad/publication/world-economic-and-social-survey-archive-1970-1979/.

[9]1979 Hutchison Whampoa Ltd., Chairman's Statement, Annual Report, April 1980: 15.

[10]HSBC issued 60% of Hong Kong's bank notes in circulation in 2012.

[11]Bill Wyllie had subsequently resigned from the HWL Board at the AGM in 1982.

[12]ASW's 1980 profit after minorities and taxation but before extraordinary items of HK$16 million included the write-off of its investment in the closure of the bottling operation in late 1980.

[13]The extraordinary income was due to the sale of ASW's controlling interests in Singapore and Malaysia to Sime Darby Sdn. Berhard, and the three property holdings in Kwai Chung, Kwun Tong, and Macau.

[14]The proceeds of sales of ASW's Singapore and Malaysia agency business to Sime Darby Bhd. was used to finance the development of the property of the

Retail Godown cum ASW's corporate headquarters which were due to complete in 1982.

[15]Expatriate managers were paid multiples of salaries than local managers including education allowance for their children in attending international schools, and housing provided to their families.

Chapter 4

1982–1988: New Leadership

The First Leg of Geographical Expansion

Leadership with the Sportsman's Spirit

The 1980s were a pivotal time for ASW. In 1981, ASW was privatised after the remaining minority shareholding, 48% to be precise, of the business was acquired by and became a wholly owned subsidiary of HWL. Still, financials were far from ideal and ASW had lost significant amounts in expanding ParkNShop (PNS) in the late 1970s and early 1980s. The search for the right man who had extensive knowledge and experience in growing a retail chain from a small multiple became a priority for HWL.

John Richardson, CEO of HWL and chairman of ASW, believed that ASW could become a major revenue and cash flow driver of HWL. Hence, the new managing director of ASW had to be an "intrapreneur" who had already learned the ropes. The new taipan candidate needed to formulate and execute a strategic plan to build up ASW's retail portfolio and contribute to HWL's revenue. One would soon be found.

Ian Wade was a British retail executive who had worked his way up to become the youngest member of the board of directors of the Asda supermarket chain of Leeds in 1979. He appeared on the radar when ASW was seeking new blood to revitalize its struggling business.[1] (see Chapter 10). As the new taipan of ASW, Wade's first job was to review the organisational structure and to install a fit-for-purpose leadership team for a successful retail business with local commitments and outward ambitions. It closely resembled the spirit of cricket to a professional sportsman, which explains why Wade had chosen it as his initial career after leaving school:

> *"Cricket is an exciting game that encourages leadership, friendship and teamwork, which brings together people from different nationalities, cultures and religions".*[2]

Strategy Formulation and Execution — The First Three Year Plan

Wade began in his new position as the group managing director of ASW on March 15, 1982, in Hong Kong. Within the first 3 months, he had organised the ASW leadership team to conduct a preliminary PEST review of Hong Kong's markets and a SWOT analysis of ASW.[3] Meanwhile, Wade visited the PNS supermarkets and WTC drug stores. He held direct talks with local consumers to learn their expectations of a retail chemist and supermarket. Wade also held talks with ASW's shop managers and merchandisers about their challenges and how they could better serve Hong Kong shoppers and improve each shop's revenue and profitability. Finally, he talked to suppliers to find out how to ensure consistency in quality and what constituted the optimum inventory level for both parties.

Wade's findings revealed that suppliers and consumers in Hong Kong and the UK both shared the same concerns and preferences. The three key factors for success were universal; corporation,customers, and competitors. ASW's leadership team reached a consensus to develop a business model and adopt best practice management strategies they believed to be effective in the UK and applicable to the Hong Kong market. They all believed ASW could excel in Hong Kong but could not do so with the fragmented businesses which had evolved over the years. Their top priority was to formulate a long-term strategy for a sustainable and profitable business.

Wade refined the collective work of ASW's leadership into "ASW's Eight (Prosperity) Strategies".[4] (see Chapters 11 and 12). These strategies were similar if not identical to renowned business administration researchers such as Jim Collins who authored *Good to Great* and Harvard Business School professor Nitin Nohria, William Joyce, and Bruce Roberson who articulated the "4+2 Formula". In his proposal, Wade planned to reorganise the core businesses with a streamlined organisational structure concentrating solely on expanding retail and food manufacturing activities in the first 3 years. With continued momentum, Wade made a business presentation to the board chaired by Richardson in June 1982 and it was promptly approved. At the meeting, HWL's board decided that the Import and Pharmaceutical Division of ASW was not a core business and 4 months later, in September, transferred the Division's business to the trading arm of HWL, John D. Hutchison Ltd. (see Chapter 12).

A "Black Saturday" in 1983

A year later, after the strategy realignment at ASW under Wade, the firm would have to adjust to larger frameworks concerning Hong Kong's future and the expiration of the New Territories lease on June 30, 1997. The first round of negotiations over Hong Kong were held between Chinese and British government delegations in Beijing from July 12 to 13, 1983. In the next three rounds of talks, Britain insisted that it wished to administer Hong Kong after 1997 as the 1842 Treaty of Nanking had laid down that Hong Kong Island was ceded to the United Kingdom in perpetuity. Amid political uncertainty, the Colony's retail business was hard hit. This challenging time coincided with the period when Wade began embarking on his ASW revitalisation plan.

Then there was the currency crisis, otherwise known as "Black Saturday", which occurred on September 24, 1983. This saw the Hong Kong dollar value drop to an all-time low. Raymond Li, Executive Director of the Banking Policy Department of the Hong Kong Monetary Authority, described the currency situation in his paper as follows:

> *Following China's official statement in August 1983 that it would take back Hong Kong on or before 1 July 1997 regardless of its negotiations with the UK, political uncertainties added to the crisis atmosphere. On the weekend of 23–24 September 1983, news broke that Sino-British talks had ended in a stalemate. During these two days, the HK dollar depreciated by some 13% against the US dollar, closing September 24 at a record low of HK$9.6. Matters stabilized after the announcement and implementation of the linked exchange rate system in October 1983, which pegged the HK dollar to the US dollar at a rate of HK$7.80/US$.*[5]

With investors' confidence in Hong Kong's future under Communist China's rule after 1997 in question, ASW bore the brunt of the crisis — because Hong Kong imported most of its consumables. The drop in the

Hong Kong dollar resulted in a price hike with grave consequences in the retail market. Consumers responded by shopping less to compensate for the increased cost.

Re-entry into the Mainland, 1984

Soon after the "Black Saturday" currency crisis ended on October 17, 1983, Wade commenced exploratory negotiations with the Shenzhen authorities with a view to entering the retail market with a PNS branch. Adverse media reports circulated that Li had divested himself of his Hong Kong investments for overseas markets to avoid being swallowed by nationalisation.[6] Hence, ASW's investment in Shenzhen, a border town across from Hong Kong's New Territories, was believed to be a gesture to refute those circulating rumours.[7]

After a year-long negotiation with the state-owned local partner, the Shenzhen Branch of China Merchant Group, ASW opened an 8,600 square feet (or 800 square meter) PNS supermarket in Shenzhen's port city in October 1984. The Shekou ParkNShop Supermarket Ltd. (SPNS), China's first service joint venture, was formed with a 60:40 shareholding in favour of ASW. It served the expatriate community living in Shenzhen, and the Foreign Exchange Certificate (FEC) was their currency to purchase at SPNS.[8] International visitors to China would first exchange their own country's currency notes in a Bank of China's sub-branch office, which would then issue an equivalent amount of RMB in FECs. The formation of SPNS in Shenzhen was a timely move by the Central Government and had somewhat helped to mend the Hong Kong public's long ebbing confidence. In December 1984, the Government of the United Kingdom of Great Britain and Northern Ireland and the Government of the People's Republic of China signed the Joint Declaration on the Hong Kong Question ("the Joint Declaration") in Beijing.

Wade decided in the mid-1980s that China would spur his cross-border plans for Watsons. ASW's board members had reservations, but fortunately for Wade, he had the support of the chairman Mr. Li Ka-Shing. In 1989, two WTC stores were opened in Beijing and Guangzhou.

Ilha Formosa — The Beautiful Island of Taiwan[9]

When Japan lost the Second Sino-Japanese War (1937–1945), Taiwan's sovereignty reverted to China when Imperial Japan surrendered to the

Kuomintang (Republican) Government of Chiang Kai-Shek on September 9, 1945 in Nanking.

Historically, ASW's opium substitutes were one of the top three brands in Taiwan in the late 19th century.[10] A local apothecary owned by the merchant family of Li Jun Chih visited ASW in Hong Kong and sought to import the Scotts brand of Fish Oil from ASW in 1926 (ASW was Scotts's Asia distributor in the early 20th century).[11] The Li family renovated their three-storey high shop-house with a prominently displayed ASW dragon, pagoda and unicorn logo on its façade — but without the prior consent of ASW. Instead, the Wu Shi Chuan Apothecary was appointed as an ASW distributor in 1927 (Figure 1).

ASW filed a complaint in the High Court in Tokyo, Japan in 1928 — seeing the Li family eventually lose their case in 1934.[12,13] The Wu Shi Chuan Apothecary continued as the main importer of ASW until Japan occupied Hong Kong on December 25, 1941. ASW's exports to Taiwan were halted at once when its manufacturing plant in Hong Kong was abandoned by the Japanese imperial army.

The strategic decision to enter the Taiwan market was made by Wade, and followed-up by Rodney Miles, who was then Retail Director — Non-Food. It was fully supported by Simon Murray, who succeeded John Richardson in 1984. After an absence of almost 45 years in Taiwan, ASW opened its first WTC store in Taipei in August 1987. Two more WTC stores opened in the last quarter of that year, too.[14]

The first couple of years would present market-entry opportunities and challenges for ASW in Taiwan. Miles recalled the rationale to pick Taiwan as the first overseas market to enter:

> *In 1987, Taiwan had 20 million or four times of Hong Kong's population. With a similar urban culture and shopping habit among young working females, we had the confidence to replicate Hong Kong's success in Taiwan. The decision to enter Taiwan in 1987 was a straightforward one.*[15]

Philip Ingham, then Director and General Manager of Watson's The Chemist (Taiwan) Investments Limited was quoted in an interview:

> *From 1982 to 1985 we expanded in Hong Kong and reached about 60 stores for its six million people. To maintain the pace of expansion, Watson's had to go abroad. We started by looking at Taiwan and*

Figure 1. ASW's Retail Chemist Façade, Taipei, Taiwan @ 1928. ASW set up its direct operations in Taiwan in 1987.

Source: Courtesy of Phoebe Shih.

> *Singapore. After two years of detailed research, we concluded that Taiwan could accept Watson's concept, more importantly, because of the developments starting to happen here — increases in consumerism, reductions in tariffs and regulations, and a growing dependence on the service sector. We have upbeat music in the stores and frequently change product displays to regularly encourage people to come in. We're trying to create an image that is modern, fashionable, vibrant, and energetic. We target youth, particularly females. Something like 80 per cent of our*

customers are female, primarily 15 to 40 years of age, which is slightly different from what we had initially planned.[16]

In July 1987, ASW was allowed to set-up a wholly owned subsidiary without the legal requirement for a local partner, due to the end of martial law which had been imposed since 1949.[17] The initial success of ASW aroused interest in the local press which reported the high retail price of the Dettol® brand of antiseptic soap in December 1988. ASW sold the Dettol® soap at NTD 120 per bar weighing 125 grams, with the same selling at Watsons shops in Hong Kong for NTD 21 (or HK$5.4) in December 1988.[18] ASW promptly revised the price to NTD 65 (HK$16.7) to avoid a backlash by angry local consumers.[19] Still, the brand played on.

Hello, Lion City, Saya Kembali Lagi — I'm Back Again

ASW had a long history in Singapore.[20] Its primary consumables were exports of soda water, opium substitutes, and family medicines. Since the late 19th century, the Watson's brand of opium substitutes was the top export item of ASW until the early 1930s when commodity prices of rubber and minerals of Southeast Asian countries hit rock bottom during the Great Depression years of 1929–1939. In 1957, ASW seriously resumed exporting its range of soda water to Southeast Asian countries.

ASW subsequently stepped up its investment in Singapore and Malaysia with an import and pharmaceutical distribution business in 1973 in line with HWL's geographical expansion strategy. With the change of ownership in 1979, ASW divested its business in Singapore and Malaysia to Sime Darby Sdn. Berhad at the end of 1980 and moved back to focus on its retail business in Hong Kong.

It was not until late 1984 that ASW looked to re-enter the Singapore and Taiwan markets when Wade presented his second 3-year business plan for the 1985–1988 period. Both Simon Murray and Li Ka-Shing supported Wade's initiative. ASW's management took the next 3 years to grow Hong Kong's retail drug store and supermarket businesses to a critical mass. They then moved forward with the overseas expansion plan, eventually seeing Dennis Cassey joining ASW as its managing director for Singapore and Malaysia in early 1988.[21]

That same year saw the first WTC Shop, located in a 4,000 square feet store at Marina Square shopping mall, opened in April 1988 (Figure 2). For this location, WTC had to fight hard with the Guardian chain of pharmacies which had commanded an entrenched position since 1972. ASW's primary target customers were younger consumers in their teens and early 20s, mostly professional and free-spending females. Moreover, South and Southeast Asian tourists started travelling outside of their countries in the late 1980s. Singapore was the natural choice destination for their shopping, as there was a lack of quality brands in their own countries back then.[22]

"*Mônaco do Oriente*", 1987

Beyond Singapore and Taiwan, another market in the 1980s mandated a gamble for ASW — Macau. Considered the gateway of the Roman Catholic Church to China and Japan with St. Paul's College and St. Paul's Church built there from 1602 to 1640 by the Jesuits, Macau was unique

Figure 2. Watsons Marina Square Health & Beauty Shop, Singapore Since 1988.

Source: Author's Image Bank.

in Asia.[23] With the loss of its entrepot status in the opium trade to the British after the First Opium War (1839–1842), Macau diversified into the coolie trade and legalised gaming activities to generate revenue to support its administration of the territory in 1849 (see Chapter 5).

ASW's brand of consumer products including its soda water, anti-wormer bonbons, and a range of proprietary medicines and imported wines had been sold in Macau since the 19th century at a handful of local Portuguese-owned pharmacies.

With the city's small population of up to 200,000 in the 1950s, ASW was not keen to set up shop there in competition with the Portuguese retail pharmacies. However, ASW stepped up its marketing campaign in Macau when it launched Watsons Water® at the 1985 Macau Grand Prix. In 1986, ASW's sponsored racer, Andy Wallace, who drove Car #10, won the 33rd Macau Grand Prix trophy (Figure 3).

Wade took the opportunity to open their first health and beauty store in 1988 in Macau in anticipation of the opening of the Macau Jockey Club a

Figure 3. Andy Wallace, Watsons Water Sponsored Car # 10 at the 33rd Macau Grand Prix in 1986.

Source: Courtesy of Motofan.

year later in 1989. This subsequently led to more WTC openings with Macau's gaming industry becoming more attractive to visitors from Southeast Asia.[24] Basically, the bet for ASW on getting into Macau paid off.

Driving Economy of Scale in the Retail and Manufacturing Division

When ASW became HWL's wholly owned subsidiary in 1981, the retail and trading division's financial results were consolidated and not reported separately (Figure 4). However, Wade's first year's result in 1982 showed a significant year-on-year improvement with its manufacturing division's sound performance. The full conversion from glass bottles to aluminium cans and tetra packs for Watson's Water range, Mr Juicy, cordials, and other beverages, plus great sales of Mountain Cream ice cream, all contributed to the division's gains. ASW's PNS

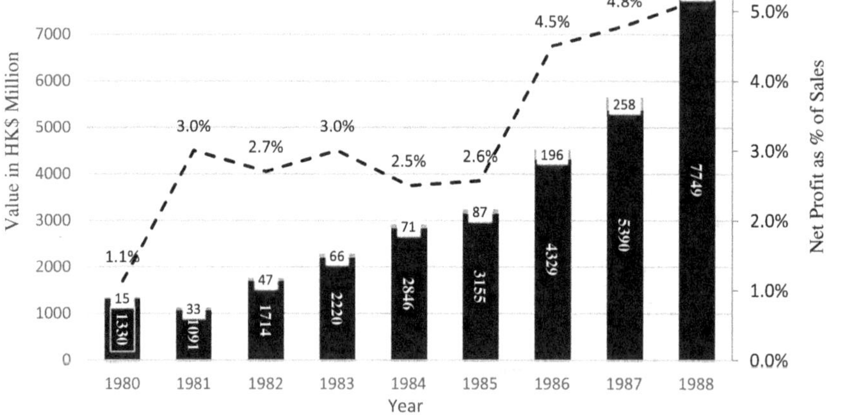

Figure 4. 1980–1988 Performance of Trading and Retail Division.

Source: JDH Annual Reports.

supermarkets and WTC stores grew from 15 and 5 in 1981 to 78 and 30 in 1983, respectively, despite the currency crisis in October 1983 (Figure 5).

Further into the decade, 1984 proved to be an eventful year for Hong Kong and HWL. In fact, the Sino-British Joint Declaration was signed in December 1984. The change of top management at HWL from John Alan Richardson to Simon Murray occurred in August 1984. However, ASW's expansion continued with Li fully supporting it. With increasing exports of beverages and other high-quality food products to the Mainland, the first PNS Supermarket was opened in Shekou, Shenzhen in October.

By the end of the year, ASW's Manufacturing (Food) Division enjoyed 80% of the Hong Kong market for distilled water, 65% for fruit juice, one quarter for canned drinks, and one third for ice cream. The business really took off in 1985, with the number of retail outlets doubling within 4 years from 31 at the beginning of 1985 to 75 in 1988. The growth came from an increasing number of young professionals in Hong Kong opting for lifestyle shopping. Also, a growing number of Mainland business tourists

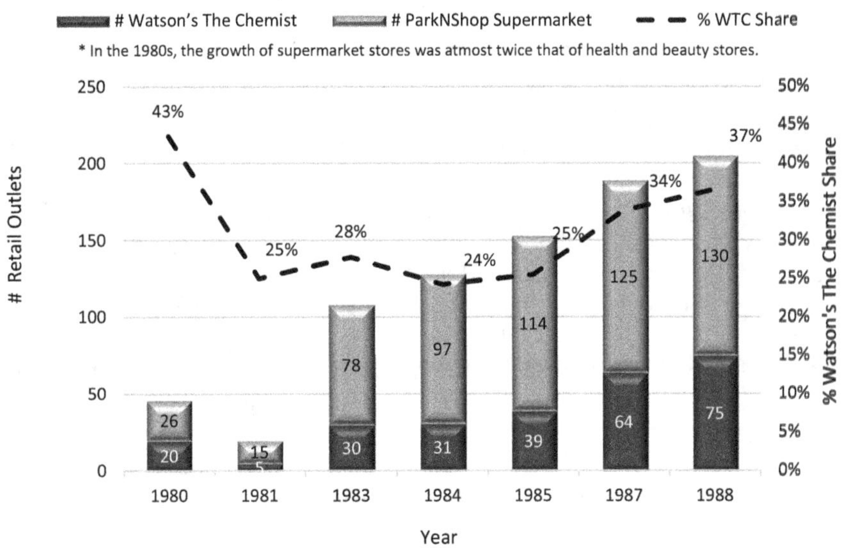

Figure 5. 1980–1988 Retail Supermarket and WTC Stores.

Source: JDH Annual Reports.

visiting or transiting through Hong Kong shopped for their families and friends back home due to the city's reputation of choice and quality reliability.

After 4 years of learning the Mainland ropes, ASW made a strategic move to open more PNS supermarkets in the Mainland. The seasoned retail leadership team put together by Wade was able to turn around ASW with speed and style in one full stroke. It opened many outlets in strategic high-street locations with foot traffic, instead of only focusing on affluent but quiet neighbourhoods.

With successful branding targeting the middle-class baby-boomer generation, ASW's health and beauty retail arm, WTC retail outlets, rapidly grew from 5 in 1981 to 75 in 1988 and became the Number 1 health and beauty chain in Hong Kong.

Endnotes

[1]HWL was embarking on a growth strategy of which the retail sector was chosen as one of its pillars of investment.

[2]Preamble to the Laws: Spirit of Cricket, Laws of Cricket, Marylebone Cricket Club, London. Accessed November 15, 2019. https://www.lords.org/mcc/laws/preamble-to-the-laws-spirit-of-cricket.

[3]Political, Economic, Social, and Technological (PEST) analysis and Strengths, Weaknesses, Opportunities, and Threats (SWOT) analysis are management tools employed by many business organisations to assess the health of the business sector and if the organisation was on track with the market changes.

[4]The Chinese word "eight" sounds phonetically the same as "prosperity". Hence, the "ASW Eight Strategies of Success" were simply dubbed as "ASW's Prosperity Strategies".

[5]Raymond, Li, Banking Problems: Hong Kong's Experience in the 1980s, Bank for International Settlements, Monetary and Economic Department, 1999: 130. https://www.bis.org/publ/plcy06d.pdf.

[6]Many held the view at the time that Hong Kong would replicate what had happened in Shanghai when the Chinese Communist Party came into power in October 1949.

[7]Shenzhen, across the Lowu bridge opposite Hong Kong, was established as Mainland's first Special Economic Zone in 1980 which offered tax-free incentives for overseas investors to set up manufacturing base there. In the same year, China adopted a dual currency system with the Bank of China responsible for the issuance of Foreign Exchange Certificates (FECs), based on its foreign currency reserve held by its treasury. *Renminbi* (RMB), the official currency was issued by the People's Bank of China (PBOC).

[8]SPNS was a breakthrough as almost all JVs at the time were equity, manufacturing oriented with an emphasis on technology transfer for industrial products or machinery. The expatriate community could only use FECs for shopping for imported goods at the state-owned Friendship Stores, restaurants, hotels, and now at the Sekou PNS Supermarket Ltd. The Bank of China abolished the FECs and merged with the Chinese currency in 1994.

[9]The National Geographic, *Formosa the Beautiful*, The National Geographic Society, Washington DC, March 1920.

[10]"Urgent Supply of Opium Cessation Remedies", *Taiwan News Daily*, April 3, 1897 (30th Year of Meiji Era): 1.

[11]"Chi Kan Express", *Taiwan News Daily*, March 3, 1926 (15th Year of Taisho Era), p. 4.

[12]"A.S. Watson Won the Trade Mark Infringement Law Suit", *Taiwan News Daily*, May 13, 1934 (9th Year of Showa Era).

[13]"Shennong's Pharmacy", *Taiwan News Daily*, July 15, 1927 (2nd Year of Showa Era), p. 4.

[14]"Opening of ASW in Taipei, Hong Kong Chain Shop Entering Taiwan", *Wealth Magazine*, Taipei, July 1987 (76th Year of the Republic of China), p. 280–281.

[15]Personal interview of Rodney Miles, November 26, 2019.

[16]"Making It In Taiwan", *Taiwan Today*, March 1, 1990. https://taiwantoday.tw/news.php?post=13126&unit=8,29,32,45.

[17]When President Chiang Ching-Kuo of the Republic of China Government in Taiwan declared the end of martial law on July 15, 1987, foreign exchange controls and trade restrictions for a mandatory local joint-venture partner were eased immediately.

[18]"Price Reduction of Antiseptic Soap from Yuan 120 to 65 Day After Tomorrow", News in Focus Section, *United Daily News*, Taipei, December 18, 1988 (77th Year of the Republic of China), p. 3.

[19]The price difference was due to the mandatory requirement that imported products were only to be sourced from the official distributor who marked up the products along with the high import duty and value-added tax in Taiwan. ASW sourced directly from the manufacturer, Rickett & Colman without any mark up by a distributor or customs duty and retail sales tax.

[20]According to legend, Singapura — derived from the words "Singa" for Lion and "Pura" for City — was named by Sang Nila Utama, Emperor of the Siriyavan Empire, as the new capital when he and his royal party landed on the island of Temasek ("sea town" in Javanese) in 1299.

[21]Dennis Casey was the deputy managing director of Underwoods Department Store in the UK before he joined WTC in early 1988.

[22]The public perceived Watsons as a trendsetter in Singapore's retail health and beauty market. Watsons shop front design, the layout, and the kind of products it carried were a breath of fresh air to the *Lion City*'s young consumers. Watsons opened eight stores to serve *Singapura*'s urbanites within the first full year.

[23]Macau was the first European settlement in China which the Portuguese leased the territory as a trading post from the Ming government in 1557. From 1848 to 1873, Portuguese Macau was a hub for transshipment of contract labourers from Southern provinces of China to the British colonies in Australia, the Caribean Islands, Malaya and Singapore, and the Dutch Indies of Indonesia and as far as Cuba, North and South America.

[24]In 1987, Macau's population reached 300,000 and tens of thousands out-of-town tourists; in particular those from Hong Kong flocked to Macau for their regular mid-week and weekend gaming visits.

Chapter 5

1989–1998: Overheating Economy

The Asian Economic Crisis

Back to Beijing — The Second Stop in the Mainland

After almost 90 years of absence from Beijing since the Boxers or the "Righteous and Harmonious Fists" burnt down ASW's retail chemist in the summer of 1901, WTC returned to the capital with the opening of a retail health and beauty shop in The Palace Hotel on May 30, 1989.[1]

Wade's decision to open a WTC store in Beijing's high-end hotel was a visionary chess move. Its targeted customers were visiting business executives and a small but burgeoning circle of well-off local families. The WTC store was inaugurated by Wade 4 days before the Tiananmen Square Incident on June 4, 1989.[2] It was closed briefly, but later reopened once business executives returned to the hotel a few weeks later.

Rodney Miles was designated as the project manager to oversee logistics and ensure regular shipments could be delivered to the Beijing WTC store with clearance by the State Customs Administration without delay.[3] Miles recalled the decision to open the first WTC store in Beijing instead of other cities:

> *It was a rare opportunity to build Watson's brand as a modern, premium, health and beauty store in the Mainland. Both Ian Wade, the managing director of ASW, and Simon Murray, the managing director of HWL, were all very aggressive in overseas expansion. Watson's Beijing flagship store was positioned as a leader in this sector.*[4]

The WTC store in Beijing became ASW's business model in the Mainland with rental being based on a percentage of sales generated from the shop. This financial arrangement minimised the recurrent expenditure of running a retail business in a new and uncertain market.

Step-Up Investment in the Mainland

In the second half of 1989, ASW accelerated its regional expansion strategy by focusing on Singapore and Taiwan. It was also taking a cautiously optimistic approach to the retail market in the Mainland. HWL's 1989 consolidated financial statement showed that corporate results from sales and profits after tax reached figures of HK$17,685 million and HK$4,105 million, respectively.

In HWL's 1989 annual report, the Trading and Other Services Division, which included ASW, contributed HK$10,089 million and HK$1,050 million or 57% and 25.6% in revenue and profit after tax, respectively. HWL's Hong Kong market contributed 90.8% in sales and 87.4% in profit after tax to HWL's 1989 performance.[5]

The over-reliance on Hong Kong as the single source of income was a genuine concern of any established and publicly listed company.[6] It might seem ironic that while HWL was aggressively seeking opportunities to invest in Southeast Asia after the 1989 Tiananmen Square Incident, it was also at the same time stepping up its investments in the Mainland. In fact, the group stepped up its investments in the Mainland soon after Jiang Zemin, the Party Secretary of Shanghai, was elected as the General Secretary at the Fourth Plenary Session of the 13th Central Committee of the Communist Party of China on June 24, 1989.

In the second half of 1989, the property market in the tier one cities of Beijing, Shanghai, and Guangzhou dropped to its lowest point. To revitalise the stagnant economy and regain investors' confidence from Hong Kong and Taiwan, the central government, led by General Secretary Jiang, empowered the municipal governments in Beijing and Shanghai to provide attractive incentives to selective investors such as HWL to develop commercial and residential properties in prime locations. Simultaneously, investment-inducing measures such as tax incentives were on offer to attract businesses from Hong Kong, Taiwan, and Southeast Asia. ASW followed all these closely. After all, it had many new products to roll out — from thirst-quenching water to sumptuous ice cream.

W's Star Products — Distilled Water and Mountain Cream®

Indeed, water and ice cream were ASW's star products for the Mainland. ASW first launched its brand of soda water in 1876. The supply of potable water by the public works was still at its infancy at the beginning of the 20th century in Colonial Hong Kong. When ASW's North Point production site was ready for use, the Watson's Water brand was marketed in 1904 in direct response to increasing demand for clean drinking water from inhabitants living in the newly leased Kowloon and New Territories.[7]

Much later, they acquired the Finland Ice Cream brand and the industrial site in Kwun Tong in August 1973. This marked ASW's entry into the frozen food manufacturing business to extend the horizontal integration of its PNS retail business.

A notable turn in this success story occurred when Dr I.A. Jagtiani, a manufacturing chemist, became the Director of Food at ASW in 1980. He began to develop a business strategy for ASW and picked distilled water and Mountain Cream ice cream as the dual "Star" products to sustain its profitability into the 21st century.

Jagtiani further grew the Watsons Water brand as a "cool, sporty and trendy" thirst-quenching refreshment. He did so by reaching out to the mass market with students and sports enthusiasts as immediate supporters. Inspired by Wade, Jagtiani achieved this through aggressive marketing and sponsorship of the annual Hong Kong Tennis Open and the Macau Grand Prix motor racing events in 1985. He used the same channels for the Mountain Cream brand of ice cream by covering the corner shops, school canteens, and supermarkets.[8] With its extensive distribution channels, ASW became the distributor of Dreyers, a premium brand of ice cream, for Hong Kong and the Mainland market in 1985. ASW also built a plant in Guangzhou and a sales network in Southern China in the late 1980s.

After a decade of success in Hong Kong, ASW evaluated the beverages market and prepared its entry into the UK's water segment as its first port of call in its globalisation journey. The "Powwow" brand was developed in September 1998, and a year later ASW embarked on an ambitious acquisition plan to establish its foothold in the UK's mineral water segment (see Chapter 6). The momentum was electrifying — literally.

Fortress — Electrical and Electronics Retailing

The Fortress Group was a local electrical and electronics retailer founded in 1975 by Hong Kong Electric (HKE), one of the two monopolies in Hong Kong's electricity supply. In 1983, Jardine Matheson sold HKE to HWL, and in 1991, Fortress was sold internally by HKE to ASW.[9] This enabled the company to enrich its retail portfolio in preparation for future corporate manoeuvres (Figure 1). In the same year, Fortress's flagship store opened in the newly completed shopping mall at the Whampoa Garden, the huge residential project developed at the former Whampoa Dockyards by HWL. The Fortress Whampoa Garden store had a catchment market of 10,000 apartments or 40,000 residents. The shop was the first electronic and electrical appliance store to offer a one-stop shop for branded products. The latter covered the full range of audio-visual and home entertainment equipment, mobile phones, and telecommunication equipment, cameras and computing, plus home and kitchen appliances.

Besides bulk-purchasing of white goods from leading multinational brands, Fortress also introduced its value strategy with private label brands for fast-moving regular and seasonal electrical appliances. Its sales representatives were better trained and could provide sound advice to consumers who opted for quality service in their purchase experience, such as for air conditioners, electrical fans, heaters, and humidifiers.

Given its recent success in Hong Kong and WTC's success in Taiwan since 1988, Fortress entered the Taiwan market in 1998 and promptly opened three shops. But it soon found out that the Taiwanese market was not one where Fortress could build a sustainable and profitable business. The challenge was that there were local retailers aplenty who worked on low single-digit profitability, and Fortress was not in a competitive position to attract the price-conscious families. Additionally, the tens of thousands of "mom and pop" electrical appliance shopkeepers served their neighbourhood with a "seven-eleven" opening schedule. And, unlike Hong Kong buyers, cost-conscious consumers in Taiwan (in particular working homemakers with a family to support) had a much higher

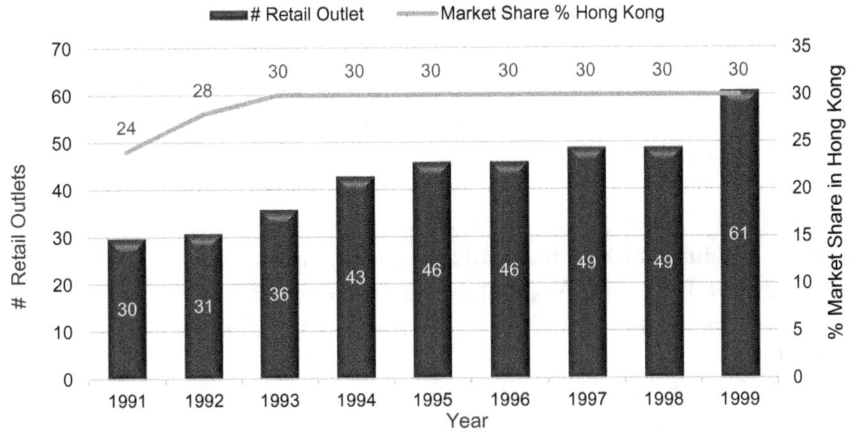

Figure 1. Fortress Retail Outlets and Market Share in Hong Kong, 1991–1999.

Source: HWL Annual Reports.

tendency to send their broken old models of electrical appliances for repair instead of buying new, premium quality, imported brands from Fortress. The company did not stay long and returned home with ample insights into the true needs of Taiwanese consumers. Yet, this did not prevent ASW from maintaining an appetite and vision for more global expansion.

Expansion in the South Sea Markets

ASW had first exported its opium substitutes, soda water, and proprietary medicines to Southeast Asia in the late 19th century for consumption by Chinese labourers in their hundreds of thousands who had been working in tin mines and plantation fields since the mid-18th century.

When the Korean War ended in 1953, ASW began to invest in Malaysia and formed a local joint venture to manufacture soda water and generic pharmaceuticals. The business did not take off due to the communist insurgency in the mid-1950s. However, ASW resumed its pharmaceutical agency business in the mid-1970s to distribute imported ethical pharmaceutical products.

Once again, the local company was too small to justify meaningful corporate management time and, in 1980, ASW sold the business to Sime

Darby Bhd. Following this, ASW opened its first retail health and beauty store in Singapore in 1988 and later on in Johor Bahru, the state capital of Johor across Singapore's Causeway, as soon as it achieved profitability in the Lion City in early 1994. Spurring on, ASW opened three more WTC stores within a year (Figure 2).

The expansion in Malaysia was full of challenges as there were strong local players, namely the Apex Pharmacy (Apex) and the Guardian Pharmacy (Guardian) chains of dispensing chemists.[10]

But after 3 years, 29 WTC stores had been opened across the country, becoming the leading retail brand with Apex and the Guardian shops trailing behind.

When the Asian economic crisis hit Malaysia in 1997, its economy dropped to rock bottom within a few months.[11,12] Cash flow soon became a problem for Apex Pharmacy, part of the Apex Health Care Bhd. Group. The owner struggled a few more years and eventually sold off its 20 retail pharmacies and 35 sales counters trading under the Apex brand to ASW for RM 12.2 million (HK$6.1 million) in May 2005. The government initially disapproved of the deal due to anti-trust concerns, and the

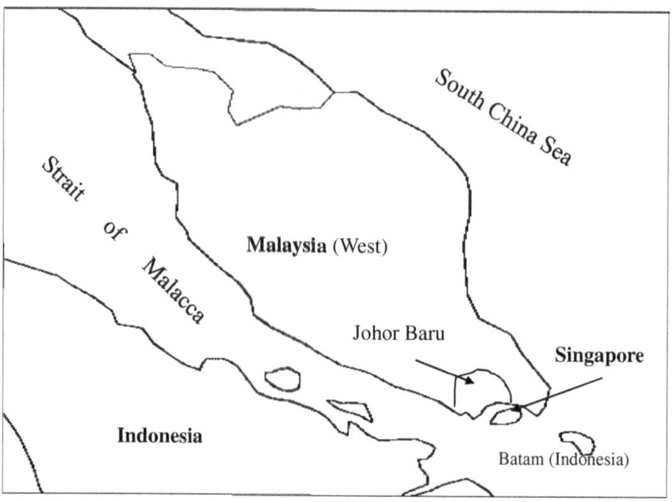

Figure 2. Johor State of Malaysia and Singapore.

Source: Author's Image Bank.

transaction did not materialise within the year. The majority of WTC retail outlets were opened in Malaysia's western part as it was more urban than the eastern states of Sabah and Sarawak on the island of Borneo.

Looking further at Southeast Asia in the 1990s, the Thai health care system was a hybrid of public and private medicine. Medical doctors worked at the public hospitals in the day-time, but moon-lighted out of their home clinics in the evenings. Daily wage workers could not wait for hours in the long queues at the public hospitals for a 15-minute out-patient consultation and then wait for another hour for the dispensed medications, but they could visit their neighbourhood clinics in the evenings with convenience. Retail pharmacies operated like a 19th-century apothecary at "seven–eleven" hours all year round. They supplied a wide range of remedies from antibiotics, lipid-lowering statins or steroid ointments for eczema or haemorrhoids to generic sildenafil citrate tablets to improve sexual function without the need of a physician's prescription. These retail pharmacies met the expectations of Thai families and workers at the time.

Seeing the growing middle-class families, with female college graduates entering the workforce *en masse*, PNS entered Thailand in 1990 with its first supermarket in Bangkok. After struggling for a year, PNS closed shop as Thai consumers preferred wet markets for their daily fresh supplies. The open, self-service, packaged, and frozen food concept was too early for the then up-and-coming middle class, as it had been in Hong Kong 20 years before. In short, the timing was not right.

But 1996 was a busy year in the Thai retail health and beauty market. Boots the Chemists (BTC) from the UK, the first foreign-owned pharmacy chain, opened its first retail store in Bangkok that year.[13] Six months later, ASW opened the first WTC retail store, also in Bangkok. It is interesting to note that the local joint venture partner of ASW and Boots was none other than the Chirathivat family of the Central Group.[14] They owned Central Retail Food (CRF) which operated the supermarkets and the Central Department Store chain (CDS). So, ASW's partner was CDS and BTC's partner was CRF — two sides of the same coin indeed.

In fact, WTC opened three stores in Bangkok alone in the first year. Of course, BTC and WTC were direct competitors — and the 1997 Asian economic crisis hit them hard. However, BTC and WTC stores were not in direct competition with the independent chemists whose income was instead based on counter-prescribing.

Asian Economic Crisis and the Change of Priority

From 1989 to 1998, the per capita GDP growth rate of Asian countries was in the range of 6–8% annually (Figures 3 and 4).[15] ASW's chain stores grew by leaps and bounds from 260 outlets in 1989 to 788 outlets at the end of 1998 — about three times across seven countries (Figures 5 and 6). In 1995, the number of WTC health and beauty retail outlets had exceeded PNS supermarkets in Asia. Taiwan had the highest growth figures, with 133 WTC retail drug stores by 1996. Meanwhile, Hong Kong boasted 82, and Singapore hosted 43.

But this boom came to a sudden stop on July 2, 1997. Southeast Asian financial systems had a shared weakness inherent in export driven economies. Commodities and industrial products with little or no domestic markets were very vulnerable. Their open market approach became easy prey to global hedge fund managers. Thailand was the first country to be raided by these ruthless global hedge fund managers. They drove down stocks' values, properties, and forex reserves in these markets unmercifully — almost overnight due to panic selling.[16,17]

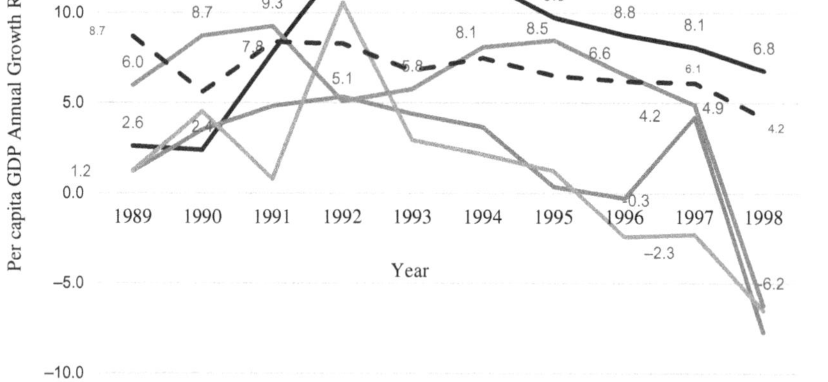

Figure 3. 1989–1998, Per Capita GDP Growth Rate of East Asian Markets (Annual %).

Source: The World Bank.

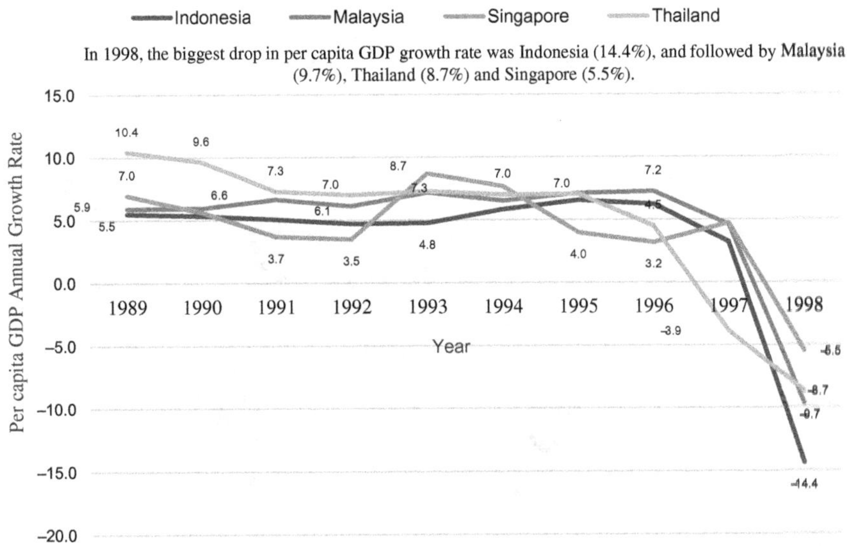

Figure 4. 1989–1998, per capita GDP Growth Rate of Southeast Asian Markets (Annual %).

Source: The World Bank.

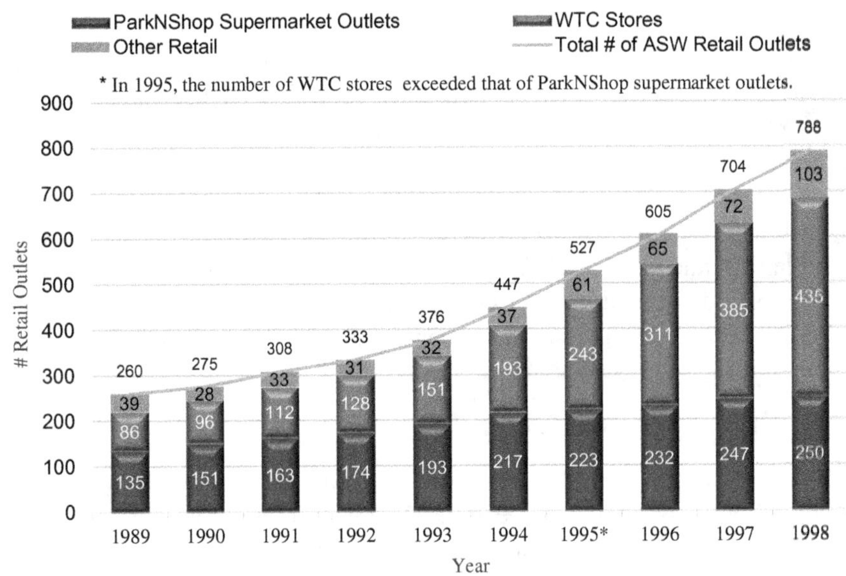

Figure 5. 1989–1998 ASW Stores by Sub-Category.

Source: HWL Annual Reports.

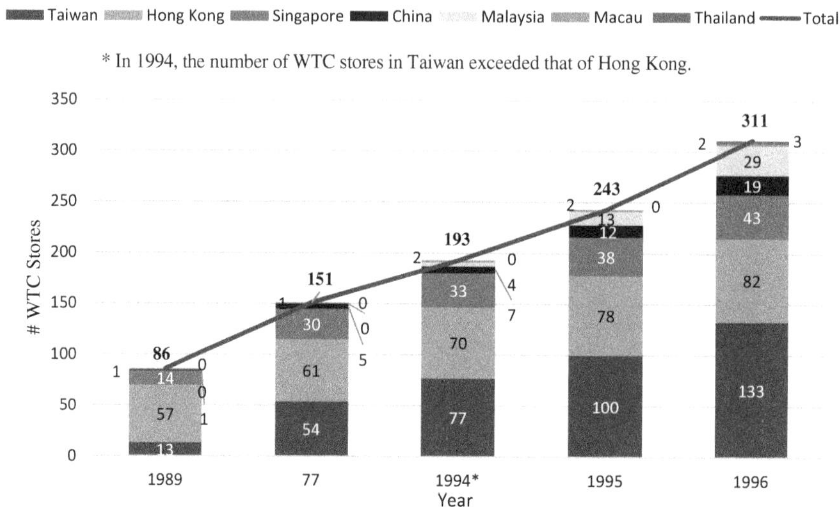

Figure 6. 1989–1996 WPC Stores Distribution by Country.

Source: HWL Annual Reports.

With a 20–35% drop in the forex, GDP per capita annual growth rate of nearly all countries and regions in Asia dropped into the negative range in 1998. This resulted in recession, and ASW faced a dramatic drop of 37% YOY in EBIT to HK$845 million in 1998 following the 1997 Asian economic crisis.[18,19] This was also the third time ASW had a substantial drop of profits following the "Black Saturday" forex crisis of 1983 and the Tiananmen Square Incident of 1989. Unlike ASEAN countries, the Mainland's and Taiwan's financial systems were "closed" to outside investors and their foreign currencies were not freely convertible in open markets. Hence, they were able to come out relatively unscathed.

The Roller Coaster Decade

Soon after the June 4, 1989 Tiananmen Square Incident in Beijing, Hong Kong's economy took a nose dive. Wade took initiatives to stabilise ASW's business and struck a balance between sustainable profit growth and weak sentiments as the public tightened their belts for the rough ride ahead. He gathered a working group to look at every business category and decisively embarked on a rationalisation exercise which brought the business back to solid ground within a year.

Wade and his leadership team further improved WTC's brand strategy, which saw profit margins doubling compared with original brands from Europe, Japan, and the US. The leap in gross profit margins set the tone for ASW's sustainable retail strategy in Asia with almost half of WTC's product portfolio comprising Watson's or private labels exclusively sourced for WTC stores. Between 1989 and 1998, ASW continued to expand with admirable margins. The company saw a whopping 203% increase in profits from its 788 retail outlets (increased from 260) over this period. At the same time, WTC outlets jumped from 33% to 55% in their share of total in the retail portfolio of HWL and brought in better profit margins for the retail and manufacturing division as a whole.

The return of the sovereignty of Hong Kong from the United Kingdom to China after 156 years of colonial rule on July 1, 1997 was a smooth one. ASW noted this well, also seeing opportunity to show a special Hong Kong brand to Europe. Soon after the Asian financial crisis, ASW set its eyes on England.

In 1999, ASW's waters department started its venture into the UK by building a new European brand, "Powwow". It would replicate Watsons Water's success in the office-delivery business in Hong Kong. ASW had been very successful in Hong Kong, setting the "Powwow" brand on course to become the "gold standard" beverage for office workers, students, and athletes. By 1998, HWL's Hong Kong's domestic market sales and EBIT contributions were reduced from 91% and 87%, respectively, to 57% and 70% representing a drop of 34% and 17%, respectively, from 1989 figures. Marching on, Wade's vision was to develop ASW's business with a geographical diversification strategy spanning 17 years to 2006; one-third of its contributions would come from each of China, Asia, and Europe. The strategy was ultimately prescient.

Endnotes

[1]The Palace Hotel was the first luxury hotel with a dozen high-end premium shops including the WTC, which was the only stylish health and beauty store that catered to the visiting business executives and the few privileged locals. Initially owned by the People's Liberation Army General Staff Department, later its shareholding was transferred to China Everbright Group, a state-owned enterprise, in

1999. The Peninsula Hotel Group (PHG) of Hong Kong assumed its management in 1996 and it was renamed as The Peninsula Beijing in 2006.

[2]The Tiananmen Square Incident was a short-lived student and labour movement in Beijing in the second quarter of 1989, which was ended on June 4, 1989.

[3]One railway cabin-load of health and beauty items was shipped from Hong Kong to Beijing monthly. Each shipment was required to be inspected by customs officers and border quarantine inspectors before delivery to the shop.

[4]Personal interview of Rodney Miles. November 26, 2019.

[5]In January 1990, HWL took the timely opportunity to wrap up the JD Hutchison sale to IPG which was estimated at HK$870 Million.

[6]In the absence of a public pension or retirement fund, shareholders of the major companies such as CPL, HWL, and HSBC consisted of any small investors who relied upon the annual dividends of their investee companies as the main source of their retirement income. Both Li and Taipan Murray decided that geographical diversification outside of Hong Kong was the top priority for HWL. This was also necessary to ease the concerns of small investors that the risks had been spread out evenly.

[7]The first impounding reservoir was constructed and put into use in 1910. https://www.wsd.gov.hk/en/about-us/our-milestone/index.html.

[8]Lo, York, *Finland, London and Swiss — 3 Ice Cream Brands from the 1960s*. April 13, 2018. https://industrialhistoryhk.org/finland-london-and-swiss-3-ice-cream-brands-from-the-1960s/.

[9]1980–1999, Economic Challenges, Business Repositioning, New Markets Exploration, *History of The Group*, Jardines CorporateWebsite. https://www.jardines.com/en/group/history.html.

[10]Both Apex and Guardian had good brand recognition after they opened in 1961 and 1968, respectively.

[11]The Malaysian currency halved and its stock market dropped by 60% when global hedge fund managers short-sold the Ringgit and its stocks. Malaysian economy eventually emerged from the crisis in 2004, almost 8 years later.

[12]Ariff, Mohammed *et al.*, The Malaysian Financial Crisis: Economic Impact and Financial Recovery, *The Developing Economies*, XXXVII4 (December 1999): 417–438. Accessed February 26, 2020. https://www.ide.go.jp/library/English/Publish/Periodicals/De/pdf/99_04_03.pdf.

[13]Boots is the largest pharmacy chain in the UK with over 2000 retail outlets in early 2022. It started off as a herbal shop opened by John Boots in Nottingham in 1848. In 2006, Boots merged with Alliance Unichem and was acquired by Walgreen in 2014 with a new corporate name as Walgreen Boots Alliance.

[14]The Central Group is owned by the Chirathivat family, whose ancestors migrated from Hainan Island, China to Bangkok in 1927.

[15]GDP per capita (current US$) — East Asia & Pacific, South Asia, Europe & Central Asia, Singapore, Hong Kong SAR, China, Malaysia, Thailand, China,

Data, The World Bank. https://data.worldbank.org/indicator/NY.GDP.PCAP.CD?view=chart.

[16]The Thai government was forced to float the baht due to lack of foreign currency to support its urgency peg to the U.S. dollar.

[17]Laplamwanit, N., *A Good Look at the Thai Financial Crisis*, Columbia University, New York. Accessed November 25, 2019. http://www.columbia.edu/cu/thai/html/financial97_98.html.

[18]The increase of 1 % or HK$92 million turnover in 1998 was primarily due to the opening of 55 new Watson's The Chemist retail stores in Asia.

[19]HWL and P&G established a 33:67 joint venture, Procter & Gamble — Hutchison Ltd., to produce household consumables in 1988 in Guangzhou, Mainland China. In 1997 and 1998, HWL sold 10% of its shareholding in P&G-H to a P&G subsidiary and the remaining 20% in 2004. The 1997 and 1998 EBIT of the retail, manufacturing, and services division had an exceptional profit of HK$ 1,430 million in 1997 and HK$ 3,322 million in 1998, which were excluded from the reported EBIT for both years.

Chapter 6

1999–2001: Y2K, SARS and Dual Springboards into the UK: Powwow and Savers

The New Millenium

While markets in China, Asia, and Europe were being fathomed by visionaries like Wade, the end of the 20th century presented unique challenges for ASW. The global hedge fund managers' sudden onslaught in Thailand had a cascading effect. This had set back economies in Southeast Asia by at least 3–5 years. Before the Asian economic crisis occurred on July 2, 1997, Thailand's GDP had hit heights of US$183 billion. These sky reaching figures dropped 38% in 1998 alone. Basically, it pushed the country back to 1992 GDP earnings of US$111 billion.[1]

Beyond China and Asia, ASW began to advance into Europe in the late 1990s. Following ASW's entry into the UK market in September 1999 with the customized Powwow water brand, it moved to acquire Savers Health and Beauty in July 2000.[2] (Figure 1) Soon after, Powwow and Savers served as dual springboards for ASW's ambitious globalization plans for continental Europe (Chapter 7).

The "Y2K Millennial Bug" situation temporarily boosted the global economy for this expansion, ironically enough.[3] Per capita GDP growth rates saw global markets increase year on year in 2000: East Asia at 2.6%–8.2%, Southeast Asia at 2.2%–7.2%, Western Europe at 3.0%–4.2%, and 4.2%–4.6% in Eastern Europe. This was short lived, but notable for businesses internationally.[4]

Figure 1. Savers Discount Drug Store, W12 Shopping Centre London, One Busy Saturday afternoon in September 2010. Savers was the first health and beauty retail chain acquired by ASW in 2000.

Source: Author's Image Bank.

These positive sentiments in 2000 soon disappeared. The global economy became negatively impacted by the spillover effects from the September 11, 2001 terrorist attack in New York City. GDP growth once again took a nosedive. However, HWL and ASW continued to grow, despite overall slowdowns between 1999 and 2001.

By 1999, HWL's revenue reached HK$72.4 billion and the retail, manufacturing, and others division of HWL brought in 1/3 (HK$23.8 billion) in revenue and 8% (HK$1.3 billion) in EBIT with a year-on-year growth rate of 10% and 56%, respectively — an astounding performance indeed (Figures 2 and 3).

In fact, the rather unusual name of "Powwow" was created by the advertising agency Wolff Olins. This brand was used for the mineral water business that ASW ultimately developed for the European market.[5,6] Within a year, a total of twelve companies that were bottlers of mineral

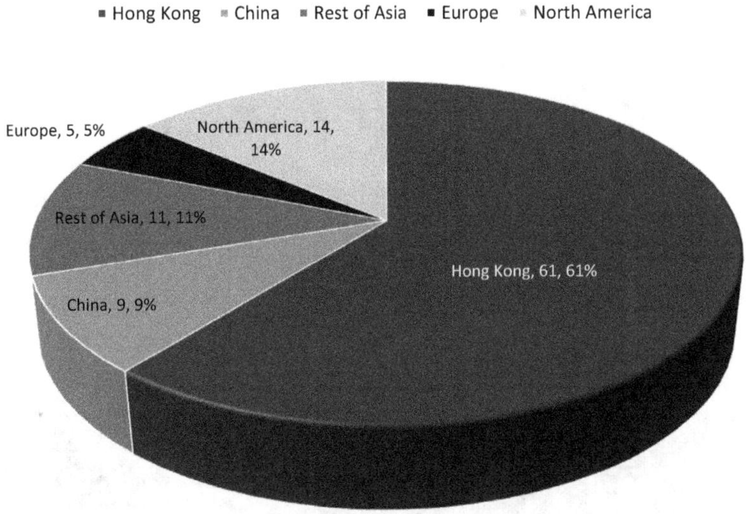

Figure 2. 1999 HWL Revenue at HK$ 72.4 billion — Geographical Region.

Source: HWL annual reports.

water, dispensers, and their ancillary equipment and supplies (including Braebourne Water) had been acquired by ASW.

A Springboard into the UK Market: Powwow

ASW's first manufactured aerated water in 1876. It has since been a leader in both the distilled water and aerated water market. In the early 1980s, ASW expanded its channel of distribution by launching the bottled and carboy water business (also known as home and office delivery or HOD) for delivery to homes, offices, schools, and sports centres under the leadership of the former director of food and manufacturing, Dr I.A. Jagtiani.

In the UK, there was little evidence of usage of pure water either commercially or domestically as the national drink was tea or coffee, and the situation was similar in many parts of Europe. Nevertheless, drawing from the success story in Hong Kong, Wade developed a water brand strategy in 1998 to enter the UK market over the ensuing 12 months. Watsons Water (UK) Holdings Ltd. (WWH) was incorporated in the UK

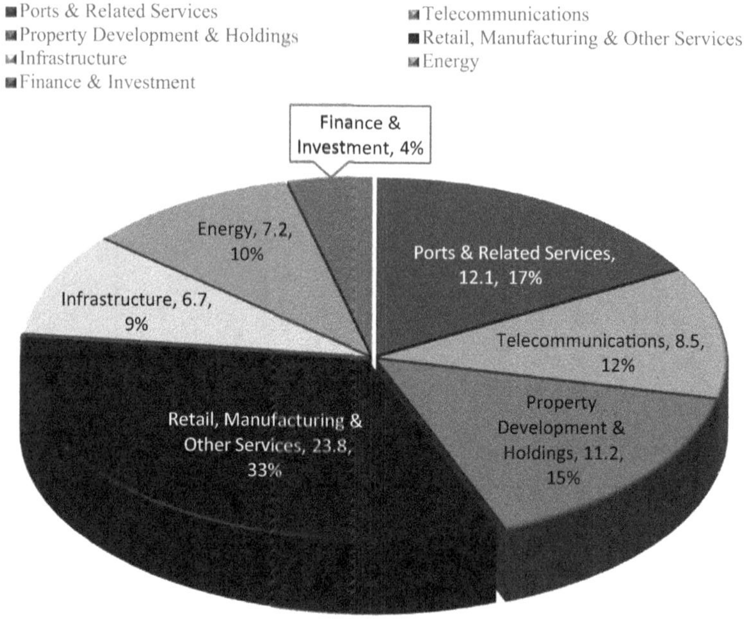

Figure 3. 1999 HWL Revenue at HK$ 72.4 Billion — Business Division.

Source: HWL Annual Reports.

in September 1998. Three directors, Ian Wade, Robert Finnigan, and P.H. Mak, were charged with the kick-off of this new intercontinental project.

ASW's local market survey showed that consumers and office workers would prefer mineral water as a "cool drink" rather than tea or coffee during their morning and afternoon break time. In the fourth quarter of 1998, the acquisitions of the Crystal Spring Water (CSW), a company specializing in bottled water based in Long Hansborough, Oxfordshire, and Braebourne Waters, a Midlands-based company, provided an immediate gain of 17% HOD market in the UK.

Finnagan, who was the financial director of ASW's manufacturing business in Hong Kong, was appointed as the chief executive officer of ASW Water (Europe) to oversee the launching of the HOD in the UK soon after the acquisition of CSW in 1998. This began a 4-year rapid growth and eventual exit of the HOD business (Figure 4).

Figure 4. Powwow Business Milestones.

This was done with a total investment of £46 million (or €73.6 million), with the first year's turnover at £21.6 million (€34.6 million) in 1999.[7,8] Other than the first full year in which Powwow recorded a loss of £700,000, the water business recorded £31.8 million and £2.5 million in revenues and EBIT in 2001 alone (Figure 5).

Within 3 years, the Powwow brand became an industry leader in Europe and in 2002, sales were recorded at £78.2 million (€120 million). It boasted 1,500 employees in seven countries: Denmark, France, Germany, Italy, the Netherlands, Portugal, and the UK. The latter alone contributed £35.5 million (€55.4 million) which was equivalent to 46% of Powwow's total turnover. However, it took a few more years to grow this water business into absolute levels of profitability (Chapter 7).

A Second Springboard into the UK: Savers Discount Drugstores

Savers was founded by Richard Tonks in Durham in December 1987 as a discount store of toiletries and family medicines under the general sales list — which did not require the presence of a pharmacist. Tonks secured

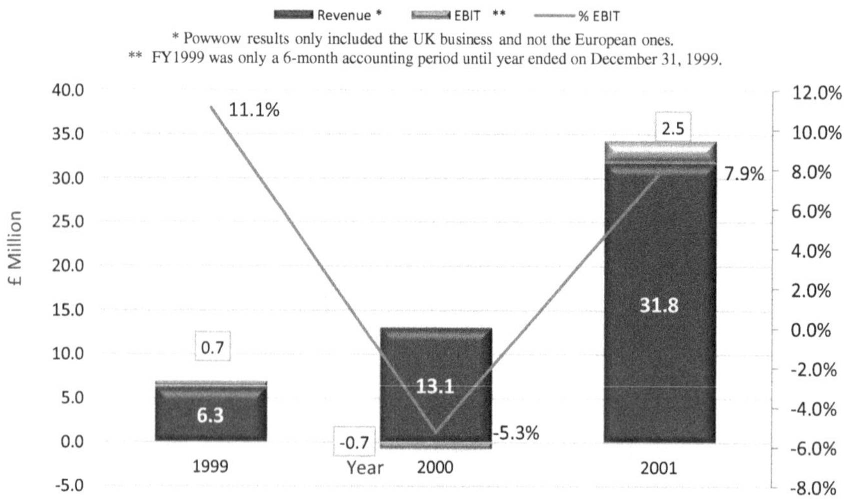

Figure 5. 1999–2002 Powwow Ltd. UK business performance.

Source: Powwow Ltd. Directors' Report and Financial Statement.

a total of £150,000 in investments from venture capitalists.[9,10] Savers' target customers were mainly in second and third-tier cities in North England.

In January 2000, Savers acquired the 115 Supersave discount drugstores under the Llyods Chemists of the GEHE UK Limited ("GEHE") for £5.4 million, or £47,000 per store.[11] A new distribution centre was opened simultaneously in Darlington, just 37 km from Durham, at the end of January 2000 as they had to cope with a more extensive distribution volume (Figure 6). The gambit paid off. Savers' fiscal year 2000 turnovers and EBIT were £51.5 million and £5.1 million, with a year-on-year increase of 71% and 173%. Overall, year-on-year EBIT percentages also increased from 6.2% to 10%. By May 27, 2000, Savers had grown into a 125-store chain with 41 existing outlets,

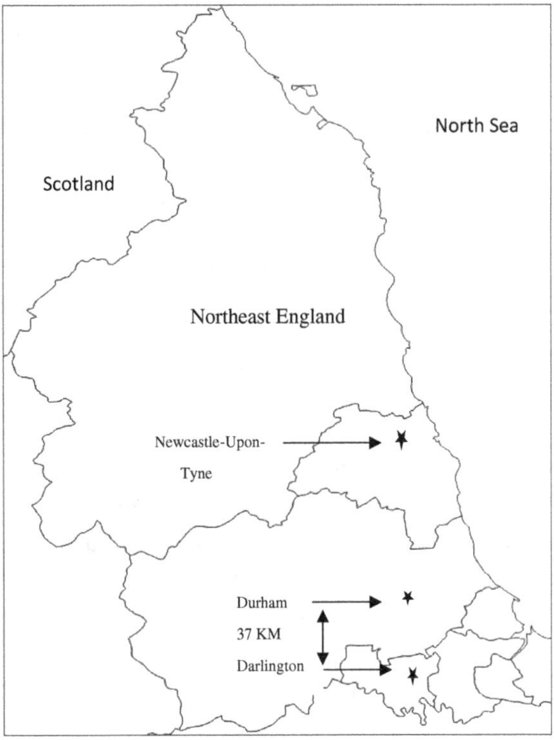

Figure 6. Savers's Durham Headquarters.

Source: Author's Image Bank.

plus 23 new shops together with 61 completed conversions of Supersave stores acquired from GEHE. This enviable uptick was due to the economy of scale and gross margin improvements in volume discounts from suppliers.[12,13,14] Mr Michael Ward (chief executive, GEHE UK) said:

> *Over the past two years, considerable time and effort has been invested in Supersave and this has improved the business performance of the stores. The decision to sell the Supersave outlets enables us to focus our core pharmacy business.*[15]

In September 2000, 165 Savers stores were sold to ASW for an undisclosed sum. It has been estimated that the purchase price of Savers was £23.7 million.[16] Savers was described in the WatsOn as follows:

> *Its deep discount format accentuated by simple store design, strong logistics and low operating cost, were in sync with the existing values of ASW providing added incentive for its acquisition. Savers' focus on fast-moving toiletries products has struck a chord within the marketplace, spurring significant growth in store numbers over the past two years.*[17]

A war chest to acquire Savers was provided by HWL to accelerate its globalization plans in the retail non-food segment in the UK and Europe at the turn of the 21st century. HWL's divestment of the 44.81% stake in the Orange telecommunication business in the UK to Mannesmann AG of Gery in October 1999 also brought windfalls — to the tune of HK$113 billion (US$14.6 billion).[18]

When the Savers opportunity knocked on Wade's door in 2000, he acted decisively. Wade also utilized the "Y2K Millennial Bug" market uncertainty situation in Europe to ASW's advantage in the negotiations for Savers.

With deft persuasion and proper figures, Wade convinced Canning Fok, Group Managing Director of HWL who succeeded Murray in 1993, of the merits of doing so. With Li's blessing, ASW snapped up Savers in October 2000. This daring and bold move was the beginning of a series of mostly successful acquisitions by Wade in the following 6 years that defined ASW's top three position in the global retail drugstore segment. As most of ASW's top management had solid experience in the British retail sector as well as Hong Kong or Asia during their time with WTC, it was a relatively level playing field for ASW in the UK. This was a better move than entering the health and beauty sector in a totally foreign terrain with costly learning by trial and error. Since the acquisition by ASW in late 2000, the business strategy of Savers was based on three principal drivers as follows:[19]

- Store locations in secondary sites with lower rents.
- Prices of branded products significantly below the competition.
- High store standards providing a convenient, enjoyable experience.

As the story goes, Richard Tonks, managing director of Savers, continued his position for two more years by integrating the Supersave drugstores and working closely with Philip Ingham, the managing director of ASW Health & Beauty (UK). The latter was appointed in August 2000 to oversee the transition of Savers into the ASW group. It was a heady time.

During the first year after ASW's acquisition, it was a mixed bag with only 7 months of sales recorded. However, its turnover and profit growth became significant if extrapolated for 12 months. In the UK, the "Y2K Millennial Bug" hype disappeared quickly. This was followed by a slowdown in economy with Y-O-Y per capita GDP growth dropping from 3.4% to 2.8%. Besides that, rental costs and wages also went up above inflation ceilings. This exerted pressure on revenues and margins for Savers and resulted in a flat revenue and a drop of EBIT. It was as frosty as the Mountain Cream ice cream they sold, but hardly as sweet.

Divestment of Non-Core Business: Mountain Cream

Of course, the Mountain Cream brand was about to be sold off. ASW's entry into the frozen food manufacturing business was through the acquisition of Finland Ice Cream Limited, a Hong Kong-based manufacturer founded in 1973. Its assets included the 10,400 square-foot plant in Kowloon. ASW developed the Mountain Cream brand in 1980 to gain a larger market share in Hong Kong as the Dairy Farm Company had dominated the ice cream market for close to a century. Through the same distribution channels, ASW became the key importer and distributor of Dreyers, a premium brand of ice cream, for the Hong Kong and Mainland markets in 1985.[20] This product positioning strategy replicated what ASW did in 1927 when it became the bottler of Coca Cola® while marketing its cola brand in the Hong Kong, Shanghai and Guangzhou markets.

Wall's, a subsidiary of Unilever's Anglo-Dutch group, established its China ice cream business and a distribution network across 70 cities, mostly in central and northern provinces in 1994. ASW's ice cream business was a strategic fit for Wall's position to become the China leader when the Unilever Group acquired it in January 1999.[21] The economy of scale made the merger much more efficient when dealing with global brands like Nestle or Haagen-Dazs.[22] The timing for ASW to divest itself of the Mountain Cream brand was excellent. After all, ASW's strategic plan was to become a global company by focusing on its core businesses — the retail health and beauty sector and the HOD water business. So the Mountain Cream ice cream brand was sold to Unilever for US$95 million, and it was mentioned briefly in the 1999 HWL Annual Report that:

> *During the year, the manufacturing division disposed of its ice cream businesses in Hong Kong and the Mainland profitably.*[23]

Endnotes

[1]GDP current data, Thailand. The World Bank. https://data.worldbank.org/indicator/NY.GDP.MKTP.CD?locations=TH.

[2]In 2000, Savers was a chain of 173 discount drug stores with its headquarters based in County Durham, Northeast England.

[3]"The Y2K Millennial Bug" otherwise known as the Y2K (Year 2000) problem was a widely held assumption that a 20th-century date in common computer programmes could cause various errors, such as the incorrect display of dates and the inaccurate ordering of automated dated records or real-time events which had never arisen.

[4]GDP per capita (annual growth %). The World Bank. https://data.worldbank.org/indicator/NY.GDP.PCAP.CD.

[5]Knapp, Pat Morrison, Powwow, a water cooler company which introduces fresh new business approach, Designing corporate identity: graphic design as a business strategy, Rockport, 2001:102–105.

[6]The Orange brand created by Wolf was the second mobile telephone operator HWL invested in the UK in 1991 after HWL's first telecom venture of Rabbit failed due to licensing issues. Orange was acquired for US$33 billion by the German industrial cum telecom giant, Mannesmann AG, in October 1999.

[7]The Crystal Water Company Limited. Accounts for the year ended April 30, 1999. Companies House, London. https://find-and-update.company-information.service.gov.uk/company/02334804/filing-history?page=2.

[8]Exchange rate of £1 = €1.6 on December 30, 1999. https://www.poundsterlinglive.com/bank-of-england-spot.

[9]Prior to the setup of Savers, Richard Tonks was the operations director of Tip Top discounted chemist chain.

[10]"Tip Top in franchise move", Chemist & Druggist, London, August 1, 1987:231. https://archive.org/details/b19974760M5820.

[11]Savers Health and Beauty Plc., Directors' report & financial statements, register number 2202383, May 27, 2000:1, 5, 8, 19. https://find-and-update.company-information.service.gov.uk/company/02202838/filing-history.

[12]Overview, 1999 Gehe annual report: 61. www.Mckesson.eu.

[13]*Ibid.* (Note 11).

[14]Llyods Chemists Limited, Directors' report and financial statements registered number 1335858, December 31, 2000:5, 8. https://find-and-update.company-information.service.gov.uk/company/01335858/filing-history.

[15]Llyods sells 115 Supersave drugstores. The Pharmaceutical Journal, January 15, 2000.

[16]An estimation of 10-time multiple of Savers 1999's EBIT of £1.85 or £18.5 million plus the £5.2 million purchase price of Supersave at a total of £23.7 million.

[17]ASW health and beauty stores — Worldwide, WatsOn, No. 55, April 2002, ASW:15. https://www.aswatson.com/wp-content/uploads/2021/06/55-watsON-e.pdf.

[18]*Hutchison Whampoa accepts offer for its 44.81% stake in Orange Plc. from Mannesmann AG for HK$ 113 billion in cash, notes, and shares*. Press Release, CK Hutchison Ltd., October 21, 1999. https://www.ckh.com.hk/en/media/press_each.php?id=8.

[19]Savers Health and Beauty Limited, Annual report for the year ended December 31, 2006. (Note 11).

[20]ASW had also established an ice cream plant in Guangzhou and a sales network in the Southern provinces in the late 1980s.

[21]Unilever to acquire Chinese ice cream business, Food Online, January 19, 1999. https://www.foodonline.com/doc/unilever-to-acquire-chinese-ice-cream-busines-0001.

[22]ASW and Wall's ice cream businesses were complementary in terms of pricing, product range, geographical coverage, manufacturing capability, and channels of distribution.

[23]Operations review, retail, manufacturing and other service, 1999 HWL report. https://doc.irasia.com/listco/hk/hutchison/annual/99/review.pdf.

Chapter 7

2002–2003: A Quantum Leap for the Continent

Kruidvat, Superdrug

A Rare Opportunity to Enter Europe, 2002

It was August 2002, ASW was preparing for superb market penetration into Europe. That sultry month, ASW took over the Krudivat Group in continental Europe. This made ASW the most significant revenue contributor within HWL's direct investment portfolio, contributing 43% in revenue. The Kruidvat Group at that time held a handful of directly owned and managed retail brands. These included ICI Paris XL, Kruidvat, and Trekpiester in the Benelux countries, and Superdrug in the UK with a total of 1493 stores (Figure 1) The Kruidvat Group was also a 40% owner of Dirk Rossmann GmbH (DRG) in Germany, which owned drug stores in Germany as well as 324 stores with operations in Poland, Hungry, and the Czech Republic.

Jacobus Cornelis (Co) de Rijcke lived from 1924 to 1997. He was married to Dini Maria (1936–2019), the daughter of Willem Groenwoudt. In 1927, Groenwoudt started the first supermarket in Bussum, a municipality in the southeast of the province of North Holland in the Netherlands. When Groenwoudt retired in the 1950s, Co de Rijicke took over the management of eight Groenwoudt supermarkets. Over the course of the next 40 years, Co de Rijicke grew Groenwoudt into a chain of a few hundred stores through the acquisition of many regional chains, such as De Ru, Minten, and Beerkens and the Nieuwe Weme chain of supermarkets.

Figure 1. Kruidvat Group's Retail Health and Beauty Brands: ICI Paris XL, Kruidvat, Superdrug in the UK, and Trepleister in the Benelux. The acquisition of the Kruidvat Group was a strategic one which put ASW in the league of CVS, Alliance Boots and Walgreen as a global health and beauty chain.

Source: Author's Image Bank.

With Dick Siebrandt, Co de Rijcke opened the first Kruidvat discount drug store in Bussum in 1975 with the advertising slogan "Always Surprising, Always Inexpensive". By 1983, it grew into a 100-store chain across the Netherlands (Figure 2). The Kruidvat Group opened the first branch outside of the Netherlands in Belgium in 1992. Four years later in 1996, Kruidvat acquired the Belgian ICI Paris XL perfumery chain (Figure 3).

Co de Rijicke passed away suddenly on May 1, 1997, without an immediate successor as his only son, Pieter Willem, was only 21. The De

Figure 2. 1st Kruidvat, and Trekpleister Stores, Netherlands.

Source: Author's Image Bank.

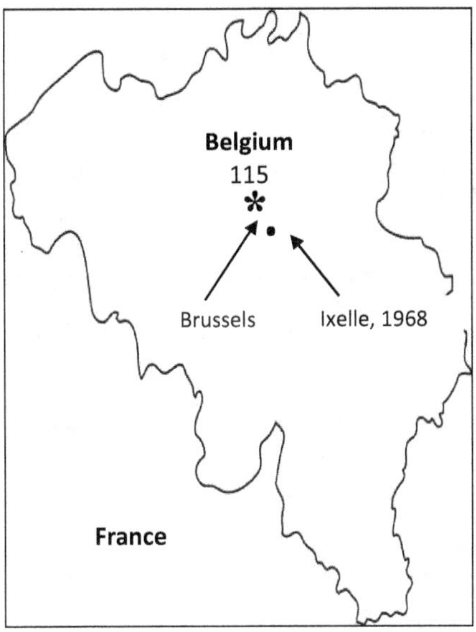

Figure 3. 1st ICI Paris XL Shop, Ixelle, Belgium.

Source: Author's Image Bank.

Rijicke family soon hired Dick van Hedel, previously a senior executive at Nutricia, as the Groenwoudt Group president in July 1997.[1]

After acquiring the Trekpleister Drug Store Chain in early 1998, the Groenwoudt Group became the leading drug store chain with a combined market share of 38% in the Netherlands. Van Hedel held a strategic view that the drug store business would be more sustainable and profitable than the supermarket business in the 21st century. His recommendations to the De Rijicke family were well accepted.

This sage advice led to the Groenwoudt Group's 2000 sale to the Laurus Group — the product of the De Boer Unigro and Vendex Food Group merger. With ample cash on hand after the supermarket business' disposal, the Groenwoudt Group changed its name to Kruidvat. It started to focus on the health and beauty business in both continental Europe and the UK (Figure 4) and soon acquired the Superdrug chain from Kingfisher Plc. (previously called Woolworths). In July 2001, however, it became apparent that the heir-apparent Pieter Willem was not keen to take over the Krudivat Group anytime soon.

1974–1975	• Dick Siebrand was the first employee to help Co de Rijicke in opening the first Krudivat Drug Store with classical music CDs placed next to the shelves of Bayer@ Aspirin.
1983	• The Krudivat business model grew to a 100 neighbourhood drug stores in the Netherlands after 8 years in operation.
1992	• First Krudivat Drug Store in Belgium.
1996	• 50:50 joint venture with Dirk Rossmann GmbH of Germany to expand in Central European countries of Poland, Hungry, and the Czech Republic. • The Belgium-based ICI Paris XL *(This is Paris!)* perfumery chain was acquired by the Krudivat Group.
1997	• Co de Rijicke, founder and chairman of Krudivat, passed away in May. • Van Hedel joined as president of Groenwoudt Group in July.
1998	• Acquisition of 175 Trekpleister stores and 1,600 employees in the Netherlands.
2000	• After disposal of the supermarket business, the Groenwoudt Group changed its name to the Krudivat Group.
2001	• Acquisition of 700 Superdrug stores at £252 million in the UK in October.
2002	• Sale of Krudivat Group of 1900 stores at £1.3 billion to ASW in August.

Figure 4. Chronological Events of the Krudivat Group.

Source: HWL Annual Reports, Media Reports, WatsOn etc.

Kruidvat's Milestones — Watsons the Competitor Becomes the Owner

Over the course of 28 years between 1974 and 2002, the Kruidvat discount drug stores grew from a single shop to over 1,800 retail outlets across continental Europe (Figure 4). After the merger with ASW, the consolidated group became a leading global health and beauty chain, amongst CVS, Walgreen, Alliance Boots.

News of ASW's acquisition of Savers Health and Beauty in the UK in September 2000 was timely. Van Hedel soon briefed the De Rijcke family on a robust Asian competitor that had landed at the backdoor of Europe. Van Hedel received the family's instructions to explore if ASW would be interested in taking over the Kruidvat Group without restructuring its business. This would allow Kruidvat's business philosophy to continue its legacy in Europe despite the take-over.

And Wade knew this was a rare opportunity. He wisely saw this as a change for ASW to become a global health and beauty empire in a quantum leap without the risks of driving rapid growth of Savers in the UK. Also, ASW would not have to go through multiples of acquisitions in each of the major European markets in the following decade. It was truly a global chess piece move.

A Star in the Making — Superdrug

Superdrug Stores PLC. ("Superdrug Stores") was incorporated under the name of Leading Supermarkets Ltd. in 1964. It was acquired by the Goldstein brothers, Ronald and Peter, in February 1966 with the name changed to Superdrug Stores in May. The first Superdrug Stores outlet was opened in Putney, London, as a discount store of toiletries, general merchandise, and medicines (non-prescription and non-pharmacy type) for low-income groups.

With a low price and volume strategy, it grew rapidly with 300 stores by 1981. With increasing price competition from other discount chemist and drug stores, the Goldstein brothers decided to sell Superdrug Stores to Kingfisher at £256.9 million in 1987. Its 1986 financial performance showed £203 million in sales and £12.3 million in profits before tax, representing 26% and 23.5% YOY increase largely due to an increase of 43 stores out of 254 total stores and improvement in sales per store (Figure 5).

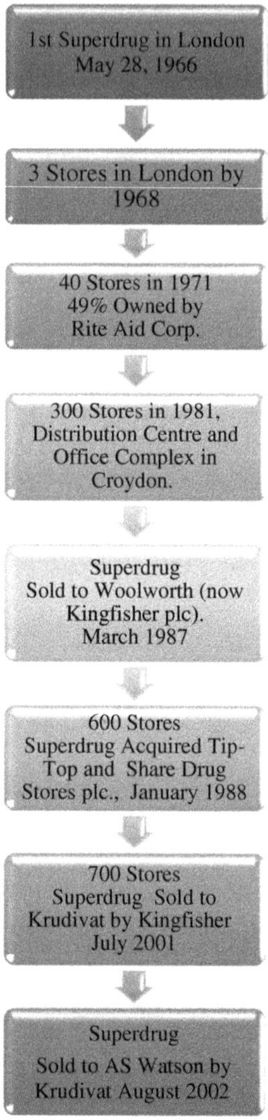

Figure 5. Chronological Events of Superdrug Stores.

In the next decade, the retail health and beauty market had become increasingly price competitive with new entrants including the leading supermarket chains extending their product offering to include volume discounts in the personal care and toiletries categories in direct competition with discount drug stores. In FY2000, Superdrug reported

£21.8 million lesser profit before tax than FY1999. The 2.6% drop in the profit before tax as a percentage of revenue (or YOY drop in profit before tax of 65.4%) was due to an erosion in gross margin by 2.1% or £18.2 million, an extra £3.2 million interest, and others making up a total of £21.8 million shortfall).

Meeting of Minds between Wade and Van Hedel

Wade was invited to a pre-Christmas dinner by Van Hedel, who had been a business friend of some years. It took place at a not at all flashy restaurant facing the River Thames in London in 2001. During the meal, Van Hedel carried the Kruidvat family's confidential message that they were disposing of their ownership of close to 2,000 health and beauty stores in continental Europe and the UK. As the dinner conversation evolved with greater intimacy and bits of business intrigue, Wade got the message that the De Rijcke family held Kruidvat drug stores' legacy in high regard. Its advertising slogan "Always surprising, always inexpensive" might be a hint of good things in a potential deal for ASW. Benelux countries' consumers had generally accepted the Kruidvat Group's discount drug stores. And it was similar if not identical to the Savers in the UK during the 1990s. This synergy appealed to Wade.

Van Hedel got the parting note from Wade that he would report these details to Canning Fok, group managing director of HWL. Wade returned to Hong Kong the next day and met with Fok, explaining that by acquiring the Kruidvat Group, ASW would speedily achieve the scale and become a significant drug store chain in Europe. Li was fully aware of the Savers acquisition in the UK a few months prior, and it did not take him long to decide to become the "new emperor" of a global health and beauty empire.

Wade also sought an audience with Li before Christmas, and he received Li's blessing on the spot. But there was a caveat. In order to get the full nod, Wade had to close the deal at a price-earnings (P/E) ratio of below ten times.[2] This was a tall order, as similar transactions were all above the ten times P/E ratio. Playing it cool, Wade dropped a note to Van Hedel before Christmas and thanked him for dinner, reaffirming that he would deliver ASW's decision in the New Year. Meanwhile, he was developing a strategy to articulate what values and synergies ASW could bring to Kruidvat's owners, employees, and customers. More importantly, he answered this question of why ASW would be the best suitor and not other investors. After a nine-month negotiation exercise, the merger of ASW with the Kruidvat Group was announced at approximately €1.3 billion on August 22, 2002. The combined sales of ASW and Kruidvat well exceeded EUR 7 billion in 2002.

Dick van Hedel, CEO of Kruidvat Group, recalled the acquisition:

> *A rarity in today's business world, the acquisition of a company by a shareholder with significant strategic value. The experience and global strength of HWL will help us achieve new heights.*[3]

Clearance by the European Commission and the Future of Kruidvat

As a mandatory requirement, the European Commission (EC) was notified of the Kruidvat Group's acquisition by ASW a week later on August 29 for regulatory clearance.

The Commission's resulting investigation showed overlapping activities in the United Kingdom where ASW owned the Savers stores and Kruidvat operated the Superdrug chain. After a month's thorough review on likely anti-trust activities on the part of ASW, the EC announced its official clearance statement on September 27, 2002:

> *The investigation also confirmed the absence of competition concerns, regardless of whether or not competition from supermarkets was taken into account. Concerning only the speciality stores market, rival chain Boots will remain the market leader in the United Kingdom, with the merged entity following in second place. This market is characterized by a string of big names such as The Body Shop and Lloyds Pharmacy, as well as a number of smaller players. If supermarkets were included in the analysis, the parties would be the fourth largest competitor, with a market share of less than 10%. Boots would still be the market leader, followed by Tesco and Sainsbury. In view of these elements, the Commission concluded that the operation will not result in the creation or strengthening of a dominant position and has decided to clear the transaction.*[4]

Wade's immediate task was to integrate the Kruidvat Group to ensure the continuity of the management and stability of the Kruidvat organisation in both the Benelux countries and its subsidiaries in the UK and joint-venture operations in central Europe with the Dirk Rossmann group. From October to December 2002, the same Kruidvat organisational structure remained intact for a seamless transition to ASW. The main exception was that Philip Ingham became the managing director of Superdrug in charge of both Savers and Superdrug (see Chapter 12). A new era for ASW had commenced.

The Kruidvat Group acquired the 700 Superdrug Stores from the Kingfisher Plc. in the UK at £252.0 million or £360,000 per shop on July 20, 2001.[5] FY 2002 was indeed a tough year. Superdrug's gross margin further deteriorated by 1.7% or £16.4 million, distribution costs increased by 1.3% or £12.6 million, and administrative expenses jumped by £8.0 million representing a YOY difference of £37.0 million.

During the 2000–2003 period, Britain's retail health and beauty market had a sea change with the leading supermarket chains further expanding their product offering to include beauty care products other than the personal care category. Like its sister, Savers Health and Beauty, Superdrug suffered profit decline, with 2002 being a loss making year and recovery in the following year in 2003 saw a profit before tax as a percentage of turnover of below 2% (Figures 6, 7 and Table 1).

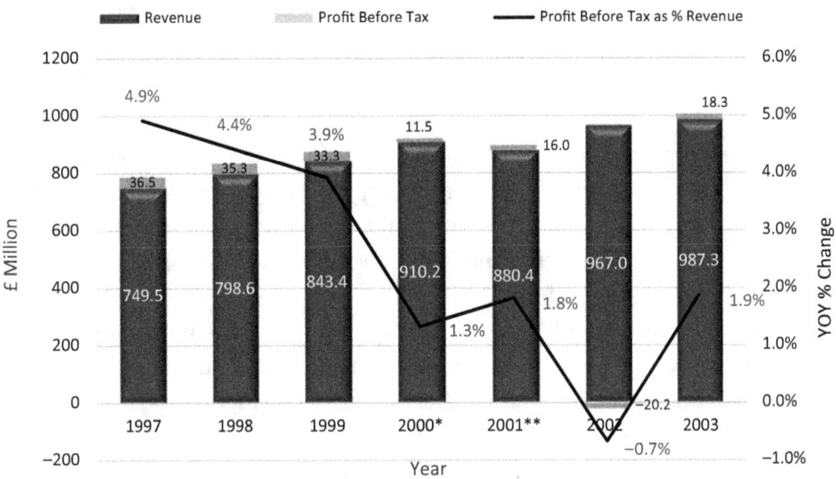

Figure 6. 1997–2003 Superdrug Stores Revenue and Profit Before Tax.

Notes: Fiscal Year ends at the end of January or beginning of February of next calendar year for FY 1997–2000.

*Fiscal Year 2000 on February 3, 2001 equivalent to 53 weeks.

**Year ended on last day of December with 47 weeks in FY 2001 instead of the normal 52 weeks account.

Source: Companies House.

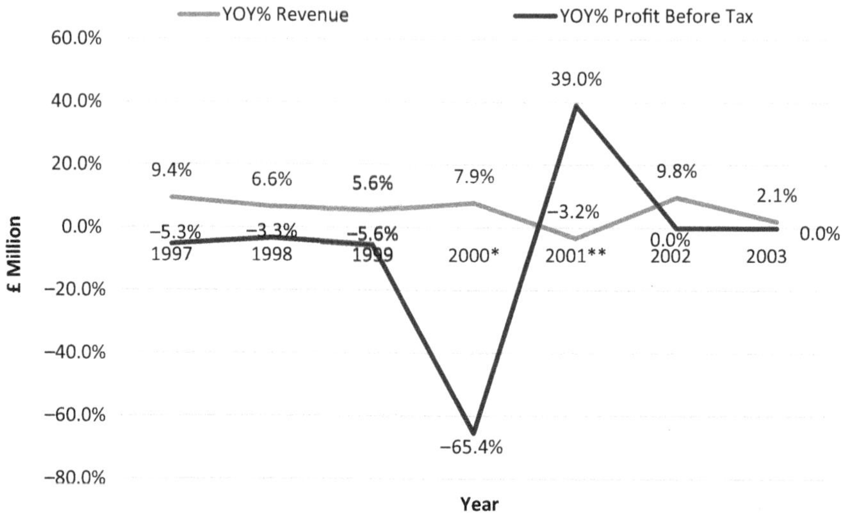

Figure 7. 1997–2003 Superdrug Stores YOY Growth %.

Notes: Fiscal Year ends at the end of January or beginning of February of next calendar year.
*Fiscal Year 2000 on February 3, 2001 equivalent to 53 weeks.
**Year ended on last day of December with 47 weeks in FY 2001 instead of the normal 52 weeks account.
Source: Companies House.

As the corporate integration of Kruidvat into the ASW group was a tall order, the HWL board decided to defer buying the interests in Dirk Rossmann GmbH for 2 years. They simply needed the focus to ensure a seamless transition following the 2002 Kruidvat acquisition and wait out the challenging market conditions.

Following the Kruidvat deal, Philip Ingham was appointed as the managing director of ASW Health & Beauty UK in January 2003. At the time, Superdrug was facing challenges of margin erosion and rising distribution and administrative costs. Actions were imperative. Wade's mission was to develop a customer connectivity strategy and perform a make-over for Superdrug as a trendy health and beauty care store. In September 2003, he inaugurated the first Superdrug store with a fresh retail format at Birmingham's Bull Ring Centre. After the make-over, Superdrug was presented as a chic female health and beauty care centre that was distinctly different from the family-oriented Boots the Chemists.

Table 1. Superdrug's 2002 and 2003 Financial Statements.

Explanatory Notes	2003 £'000	2002 £'000	YOY Change £'000	Remarks
Turnover (a)	987,288	966,953	20,335	2.1% YOY increase
Cost of sales (b)	(648,170)	(662,289)	(14,119)	2.8% YOY drop
Gross profit (c)	339,118	304,664	34,454	11% YOY increase
Distribution cost (d)	(293,247)	(282,423)	10,824	3.8% YOY increase
Administrative expenses (e)	(28,735)	(38,894)	(10,159)	4.3% YOY drop
Operating profit	28,833	(6,619)	35,452	Turn around
Interest payable and similar charges	(10,533)	(13,061)	(2,528)	19.3% YOY improvement
Profit/(Loss) on ordinary activities before taxation	18,300	(20,220)	38,520	Turn around
Taxation on profit/(loss) on ordinary activities	(6,778)	2,378	(9,156)	
(Deficit)/retained profit	11,512	(17,842)	29,354	

Notes: Prior to the 21st century, the British retail personal care market segment was dominated by discounted stores such as *Savers* and other specialist stores. At the turn of the 21st century, traditional pharmacy chains, e.g., Alliance Boots, Llyods, and lately Superdrugs, have enlarged their personal care product portfolio to compete with large supermarket chains, namely *Asda, Sainsbury, and Tesco.* which have also introduced on-site pharmacy services to shoppers.

These changes in the market place have led to intensified competition and price erosion.

Due to practice reasons, the accounting treatment of Savers and Superdrug was different. The distribution costs of Superdrug included both rental costs and payroll costs whereas Savers treated these as administration costs.

(a) Turnover

2003 performance showed a gain of £20.3 million revenue or a YOY 2.1% increase.

(b) Cost of Sales

YOY COS percentage improved by 2.8% or a saving of £14.1 million.

(c) Gross Profit

YOY gross profit percentage also improved by 2.8% with an increase of £27.6 million gross profit due to initial success in the change of product offering.

(d) Distribution Cost

Distribution cost increased by 0.5% from 29.2% to 29.7% or £10.8 million.

(e) Administrative Costs

A £10.0 million payment to the Kruidvat's family foundation as part of the acquisition agreement was recorded in 2002 only but not in 2003.

(f) Profit Before Tax

A £18.3 million profit before tax was recorded in 2003 which was back on track again.

Source: Companies House, Full Accounts.

Indeed, the relaunch of the Superdrug brand with the implementation of the customer connectivity strategy and makeover of Superdrug stores was not just timely, it was key to creating a breakthrough in those challenging times.

Trekpiester and ICI Paris XL in the Benelux

The upscale ICI Paris XL perfumery chain (ICI) was unique in the Kruidvat portfolio — it signified luxury and style. The perfume shop chain was founded in the late 1960s in Belgium. Its on-site beauty advice with a dedicated line of perfume and beauty care products was popular in Paris high street shops.

Given Kruidvat's success in Brussels in 1992, the Groenwoudt Group (subsequently renamed Kruidvat) acquired the upscale and trendy ICI 4 years later in 1996. Their idea was to replicate the business model within Benelux countries. By the time ASW acquired the Kruidvat Group in 2002, ICI had already grown into eight shops in Belgium and a 56-shop chain across the Netherlands. Trekpleister was an offshoot of the De Boer Supermarket Group (DBS). It was set up as a self-service drug store in Assen in the north-eastern Netherlands on April 3, 1980.

In 1997, DBS merged with Unigro, a grocery group founded in 1925, to become the Super de Boer. A year later in 1998, Trekpleister had grown into a 175-drug store chain. In the same year, the Super de Boer, whose strategy was to become the leading supermarket chain in the Netherlands, divested itself of Trekpleister.

The takeover of Trekpleister by the Groenwoudt group filled the void of Kruidvat Drug Stores, a southern Netherlands leader. It expanded to become a leader in the northern Netherlands, too, for national domination. After the merger, the combined market share of Kruidvat and Trekpleister rose to 36%, assuming the position as the number one drug store chain in the entire Netherlands. But ASW was hardly finished expanding across Europe — Germany was also clearly on the map.

Divestment of the Powwow Brand of Mineral Water

Following ASW's launch of its Powwow brand of mineral water in the UK in 1998, and its subsequent acquisitions of mineral water companies in Europe and the UK, its revenue exceeded £782 million or €120 million) in 2002. That same year, Nestle Waters, a major player in the bottled water business, acquired the Arrowhead brand of water in the US and had 40% of the market share.[6]

In the 2 years of 2002 and 2003, Wade was busy spending three weeks out of every month in Europe and the UK. He revitalised the recently acquired Savers business in the UK and conducted due diligence exercises with the Kruidvat Group in Amsterdam and London. It was evident to Wade that ASW's future lay in the health and beauty business — rather than the Powwow brand of the natural spring water. Soon after ASW acquired the Kruidvat Group in October 2002, Wade entered into serious negotiations with the Nestle Waters' top management. The deal was sealed on February 4, 2003. ASW sold the Powwow Group to Nestle Waters at €560 million, or 4.7 times its 2002 turnover, a figure that Wade could not decline. Frits van Dijk, CEO of Nestle Waters said:

> *Europe and the Home and Office Delivery channel (HOD) are two of the strategic pillars of Nestlé Waters' development. The addition of the Powwow network to our existing operations in Europe is a key element to forming a truly pan-European presence in HOD. In such a high potential new business, with double-digit annual growth, we ensure a good start by acquiring the right positions. In two years we have built a significant presence throughout Europe and Nestlé Waters ranks number one in the region.*[7]

The disposal of the Powwow brand in 2003 soon after the October 2002 acquisition of the Kruidvat Group sent a strong signal to the market: ASW would focus on the retail health and beauty business in the global market. After all, the water brand constituted only a small part of ASW's global revenue and profit contribution. Its decision to keep the Watsons Water brand in Hong Kong and the Mainland had taken into consideration community and sports events which the brand had been supporting. This has maintained the continuity in its support of the Inter-School Athletics Competition, Hong Kong Tennis Open, and the Macau Grand Prix — all corporate social responsibility endeavours which ASW has been promoting since 1985. In addition, the synergy of Watsons Water with WTC stores in Hong Kong dated back to 1874, and it was not an easy decision to let go of a business built over a century and a half on its home turf.

Financial Performance

In terms of financial performance, 2003 was a memorable year for the retail and manufacturing division. The year witnessed ASW becoming the largest cash flow business within the HWL group. It contributed 43% and 11.4% in revenue and EBIT, respectively, reaching HK$63.1 billion and HK$2.3 billion (Figure 8). The quantum leap was due to an increase of 1,900 stores acquired from the Kruidvat Group in October 2002 (Figure 9). The 2003 performance of the Retail and Manufacturing division saw a year-on-year increase of HK$23.7 billion (60%) in revenue, HK$1 billion (124%) in EBIT and a 4% gain in % EBIT. This also reflected a profit margin higher than that of the health and beauty business achieved in Kruidvat's Benelux countries (Figures 9 and 10).

However, ASW still had a long way to go to edge up in the retail health and beauty sector. Its real challenges were the market dynamics of the retail trade in mature markets, particularly in the UK. Challenges from

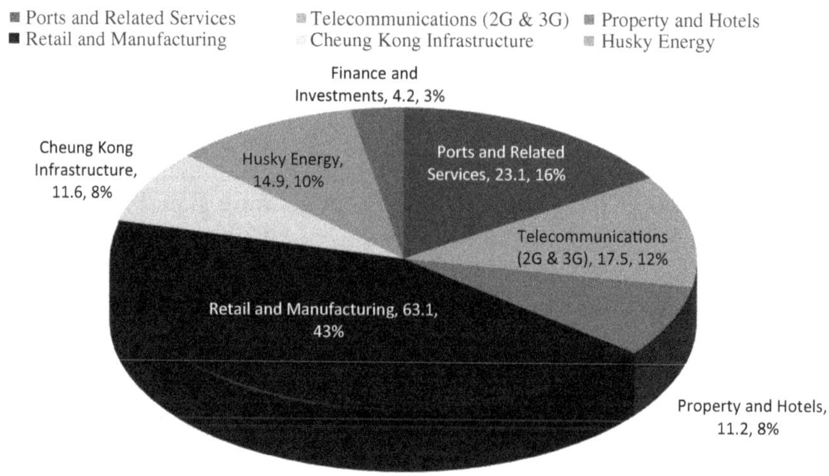

Figure 8. 2003 HWL's HK$145.6 Billion Revenue Contribution by Business Division.

Source: HWL Annual Reports.

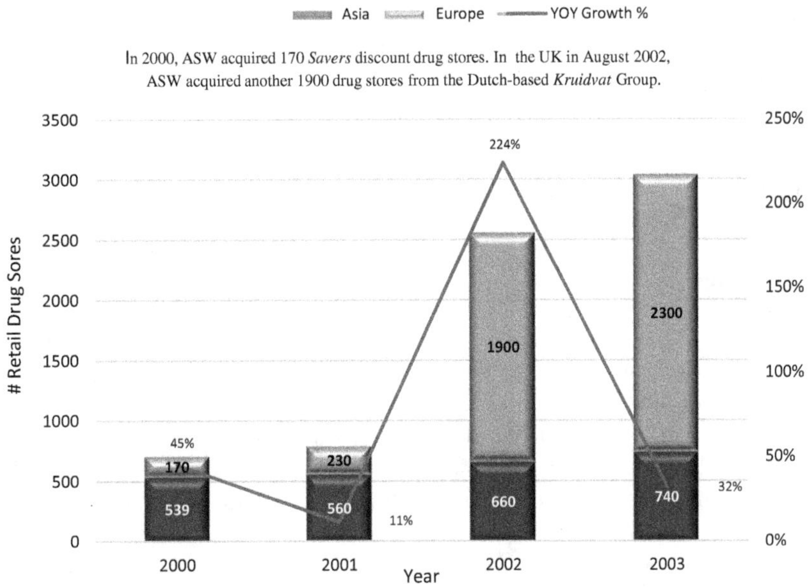

Figure 9. 2000–2003 Annual Growth of WTC in Asia and Europe.

Source: HWL Annual Reports.

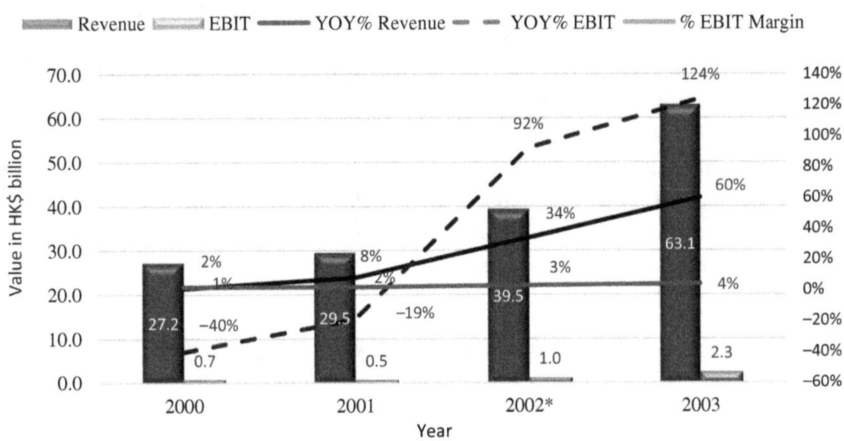

Figure 10. 2000–2003 HWL's Retail and Manufacturing Business Division Revenue and EBIT.

Note: *A quantum leap in October 2002 was recorded with the acquisition of the 1900 drug stores of the Dutch-based *Kruidvat* Group with full year impact in 2003.
Source: HWL Annual Reports.

the leading supermarket chains of Tesco, Sainsbury, and Asda who wanted to expand into health and beauty were omnipresent, and their very different cost structures which allowed them to go for such expansion with marginal additional distribution and administrative costs were advantages which were not possessed by Savers and Superdrug. In the end, Wade kept pushing the envelope and the company saw profits in the black.

Endnotes

[1]Van Riessen, P., *In Memorian: Dini de Rijcke-Groenwoudt, the Silent Force Behind the Founder of Kruidvat*, Quote, May 1, 2019. Accessed April 6, 2021. https://www.quotenet.nl/nieuws/a27328980/in-memoriam-dini-de-rijcke-groenwoudt-de-stille-kracht-achter-de-oprichter-van-kruidvat.

[2]Li, S., A.S. Watson Man at Helm Laid Foundation on Krudivat Deal, *South China Morning Post*, August 30, 2002. https://www.scmp.com/article/389770/watson-man-helm-laid-foundation-kruidvat-deal.

[3]*Hutchison Whampoa Acquires One of Europe's Leading Retail Group Kruidvat.* Press Release, Hutchison Whampoa Limited, August 22, 2002. Accessed April 6, 2021. https://www.ckh.com.hk/en/media/press_each.php?id=995.

[4]*Commission clears the acquisition of Kruidvat by A.S. Watson in the retail of health and beauty products*, Press Release, European Commission, September 27, 2002. Accessed December 12, 2019. https://ec.europa.eu/commission/presscorner/detail/en/IP_02_1388.

[5]The average sales and profit before tax per Superdrug store was £1.25 million and £23,000 per shop in 2001.

[6]Nestlé Waters acquired the Perrier Vittel Group, the two French brands of natural spring mineral waters in the same year.

[7]*Nestlé Waters and Hutchison conclude a major water business transaction in Europe*, Press Release, Nestle, February 4, 2003. https://www.nestle.com/media/pressreleases/allpressreleases/watershutchisonmajortransactioneurope-4feb03.

Chapter 8

2004-2006: Dirk Rossmann GmbH, and Enlarging the Beauty Business Portfolio

Marionnaud and The Perfume Shop, and the Emerging Markets

The Dirk Rossmann GmbH[1]

The first day was a huge success. Consumers flocked to Dirk Rossmann's drug store for low price brands of personal care products. The following year, 1973, the German government loosened controls on toiletries' retail prices. This boosted discount drug stores like DRG. Within 10 years, Rossmann grew his drug stores to over a 100, mainly in the northern part of West Germany. In 1979, DRG reached a turnover of Deutsche Mark 50 million, but its equity ratio fell below 20%.

The year 1996 was devastating for Rossmann. DRG faced bankruptcy as he was overleverageing its retail business through aggressive expansion into Central Europe. Rossmann suffered a heart attack. His personal losses were compounded by speculative trading in the stock market.[2,3] In the same year, the De Rijcke family provided a timely cash injection into DRG by forming a joint venture with Rossmann to fund DRG's growth of the discount drug store business in Central Europe. After swallowing this bitter pill, DRG had learnt its lesson and become financially savvy.

ASW waited until the end of the option period in August 2004 to exercise its right to acquire the 40% owned by the De Rijcke family, thereby establishing ASW's foothold in Central Europe. The postponement was largely due to ASW's busy integration of its newly acquired Kruidvat Group in 2002. At the same time, this also gave Wade time to dispose of the remaining non-core Powwow business. By then, DRG had developed into over 1,100 stores, with 786 in Germany alone (Figures 1 and 2).

Wade made his comments on this decisive acquisition:

> *A.S. Watson decided to purchase a stake in Rossmann Germany because the market prospects are exceptional. Germany is the largest health & beauty market in Europe and offers huge potential for further development. The Group's strategic aim is to expand its footprint in Europe, hence the option to invest in Germany offers an excellent opportunity for us. We have enjoyed a tremendous business relationship with Rossmann over the past two years in Central Europe. We believe this acquisition will reinforce the synergetic links between AS Watson's European operations and Rossmann.*[4]

Figure 1. Dirk Rossmann GmbH Drug Store, Olderwald, Germany, 2021.

Source: Author's Image Bank.

Figure 2. Toiletry Trial Pack Shelves, Dirk Rossmann GmbH Drug Store, Olderwald, Germany, 2021.

Source: Author's Image Bank.

The Global Fragrance and Decorative Cosmetics Market

In the swinging 1960s and 1970s, the distribution of high-end designer fragrances and perfumes in Europe was mainly through speciality fragrance shops such as Guerlain, Fragonard, and Serge Lutens. Their natural capitals were the fashion-conscious cities of Paris, Frankfurt, London, and Milan.

But by the 1980s and with growing affluence, European perfume and decorative cosmetic chain shops such as Marionnaud and Sephora were branching out across the continent to smaller cities, expanding the market of beauty and fragrance retailers for increasingly affluent consumers.

Facing the increasingly competitive, low margin discount drug store market in Europe, ASW had a lot of catching up to do. With Kruidvat, Savers, and Superdrug brands in its retail health and beauty portfolio, it was well placed to compete in the high profit margin fragrances and perfumes market. In fact, Kruidvat's Belgian fragrances and perfumes retail arm, ICI Paris XL, was doing well; but it would take too long to grow it out organically. ASW soon acquired Marionnaud of France in April 2005, and 3 months later, The Perfume Shop in the UK (Figures 3 and 4). This filled a void in the UK and Western Europe market, as well as the fast-growing countries in Eastern and Central Europe.

This established market trend had behaved surprisingly well between 2000 and 2006 despite the concurrent global IT bubble burst taking place then. Overall, the EU15 markets grew at an average Compound Annual Growth Rate (CAGR) of 3% under the combined fragrances, perfumes, and decorative cosmetics categories.[5] The EU 12 markets grew much faster, at 6.4%[6,7] (Figures 5 and 6). There was ample room to blossom in the EU12 markets. By 2006, the combined Europe, US, China, Japan cosmetics and toiletries market, at retail sales price, was €136.2 billion. Western Europe (EU15) contributed €62.7 billion or 46%, of which €17.0 billion or 27% was under the combined fragrances, perfumes, and decorative cosmetics market. In the same category, the newly joined 12 European Union member states (EU12) contributed €5.9 billion or 4.3%.

Figure 3. Marionnaud, Antibes, France, 2021.

Source: Author's Image Bank.

Figure 4. The Perfume Shop, London, 2021.

Source: Author's Image Bank.

In 2004, ASW became a global retail health and beauty group with over 90% of the 7,700 retail stores focusing on the retail health and beauty sector across Asia and Europe's 36 markets.[8] It was one of HWL's largest businesses, contributing HK$74.4 billion revenue and $3.65 billion EBIT, or 41.5% and 18.9% in 2004. In fact, ASW was the largest cash flow contributor to HWL.

Between 2004 and 2006, Wade and his lieutenants were able to close the loop in Asia by acquiring businesses or forming joint ventures with influential families in Malaysia, the Philippines, South Korea, and Thailand. They were either already in the retail drug store business or owners of commercial properties or department stores. But they lacked enough expertise in the retail health and beauty sector to properly drive a sustainable and profitable business. By the end of 2006, ASW reached HK$99.1 (£6.85 and €10.1) billion in turnover and HK$2.72 billion (£188 and €276 million) in EBIT (lower than 2004 due to the Marionnaud

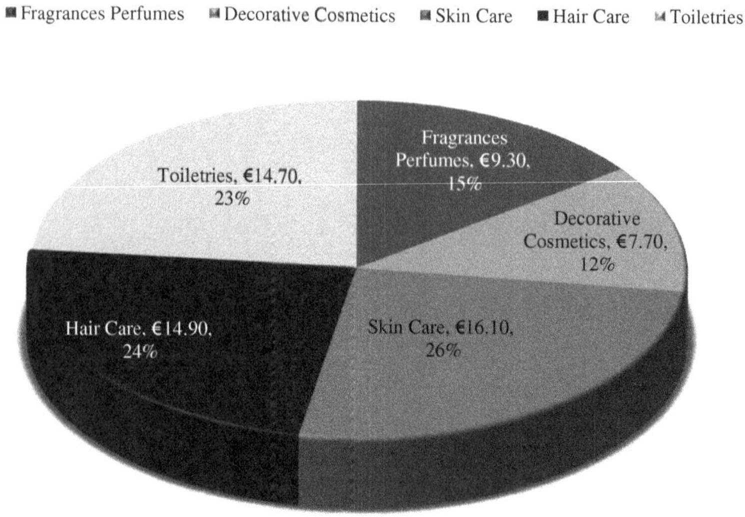

Figure 5. 2006 EU15 Retail Sales Price in €62.7 Billion by Product Category.

Source: Director General for Enterprise and Industry, European Commission.

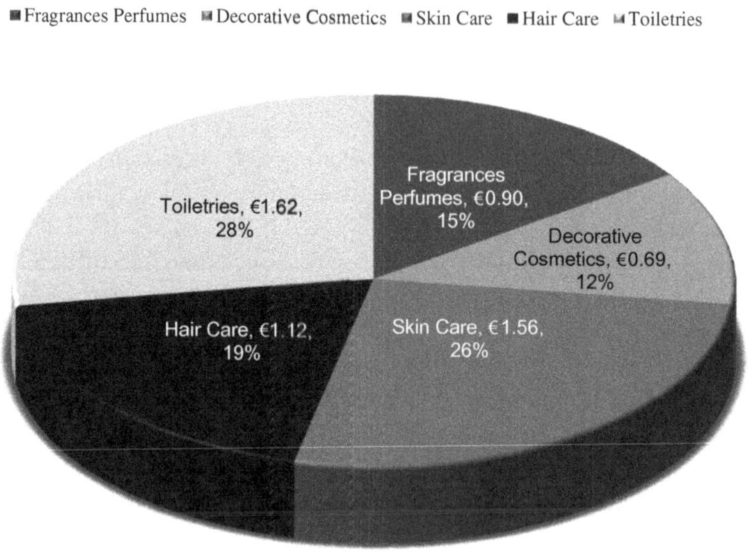

Figure 6. 2006 EU12 Retail Sales Price in €5.9 Billion by Product Category.

Source: Director General for Enterprise and Industry, European Commission.

revised figures).[9] While its turnover increased by 33%, EBIT dropped by 26% over a 2-year period.[10]

Marionnaud Perfumeries SA

Bernard Marrionnaud (1934–2015) learned his retail skills in his childhood years when helping his parents operate a stall selling drug store items in Clamart on the southwest outskirts of Paris. In 1958, at the age of 24, Marionnaud opened his first discount shop, Marionnaud Perfumeries SA, below his parent's apartment in Clamart. By 1996, Marionnaud had grown to 96 retail shops, but was trading at a loss and was sold to Marcel Frydman (1932–2015). The latter was running a profitable business with a chain of 48 discount perfumeries.[11,12]

Consolidation of the two businesses produced a ten million French Franc saving due to a streamlined organisation structure without duplicating overheads, warehouses, or delivery fleet. By listing in the secondary market of the Paris Stock Exchange in 1998, Marionnaud raised capital to fund its acquisition spree of perfume shops within 7 years — blossoming into 1,300 retail stores. In 2001, Marionnand migrated to the primary market and by the end of 2004, Marionnaud was present in 13 other markets, with the majority in Europe. Based on Marionnaud's 2003 turnover of €1.1 billion and H1 2004 turnover of €535 million, ASW made a public bid of an approximately €534 million cash offer for Marionnaud shares and convertible bonds for its sole control on January 14, 2005.

The deal was approved by the European Commission on April 7, 2005 and HWL's board subsequently approved a further capital injection of €800 million into ASW to fund its ongoing operations. However, further drama unfolded.[13,14] The French Financial Market Authority (AMF) initiated an investigation soon after Marionnaud's announcement that the group had sharply revised down its net profit for 2003 from €39 million to €12.8 million and, in April 2005, Marionnaud announced that it had suffered a net loss of €98 million in 2004 versus the already revised down profit of €12.8 million for 2003. AMF suspected that the accounts, the balance sheets, and all the financial communications concerning 2002 and 2003 were, "false, inaccurate, and misleading." For a beauty and perfume operation, this was ironically an ugly and stinky state of affairs.[15] Although ASW conducted professional due diligence on Marionnaud, it was unfortunate that the accounting flaws were not uncovered prior to acquisition.

The Perfume Shop

The Perfume Shop Limited (TPS), a wholly owned subsidiary of Merchant Retail Group Plc. (MRG), was incorporated in March 1992 in Middlesex, UK. In July 1992, TPS acquired Eau Zone Ltd.'s business comprising six retail fragrance shops.[16]

Over the next 14 years, MRG divested its other businesses and focused on the growth and expansion of TPS. This resulted in a portfolio of 110 upmarket retail fragrance shops. In the fiscal year ending March 31, 2005, TPS's full-year turnover and profit before tax were valued at £104.1 million and £16.1 million, respectively, representing a high profit/turnover ratio of 15.40% for the retail fragrance business.[17] Three months after the closure of the acquisition of Marionnaud, ASW continued with its expansion plan and offered to buy up the entire issued capital of MRG, a London Stock Market listed public company, for £221.9 million, thus adding TPS to its portfolio. This deal was sent for approval to the Office of Fair Trading on July 14, 2005.[18]

The Emerging Markets of Eastern and Central Europe

Following the collapse of the Berlin Wall in 1989, many were eyeing potential opportunities in the newly opened Eastern European markets and one of them was none other than DRG which became an addition to the ASW portfolio in 2004. DRG was particularly active in its expansion in Poland and the Czech Republic. Similar new market opportunities were opened up with the dissolution of the Soviet Union in 1991 and trade liberalisation emerging in the former Soviet republics. It was unsurprising that ASW should want to gain a foothold in these markets and hence, its aggressive bid for Drogas in 2004.

Drogas opened its first store in Lithuania in 1993 and by 2004, it was operating over 80 health and beauty stores in Lithuania and Latvia.[19] Its turnover in 2003 was €15.8 million (22.7 million lats) with a profit of €2 million (1.4 million lats) or a 12.7% profit/turnover ratio — an enviable performance indeed by industry standards.[20]

At the time of its acquisition by ASW in 2004, Drogas's valuation was over €20 million, or slightly more than ten times its P/E ratio, and ASW won the bid over other retail pharmacy chain players such as Alliance Boots from the UK. It was ASW's first entry into the Baltic

States and reinforcement of its strategy to expand its presence in Europe. The new market entry on the Continent was reminiscent of ASW's pioneering endeavours in Southeast Asia in the late 1980s and early 1990s.

Smooth Transition in the Baltics

With ASW's acquisition of Drogas and given its Far Eastern background, it was incumbent on the new owner to assure the employees and give expression to its century-old tradition of respect and nurturing, rather than the heavy-handed approach of some of the global corporations. And Wade wasted no time communicating that to Drogas's employees. David Cassey was appointed as executive director for ASW Eastern Europe in early 2004. Cassey joined ASW in 1988 and had rotations as the country manager for Singapore, Malaysia, Taiwan, and the Philippines where he had amassed valuable experience in emerging markets. His mission was to drive entry into the Baltics, Ukraine, and Russia (Figure 7).

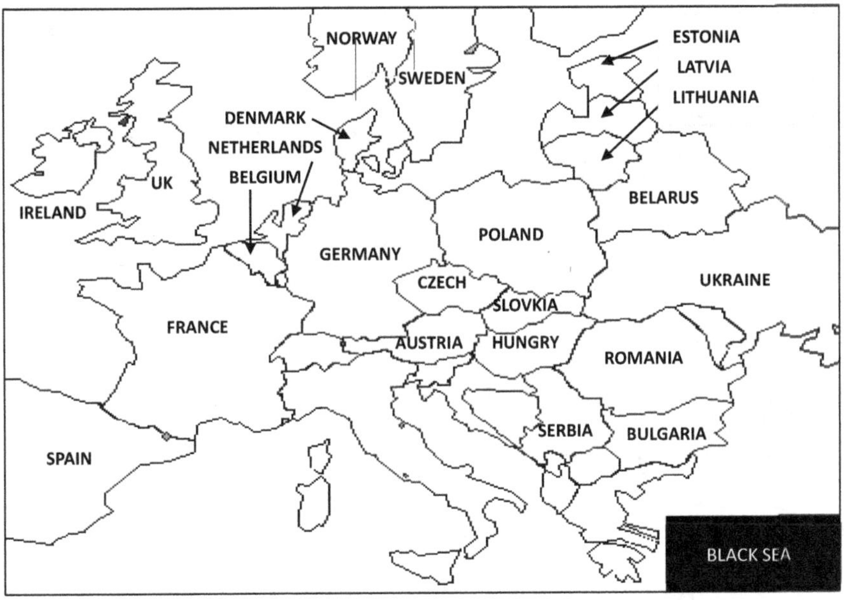

Figure 7. The Baltic, North, Central and Eastern European Countries.

Source: Author's Image Bank.

Russia, Turkey, and Ukraine were of strategic interest to ASW as part of its Europeanisation plan. After completing acquisitions in the western European markets, ASW's appetite turned to the Eastern and Near Eastern regions. Opportunities came for ASW in 2005 and 2006 with the addition of the Cosmo Group's seven shops in Turkey, the Spektr Group's 24 stores in St. Petersburg, Russia, and the DS Group's 99 stores in Ukraine. ASW gradually converted the national brands of Drogas, Cosmo, and Spektr to the Watsons brand over time (Figure 8). ASW's acquisition of Drogas was one of the first significant foreign investments in the Baltic States. When asked by the media, Rafails Deifts, owner of the Rota Group, Drogas's main shareholder, said:

> *Drogas has been the most successful of long-term development projects in Rota's history. Selling this business to AS Watson is an excellent achievement.*[20]

Figure 8. Turkey and Neighbouring Countries.

Source: Author's Image Bank.

Drogas's transition to ASW was a smooth ride as Andrej Jernev, who became the Chief Executive Officer of the new Drogas, was Rota's general manager.[21] Jernev had adopted many best practice management skills when he was a country manager at Coca Cola in Latvia.

He was able to introduce the same to Rota and earn the respect of front line store managers. In October 2005, two new stores under the Watsons Your Personal Store (WPS) brand were opened in Tallinn, Estonia's capital. The Watsons corporate brand was used instead of the Drogas brand which Estonians had perceived as an Eastern European label and not a global player like Watsons.

Eastern Promises with Turkish Delight

Turkey's population grew rapidly to 72.7 million or a 7.6 million net gain over 10 years from 2001–2010, which indicated a promising and an upcoming middle-class market.[22] Wade saw Turkey as an attractive market that could become one of ASW's growth engines. For this, Wade sought out super deals. He eventually learned of Ahmt Yanikoglu, a trained civil engineer, who had done a 4-year stint with a Turkish insurance agent and broker before founding a personal care retail store named Cosmo in 1993 with three other partners. Yanikoglu became the general manager of Cosmo in December 1994.[23] Within 12 years, the Cosmo brand had grown into a chain of seven health and beauty shops in Istanbul. It was sold to ASW in March 2005. ASW was the first foreign company to enter Turkey's drug store market. This was followed by local and international players who soon afterwards competed in this sector. Cosmo was rebranded as Watsons in the second quarter of 2005 and started expanding into other cities in 2006 at a 40–50% growth rate per annum. Yanikoglu stayed with ASW to oversee its rapid expansion until retirement in December 2017.

Northern Star — Spektr

In the early 2000s, Russia had a limited number of imported health and beauty items for sale in its state-owned retail outlets. Russia's retail sector was expected to report double-digit growth in the second half of the 2000s, with an estimated 15% year-on-year increase in retail sales in

2005. Opportunities in the Russian market were not lost to European brands such as Yves Rocher (market entry in 1990), ASW (market entry in 2005), and Alliance Boots (market entry in 2006). However, a lack of convenient locations and shopping malls and unfavourable demographics had deterred international retailers' entry.[24] Spektr was founded in St. Petersburg in 1990 and opened its first store in 2001.[25] It had grown into a chain of 24 retail drug stores by the time it formed a joint venture partnership with ASW in October 2005.

The Entrancing Ukraine

In the mid-1990s, Ukraine was one of Central and Eastern Europe's fastest growing economies with the region's second-largest population at 46.8 million. As part of the Asnova Group founded in 1992, the DC health and beauty chain also owned supermarkets and a logistics company. It was the largest retail drug store group with 99 shops in Ukraine by the end of 2004. It became an attractive target when the owner, Anatoliy Strogan, decided to sell a 65% shareholding of DC and use its proceeds for other ventures in July 2006.[26] DC was a convenience store stocked with home care and toiletries. ASW deemed it necessary to have a new strategy to transform DC into a profitable health and beauty store. The new stores became bigger and offered exclusive and trendy decorative cosmetics.

Enlarging the Asian Footprint

Since the early 20th century, many large conglomerates in Southeast Asia have been owned by ethnic Chinese families; they have been key drivers of economic growth and are actively investing in property development including shopping malls. Some are major employers in the service industry, including supermarket chains and department stores. Foreign companies with expertise in the service industry would usually team up with reputable local families as joint venture partners to help them navigate the complicated government bureaucracy. It would take months if not years to obtain various business, environmental, and sanitary licenses and tax certificates. The local partner's role is to ensure that their foreign partner does not infringe upon often antiquated and ambiguous national and local laws. The trappings of a new and foreign operating environment may

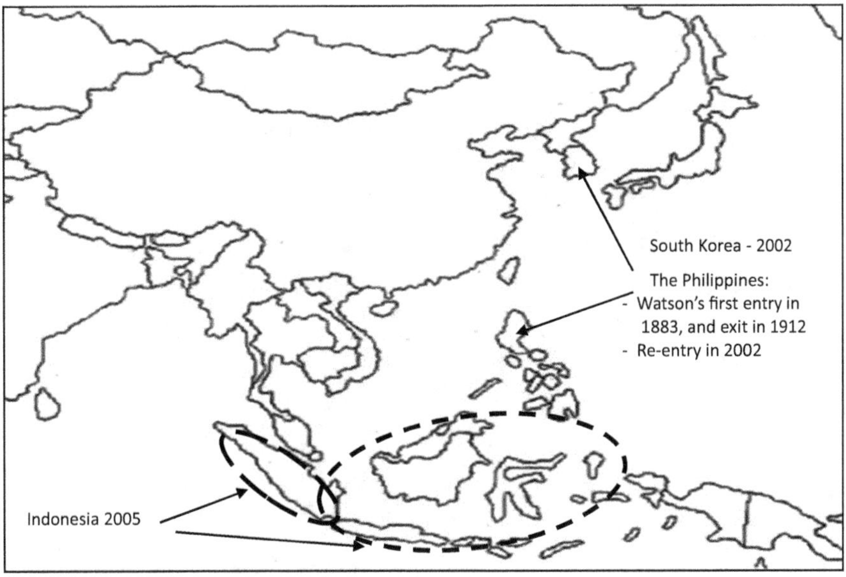

Figure 9. ASW's Joint Ventures in Asia, 2000–2005.

Source: Author's Image Bank.

disrupt business development efforts which could have otherwise been better spent. During the 2004–2006 period, ASW further penetrated the Asia market by setting up joint ventures with local families in Indonesia, the Philippines, and South Korea to enlarge its geographical footprint[27] (Figure 9 and Table 1).

Re-entry into Luzon and Beyond[28]

ASW exited the Philippines to save its core pharmacy and soda water business in the home market in 1912. After 90 years of absence from the main Philippines island of Luzon, ASW re-entered the Philippines by forming a joint venture with the Sy family of the SM Prime Holding Inc. (SM) in April 2002.[29,30] Since the government had promulgated its new foreign investment policy in March 2000 to attract overseas investment in the retail market, ASW's investment was also the Philippines's first significant foreign investment by an international retail chain store. The SM group was one of the largest companies in the Philippines, owning shopping

Table 1. ASW's Joint Venture Partners in Asia and Europe in 2006.

Region	Year Business or JV Formed/	Country/ Market	Name of Local Family/Company	ASW Shareholding
Asia	1996	Thailand	Chirathivat/Central Group	70%
	2004	Philippines	Sy/SM Group	60%
	2004	South Korea	Huh/GS Holdings	50%
	2005	Indonesia	Duta Intidaya Tbk	Master Franchise
Europe	2004	Germany	Rossmann/Rossmann GmbH	40%
	2005	Russia	Ilina/Spektr	65%
	2006	Ukraine	Strogan/DC	65%

Source: Miscellaneous.

malls, supermarkets, other retail chains, plus 61 health and beauty and drug stores.

The Sy family appreciated ASW's branding and expertise in the retail drug store industry. Having a joint venture with ASW could achieve the same goal without going through teething problems in its rapid growth phase. With ASW's direct participation in the retail health and beauty business joint venture, the Sy family could focus on more lucrative property development projects in the Philippines and China. A 60:40 retail joint venture between ASW and the Sy family was set up in April 2005. Dennis Cassey became the first managing director of Watsons Personal Care Store (Philippines) to lead this joint venture. Before that, he was the country manager of Watson's The Chemist Stores in Taiwan for 7 years.

His first job in the Philippines was to rebrand existing stores under the "Watsons Your Personal Store" brand and roll out the larger, brighter, and smarter consumer-friendly concept. In May 2006, a flagship store of 800 square meters was opened in the Mall of Asia in Metro Manila. This also included a beauty salon with hairdressing, nail spa, facial services, and beauty treatment rooms. It was the first health and beauty store in Asia to provide comprehensive personal care to its customers — essentially a lifestyle and shopping paradise for young professionals and the affluent.

A Hiccup in Malaysia

ASW entered Malaysia in 1994 with its first store in Johor Bahru, right at the Southern tip of the Malay Peninsula opposite Singapore. Within 10 years, it grew to over 70 retail health and beauty stores under the WPC brand in Malaysia's eastern and western parts.[31] However, in the first half of 2003, the retail drug store business in Asia (particularly Hong Kong, Malaysia, and Singapore) was severely hit by the SARS epidemic and surging sales of disinfectants and surgical masks simply could not compensate for the loss of other sales. In the second half of 2003, the Malaysia drug market worsened due to declining consumer confidence in retail pharmacy. This was caused by the recall of more than 300,000 packs of health supplements supplied by Pan Pharmaceuticals of Australia. Apex Healthcare Berhad (AHB), a local publicly listed pharmacy, drug manufacturing, and distribution company, was badly hit by this.[32]

Hence, AHB was under tremendous pressure from shareholders to improve its financial performance. AHB had no choice but to sell its retail arm of pharmacies and drug counters in department stores to preserve its generic manufacturing and distribution business. Acquiring 24 pharmacy shops and 35 retail counters of AHB by ASW in July 2004 at RM14 million (HK$28.7 million) presented an excellent consolidation opportunity in the Malaysian health and beauty market.[33]

The Foreign Investment Committee (FIC) of Malaysia initially declined to approve the transaction by the extended cut-off date of December 11, 2004, due to a local listed business's foreign ownership. The decision was reversed in the second quarter of 2005 through intensive lobbying by AHB's senior management with FIC officials. The acquisition was formally completed on May 31, 2005. Twenty Apex pharmacies were sold and the use of Apex's brand was licensed to ASW for 5 years to ensure a smooth transition.

Head of the Four Little Dragons — South Korea

The economies of the four "little dragons" of Hong Kong, Singapore, South Korea, and Taiwan underwent rapid changes with exceptional growth between the 1960s and 1990s. By the early 2000s, the four had developed into middle-income economies[34–36] (Figure 10). South Korea

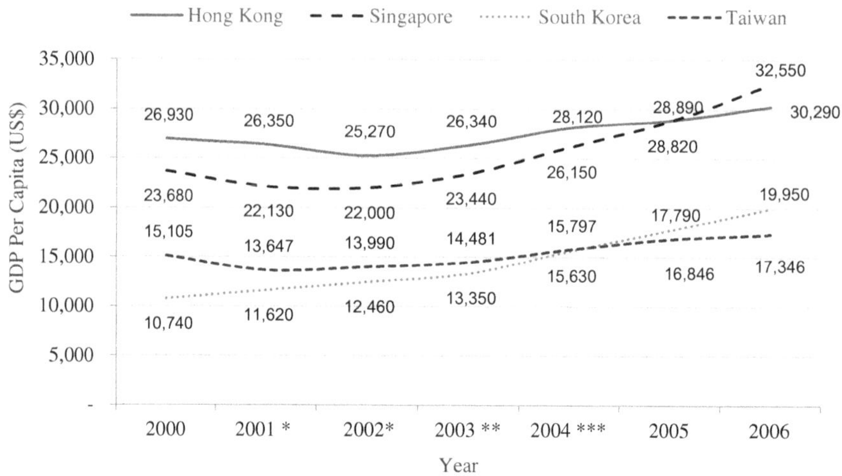

Figure 10. 2000–2006, GNI Per Capita, Atlas Method (Current US$).

Notes: *2001–2002: Drop in exports due to the slow down in world economy after Y2K for export-driven economies of Singapore, South Korea, and Taiwan. **1H 2003 hit by SARS. ***Faster growth in Singapore in 2004 due to higher exports and increase in transportation and tourism.
Source: The World Bank, NDC.

was the largest economy among the four. Although South Korea had a higher per capita GDP than Taiwan in the 2000s, it was a much protected market. In November 2004, an opportunity arose in forming a 50:50 joint venture with the LG Mart Co. LG Mart was a subsidiary of the GS Group founded by Huh Chang-soo who himself was a co-founder of the LG Group in 1947. GS Group was created in July 2002 from a merger and consolidation of LG 25 (with 2,000 convenience stores), LG Supermarket (73 stores), and other hypermarket and department stores within its retail businesses portfolio. LG Mart's 2003 revenue was US$2.9 billion.[37,38] The first GS-Watsons store was opened in March 2005 and a few months later a Watson-GS flagship store was opened in the Myeong-dong district in downtown Seoul in June 2005.[39] (Figure 5)

A Neglected South Sea Market — Indonesia

Indonesia is Southeast Asia's most populous country with 227 million in 2005. It has rich resources with coal, rubber, oil and is supplemented with agricultural and service industries. Modern-day Indonesia developed out of the Dutch East Indies, which was formed in 1800 as a colony after the bankruptcy of the Dutch East India Company. After a bitter armed conflict between the Indonesian nationalists and the Dutch colonists from 1945 to 1949, soon after the Japanese surrender when WWII ended in August 1945, Indonesia became a truly liberated land. Like South Korea and Thailand, Indonesia had strict foreign ownership laws for business investment at the time.

Hence, seeking a reliable local partner would be the prerequisite in ASW's market entry and sustainable business growth in this promising yet challenging market. ASW's entry into Indonesia was through PT Duta Intidaya Tbk (DIT) whose shareholding included 75.8% by PT Sehat Cemerlang, 14.09% by Total Alliance Holdings Ltd., and the rest by PT Bintang Indah Abadi.[40,41]

Both PT Sehat Cemerlang and PT Indah Abadi were controlled by Mr Patrick Sugito Walujo. The latter had served as a senior vice president of Pacific Century Japan, a company owned by Richard Li, the second son of Li Ka-Shing, in the late 1990s. DIT was registered in 2005, and in January 2006, the company opened its first store under the Watsons brand through a sole and exclusive licensing arrangement with ASW at the Pondok Indah Mall 2 in South Jakarta, Indonesia.

Challenges in the Hong Kong Market

Yet, despite the hurdles and opportunities presented by going global, ASW's home market of Hong Kong has always remained important. ASW relied upon it as a growth engine from the early 1980s to 2006 (Figure 10). Over 500 out of 7,700 stores, or 6%, including WTC's health and beauty retail business, PNS supermarkets, Fortress consumer electronic and electrical appliance shops, and Watson's Wine, were all located in Hong Kong. The main challenges to ASW's retail businesses in Hong Kong were the exorbitant rental costs and labour wages, which were both high and fixed. These issues have continued to this day.

In the Mainland, store rentals in shopping malls were commonly linked with sales turnover, and labour costs for sales assistants/merchandisers were mostly commission-based. In Taiwan, rentals and labour costs were much lower and controllable than in Hong Kong or Singapore[42,43] (Figure 11). The Hong Kong property market reached a peak in June 1997 and took a nose-dive due to the Asian financial crisis which started in July. It continued through the Y2K period with the trough hit hard in

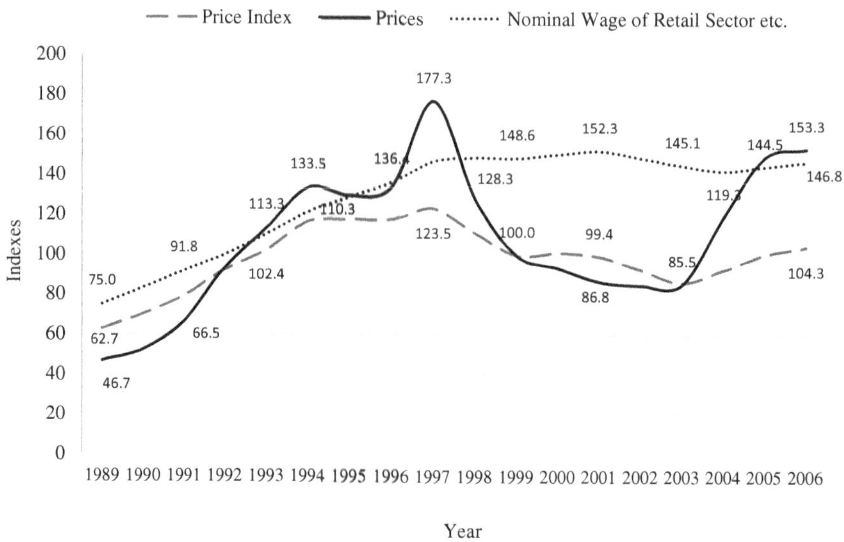

Figure 11. Hong Kong Annual Private Retail Rental and Price Indexes 1978–2006 (1999 = 100).

Note: *Prices dropped substantially from 2H 1997 to 1H 2003 due to Asia economic crisis and SARS.
Source: Hong Kong Statistics.

the first half of 2003 because of the SARS epidemic. The Hong Kong economy was revitalised in July 2003 when Mainland authorities loosened travel controls and Mainland outbound tourists visited Hong Kong in droves. The consequent social repercussions and much later COVID-19 pandemic impact will be separately discussed.

Confronting Issues and Restructuring

ASW's management had the most challenging years from 2003 to 2006 in Europe as it had 5,800 out of a total of 7,700 or 75% retail stores located there. ASW's earlier acquisitions of Savers in the UK and the Kruidvat Group in Europe demanded heavy management involvement to develop branding strategy, improve operational efficiency, and to undertake restructuring to improve profitability.

As discussed earlier, since 2003, the retail health and beauty market has become increasingly competitive with new entrants. These include leading supermarket chains expanding products and offering volume discounts in the personal care category. For example, in 2005, Savers YOY revenue grew 11%. However, gross profit margins eroded 2% from 12% to 10% due to price competition from the supermarket chains. Savers administrative costs, including operating leases and payroll costs, also increased by a total of £9.7 million[44,45] (Figures 12 and 13). Total EBIT for the year was £29 million which already included a one-time income of £20 million from the disposal of intellectual property rights from Savers to its parent company, Watson Enterprises (Bahamas) Ltd.

A new strategy was developed in late 2006 to address the poor financial performance of Savers due to a string of issues.[46,47] Prompt actions were taken by ASW's UK leadership. These initiatives included:

- Consolidation of the central and distribution functions within the UK health and beauty businesses;
- Restructuring the property portfolio with a significant number of Savers' stores being converted to other trading formats within the ASW's UK group; and
- Focusing on product offering of major brands at great prices.

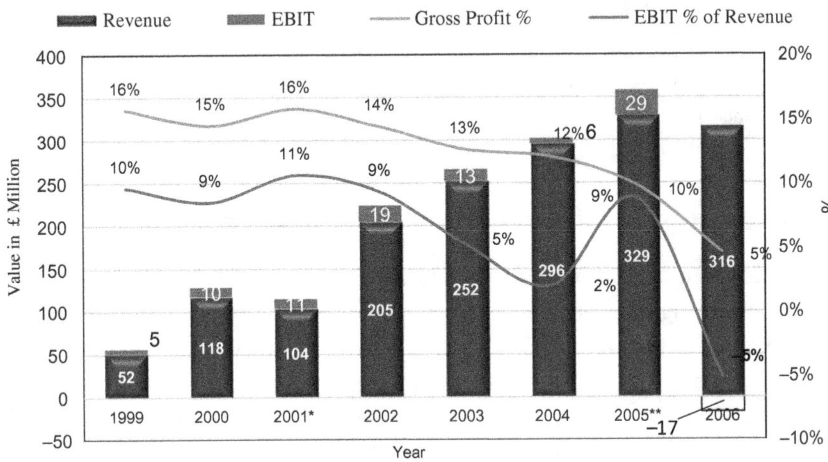

Figure 12. 1999–2006 Savers Revenue and EBIT By Value and Margins.

Notes: *Financial year 2000 had a 7-month account which began on June 1, 2000 and ended on May 31, 2001. In line with ASW financial year, commencing 2001, the 12-month account commenced on January 1 and ended on December 31.

**£29 million was shown as EBIT due to an injection of £20 million into Savers by means of intellectual property rights assignment by ASW in 2005.

Source: Companies House.

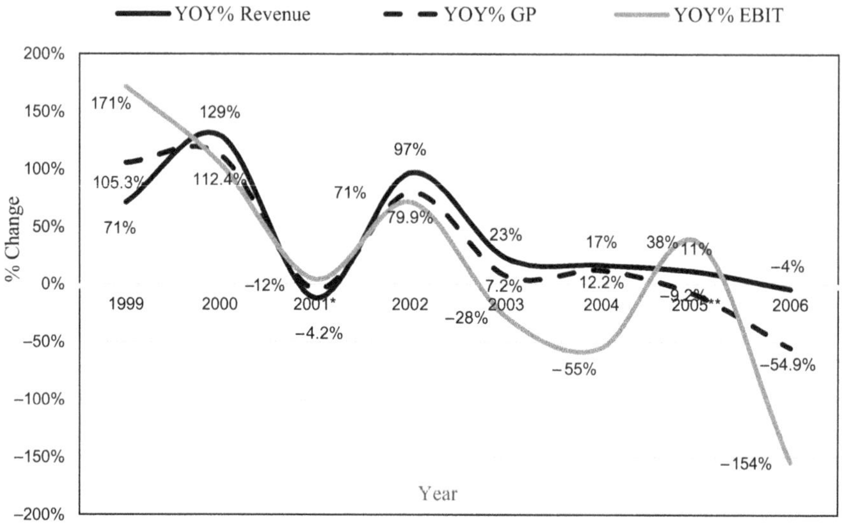

Figure 13. 1999–2006 Savers Revenue and EBIT — YOY % Growth Rates

Notes: *Financial year 2000 had a 7-month account which began on June 1, 2000 and ended on May 31, 2001.

In line with ASW financial year, commencing 2001, the 12-month account commenced on January 1 and ended on December 31.

**£29 million was shown as EBIT due to an injection of £ 20 million into *Savers* by mens of intellectual property rights assignment by ASW in 2005.

Source: Companies House.

Superdrug's Long Overdue Turnaround

Soon after acquiring the Kruidvat Group, ASW adopted a strategy to reposition Superdrug as a one-stop health and beauty store for young females in tier 1 and 2 cities versus Boots the Chemists. The latter's target customers were primarily young mothers. One year down the road, the 2004 financial performance revealed the need for an immediate overhaul of the business model in the face of continuing price erosion and increasing labour costs resulting in a 22% drop in EBIT (Figures 14 and 15). Between 2003 and 2006, Superdrug's EBIT as a percentage of sales hovered in the range of 0–2.2%.

A question to ponder: did Van Hedel, CEO of the Kruidvat Group, and the De Rijcke family foresee such a grave picture after they acquired Superdrug in the UK which motivated them to divest the entire retail health and beauty business in Continental Europe and the UK?

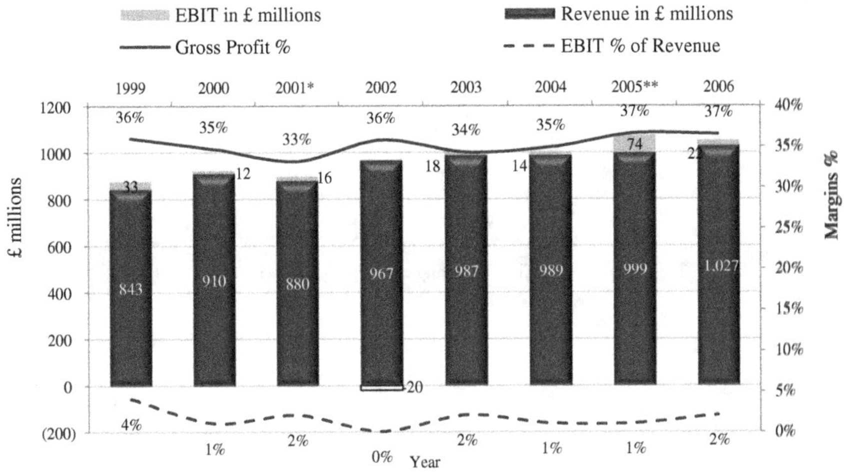

Figure 14. 1999–2006 Superdrug Revenue and EBIT By Value and Margins %.

Notes: *Financial year 2001 had a 47-week account which began on February 4, 2001 and ended on on December 31, 2001. **£74 million was shown as EBIT due to an injection of £ 60 million into Superdrug by mens of intellectual property. In line with ASW financial year, commencing 2002, the 12-month account commenced on January 1 and ended on December 31.
Source: Companies House.

In most acquisitions and mergers, restructuring costs would be budgeted in the first year after the purchase to straighten out any accounting items that needed to be fixed. This could be labour compensation, lease renovation, tax, investment in advertising and promotion, or any other factors that would negatively impact subsequent years' performance. In the case of ASW, restructuring occurred in 2005, 3 years after Superdrug's acquisition instead of upfront. It could have been a HWL corporate decision to postpone the restructuring due to the struggling 3G telecommunication business in the UK and weak sentiment in the economy during the period.

In the last 3 years of Wade's leadership at ASW prior to his retirement in 2006, Superdrug dealt with the challenges head-on and came through the trying period standing tall. Other than the long overdue injection of a one-off £60 million in the form of intellectual property rights assignment in 2005, Superdrug recorded a progressive improvement in gross profit margin and operating profit from 35% to 37% and £14 million to £22 million in one of the toughest periods of the UK's retail industry. A one-time injection of £60 million was made in 2005, otherwise its operating profit remained flat at £14 million.

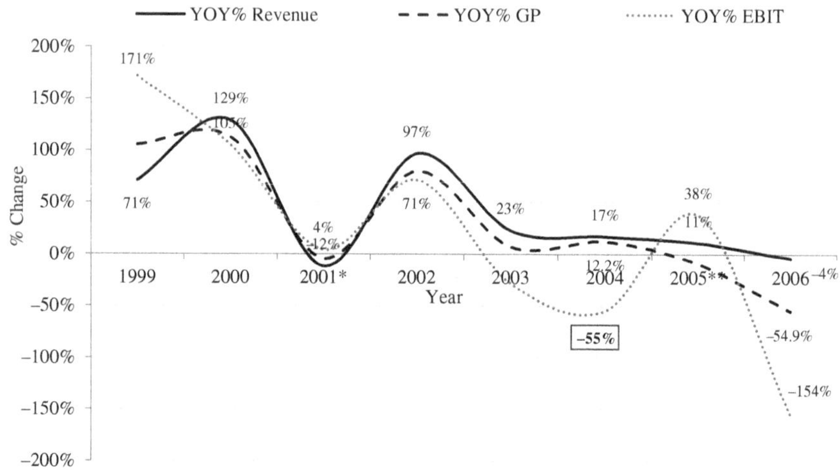

Figure 15. 1999–2006 Superdrug Revenue and EBIT By YOY % Growth Rates.

Notes: *Financial year 2001 had a 47-week account which began on February 4, 2001 and ended on December 31, 2001.
In line with ASW financial year, commencing 2002, the 12-month account commenced on January 1 and ended on December 31.
**£60 million was shown as EBIT due to an injection of £60 million into Superdrug by means of intellectual property rights assignment by ASW in 2005.
Source: Companies House.

Endnotes

[1]GmbH is a shortened German term that translates to limited liability company in English.
[2]Tonnersmann, J., *Dirk Rossmann the Unbelievable, that Everything Went Well Again*, Zeit Online, March 16, 2017. https://www.zeit.de/2017/12/dirk-rossmann-drogerie-rettung-schlecker?utm_referrer=https%3A%2F%2Fwww.google.com%2F. (Rossmann approached Hannover Fianz Group (HFG) with the latter held an initial 10% shareholding in 1980, which subsequently grew to 38%. The increase in share capital helped the financing of DRG's expansion in the domestic market and into the eastern region when Germany reunited in October 1990. Another hundred stores opened within a year in the eastern area).
[3]DRG soon furthered its expansion into the Central European countries of Poland, Hungry, and the Chez Republic. With 20 years of track record in the retailing of toiletries and household products, DRG had a good reputation as a "down to earth" discounted drug store operator. The banks were willing to extend loans to DRG to tide over the financial crisis it faced.

[4]*A.S. Watson Acquires 40% stake in German Retail Chain Rossmann*, Press Release, A.S. Watson & Co. Ltd., August 24, 2004. Accessed December 12, 2019. http://www.hutchison-whampoa.com/en/media/press_each.php?id=1493.

[5]Prior to May 1, 2004, the original 15 European Union member countries were: Austria, Belgium, Denmark, Finland, France, Germany, Greece, Ireland, Italy, Luxembourg, Netherlands, Portugal, Spain, Sweden, and United Kingdom.

[6]After May 1, 2004, 12 countries which joined as new member states of the European Union were Bulgaria, Cyprus, Czech Republic, Estonia, Hungary, Latvia, Lithuania, Malta, Poland, Romania, Slovkia, and Slovenia.

[7]A Study of the European Cosmetic Industry, Final Report, *Global Insight*, October 2007: 8. Prepared for the European Commission, Director General for Enterprise and Industry. file:///C:/Users/pchiuy/Downloads/study_eu_cosmetics_industry.pdf.

[8]Analyses by Core Business of Group Turnover, EBIT and Profit, 2004 Annual Report of Hutchison Whampoa Ltd., p. 7. https://doc.irasia.com/listco/hk/hutchison/annual/2004/analysis.pdf.

[9]ASW's lowered EBIT in 2006 was mainly due to write-downs of Marionnuad whose accounting issues were not revealed in the due diligence exercise prior to the closure of the acquisition by ASW.

[10]Analyses by Core Business of Group Turnover, EBIT and Profit, 2006 Annual report of Hutchison Whampoa Ltd.: 7. https://doc.irasia.com/listco/hk/hutchison/annual/2006/analysis.pdf.

[11]*Clamart: le parfumeur Bernard Marionnaud est mort*, Le Parisen, July 2, 2016. Accessed April 16, 2021. http://www.leparisien.fr/hauts-de-seine-92/clamart-92140/clamart-le-parfumeur-bernard-marionnaud-est-mort-22-07-2015-4964519.php.

[12]*Décès de Marcel Frydman, ex-PDG de Marionnaud, patron atypique du luxe*, 24/04/2015, Le Point, Economie. https://www.lepoint.fr/economie/de ces-de-marcel-frydman-ex-pdg-de-marionnaud-patron-atypique-du-luxe-23-04-2015-1923838_28.php.

[13]*A.S. Watson Acquired 90.69% of Marrionnaud Intends to Re-open Offer for Remaining Shares*, A.S.Watson Press Release, April 8, 2005. http://www.hutchison-whampoa.com/en/media/press_each.php?id=1665.

[14]Case No. COMP/M.3716—AS Watson/Marionnaud, Public Version, Commission of the European Communities, Brussels, April 17, 2005. https://ec.europa.eu/competition/mergers/cases/decisions/m3716_20050407_20310_en.pdf.

[15]Le Gendarme De La Biourse Epingle Marionnaud, Ecoomie, Le Monde, Paris, France, October 13, 2005. https://www.lemonde.fr/economie/article/2005/10/13/le-gendarme-de-la-bourse-epingle-marionnaud_698810_3234.html.

[16]Directors Reports and Accounts, The Perfume Shop Ltd., Registered Number 2699577, Companies Home, London, March 27, 1993. https://beta.companieshouse.gov.uk/company/02699577/filing-history?page=1.

[17]With the acquisition by ASW, the ending date of fiscal year was shortened to 40 weeks in 2005 to be consistent with December 31 as the year end date. The 2006 fiscal year of TPS would be a normal 12-month fiscal year ending December 31.
[18]Anticipated acquisition by A.S. Watson (P&C U.K.) Limited of Merchant Retail Group plc, Office of Fair Trading, London, July 14, 2005. https://assets.publishing.service.gov.uk/media/555de436e5274a74ca0000fd/aswatson.pdf
[19]In May 2004, Latvia and Lithuania joined the EU.
[20]Drogas Acquired by Hong Kong retail Giant, *The Baltic Times*, June 10, 2004. https://www.baltictimes.com/news/articles/10244/.
[21]Prior to the acquisition by ASW, Jernev was the Managing Director of Interpegro Lativa, the local joint venture partner of Coca Cola, and the General Manager of Coca Cola. Jernev had more than 10 years; experience in managing supermarkets in Latvia while working at the Interpregro.
[22]*Population Levels*, Population and Migration, OECD Data, Turkey. http://www.oecd.org/sdd/01_Population_and_migration.pdf.
[23]Our Conversation with Watson's General Manager, Ahmet Yanikoglu, *Capital*, February 25, 2016. https://www.capital.com.tr/is-dunyasi/soylesiler/talep-cok-yuksek-yeni-sirket-gelir?sayfa=2.
[24]Sanders, Paul, *Foreign Retail Groups in Russia — The Limits of Development*, Paper presented at the IX International Academic Conference of Economic Modernization and Globalization, Higher School of Economics, Moscow, April 1–3, 2008, p. 8. Time to Grow in Cosmetics, *Economist Online*, July 22, 2018. https://www.ekonomist.com.tr/kapak-konusu/kozmetikte-buyume-zamani.html.
[25]"Spektr", translated as "spectrum" in English. The original owners, Mr and Mrs Vladimir and Tatiana Ilina, who held 35% of the Spektr Group, exited their remaining shares in 2018 with ASW, making it the sole owner operator.
[26]A.S. Watson Group Adds Ukraine to Global Retail Map, Press Release, July 19, 2006. https://www.aswatson.com/a-s-watson-group-adds-ukraine-to-global-retail-map/.
[27]Other than Hong Kong, the only countries and territories that allow sole ownership in the service industry are Macau, Malaysia, Singapore, and Taiwan.
[28]Luzon is the largest island of the Philippines. During one of Zheng He's voyage to the south seas, a local Chinese resident governor was appointed as the governor for Luzon in 1405. Since then, Luzon has become a synonym of the Philippines.
[29]Henry Tan Chi Sieng Sy (1924–2019) was born in Amoy (now called Xiamen), Fujian province, China and moved with his family to the Philippines when he was 12 in 1936 when the Japanese military was beginning its invasion of China. His father started a grocery shop where he helped out at a young age. Sy completed his secondary and university education in the Philippines in 1950. He opened a shoe shop in Manila in 1948 and became the largest retail shoe chain called ShoeMart (SM) in 1958.
[30]*A.S. Watson Launches New Joint Venture with SM Group in the Philippines*, Press Release, Hutchison Whampoa Limited. April 25, 2002. Accessed January 7, 2020. https://www.ckh.com.hk/en/media/press_each.php?id=888.

[31]*Watsons Malaysia to Acquire Apex Pharmacy-Deal to strengthen Watsons' Retail Presence in Health & Beauty*, July 12, 2004. http://www.hutchison-whampoa.com/en/media/press_each.php?id=1454.
[32]Retail Section, Chairman's Statement, 2003 Annual Report of Apex Health, 15. http://www.apexhealthcare.com.my/current_annual.php.
[33]The key management of Savers and ASW UK, Ian Webley, Dennis Casey, Kevin Calvin, and Brian Ingham, resigned in June, September and October 2015 and January 2016 respectively; 2005 Annual Report of Apex Health.
[34]For the current 2020 fiscal year, low-income economies are defined as those with a GNI per capita, calculated using the World Bank Atlas method, of $1,025 or less in 2018; lower middle-income economies are those with a GNI per capita between $1,026 and $3,995; upper middle-income economies are those with a GNI per capita between $3,996 and $12,375; high-income economies are those with a GNI per capita of $12,376 or more. World Bank Definition. https://datahelpdesk.worldbank.org/knowledgebase/articles/906519-world-bank-country-and-lending-groups.
[35]GNI Per Capita, Atlas Method (Current US$), Data, World Bank. Accessed April 3, 2020. https://data.worldbank.org/indicator/ny.gnp.pcap.cd.
[36]GNI Per Capita GDP (Current US$), National Statistics, Republic of China (Taiwan), April 3, 2020. https://eng.stat.gov.tw/point.asp?index=1.
[37]*A.S. Watson Centers Korea, Establishes Watsons Health and Beauty Retail Chain with LGMart*, Press Release, November 16, 2004. https://www.ckh.com.hk/en/media/press_each.php?id=1550.
[38]Exchange Rate of South Korean Won (SKW) at December 31, 2003 was Equivalent to US$ 0.12842. https://www.ofx.com/en-hk/forex-news/historical-exchange-rates/yearly-average-rates/
[39]*Watson Opens Its First Store in Korea*, Press Release, March 10, 2005. https://www.ckh.com.hk/en/media/press_each.php?id=1651.
[40]Sidik, S., *ARTO Acquisition, This is the Record of Jerry Ng and Patrick Walujo, Market*, CNBC Indonesia, August 22, 2019. https://www.cnbcindonesia.com/market/20190822145201-17-93936/akuisisi-arto-ini-rekam-jejak-jerry-ng-dan-patrick-walujo.
[41]*Shareholder Structure and Composition,Company Profile*, Duta Intidaya Tbk, 2018 Annual Report, p. 47. https://www.watsons.biz.id/wp-content/uploads/2016/10/DAYA-2018-Annual-Report-15042019.pdf.
[42]*Private Retail Rental and Indices, Property Market Statistics*, Rating and Evaluation Department, Hong Kong. https://www.rvd.gov.hk/en/publications/property_market_statistics.html.
[43]Nominal Wage Indices for Employees up to Supervisory Level (Excluding Managerial and Professional Employees) by Selected Industry Section, HSIC Version 1.1-based statistics, Wages and Earnings, Census and Statistics Department, Hong Kong. https://www.censtatd.gov.hk/hkstat/sub/sp210.jsp?tableID=019&ID=0&productType=8.

[44]Administrative costs included operating lease and pay roll costs.
[45]*Savers Health and Beauty Limited*, Annual Reports of 2005, pp. 4–10. https://beta.companieshouse.gov.uk/company/02202838/filing-history.
[46]See note 45, pp. 1–6.
[47]The key management of Savers and ASW UK, Ian Webley, Dennis Casey, Kevin Calvin, and Brian Ingham, resigned in June, September, and October 2015, and January 2016, respectively.

Chapter 9

2007–2021: Organic Growth

One Crisis After Another

A Turbulent Era, 2007–2021

The intensification of globalisation in China from 2007 to 2021 had massive ripple effects across the world — with Hong Kong and ASW experiencing them with unique twists and turns. A key leader guiding ASW's ships through these choppy seas was Dominic Lai.

His journey with ASW saw him serve as the finance director from 1994 to 1997.[1] Before he was appointed as the acting managing director of ASW, Dominic Lai was an executive director at HWL from 1998 to 2000, overseeing the Plaza Hotel sub-division of the Property Development and Holdings Division of HWL.

Lai chose a different growth strategy from his predecessor Wade by focusing on organic growth and improving operational efficiency, mitigating the hostile external business environment's risks. Lai's first challenge was reorganising Marionnaud's business — it was dogged by inappropriate financial reporting by the former owner. Hard lessons from Marionnaud helped him install a robust operating system to prevent risks that could otherwise snowball into a disaster. Whereas room for growth in mature European markets was somewhat limited, it was natural for Lai to focus on the emerging markets — China, Eastern Europe, and Southeast Asia.

For example, in Europe, the UK was one of the hardest hit by the global financial crisis in 2008–2009. After all, its close linkage to the US financial market and the over-spilling effect of the US subprime mortgage left it particularly prone to the toxic volatility. While recovery gradually emerged in the US, and East Asia bounced back more quickly in 2010, the European Sovereign Debt Crisis (or Eurozone Crisis) triggered by Greece's failure to repay its sovereign debt occurred in 2010. This soon spread to other Mediterranean countries of Italy and Spain, with the situation taking 7 years to finally improve in 2017. Of course, the turbulence was far from over at that time — June 23, 2016 was a historical date for the UK when a simple majority voted to leave the European Union. The economic impact of COVID-19 in 2020 and most parts of 2021 were universal with some markets faring better than the others.[2,3] (Figures 1 and 2)

Business Performance Amid Globalised Turbulence and COVID-19 Pandemic

In the greater picture of globalisation and crises moments between 2007 and 2020, there were still stories of massive success, especially for middle-income urban populations in developing markets in Asia and Eastern

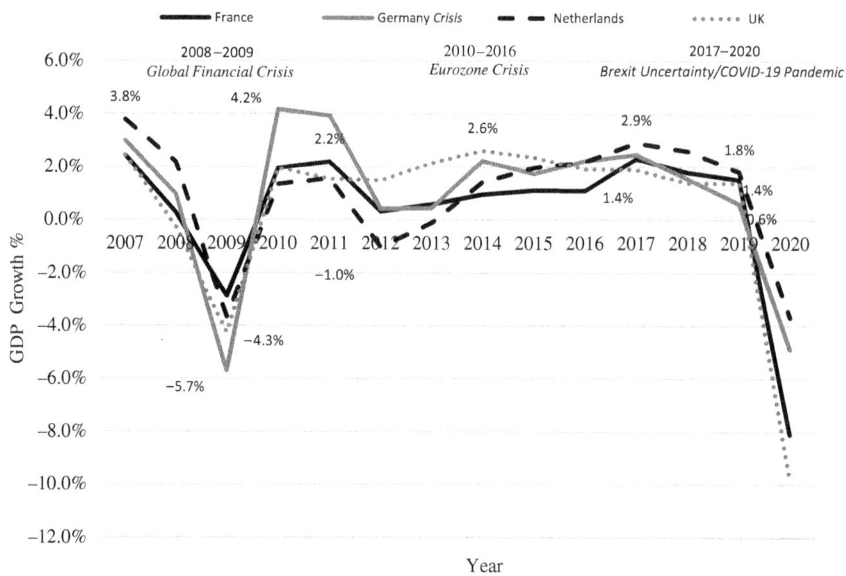

Figure 1. 2007–2020 GDP Growth Rate of Key Western European Countries, World Bank National Accounts data, and OECD National Accounts data files.

Source: The World Bank.

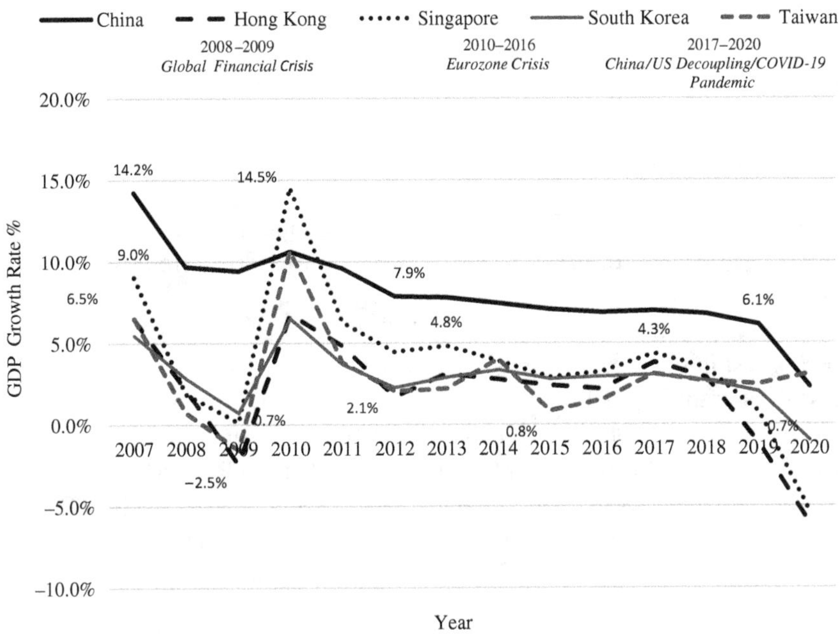

Figure 2. 2007–2020 GDP Growth Rate of Key Asian World Bank National Account data, and OECD National Accounts data files.

Source: The World Bank.

Europe. For them, growth was unabated until COVID-19. Countries that benefited the most were China, Southeast Asia, Poland and Turkey. They saw heavy government investments in infrastructure and the development of new towns. This created employment for rural residents in rapid urbanisation and industrialisation processes. Young college graduates have become ready consumers for ASW's health and beauty products.

The coronavirus pandemic's explosion in 2020 has further added new and complex challenges to the global economy. Apart from the horrific loss of life and damage suffered by families and communities, there have been severe disruptions to the supply chain with temporary plant closures and job losses globally. However, the emergency release of COVID-19 vaccines in the US just before Christmas 2020 was a sign of relief to all, with ongoing rollouts initiating a new normal in some countries and at the same time exposing global inequalities on a glaring scale.[4] Overall, this period of history will one day be examined as a turning point for humanity.

In the first decade of his leadership, Lai was treading on cautious ground to grow organically with revenue increasing from HK$99.1 billion in 2006 to HK$159.6 billion in 2020 (CAGR of 3.4%) and EBIT increasing from HK$2.7 billion to HK$10.9 billion (CAGR of 10.4%). New stores grew rapidly in developing markets in Asia, Eastern, and Central Europe from 7,757 to 16,167, at a CAGR of 5.4% (Figure 3). He commenced a restructuring exercise to improve operational efficiency by reducing inventory to free up cash flow, opening more stores and centralising the purchasing function.

These measures uplifted YOY EBIT % to 38.2% in 2010, which was the highest in the recent history of ASW (Figure 4). The Marionnaud business was transferred out of the Retail Division books to the Finance, Investments, and Others Division of HWL at the end of 2012. It was revealed in the adjustments of the 2013 HWL Annual Report's results that the Marionnaud business continued to lose HK$54 million in EBITDA or HK$309 million EBIT in 2012 — 7 years after acquisition! Although ASW's IPO did not materialise in 2013, Temasek, a Singapore sovereign

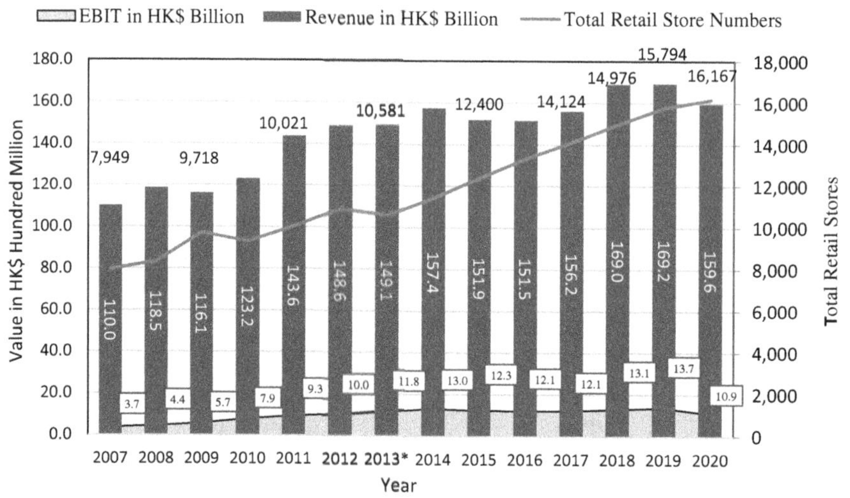

Figure 3. 2007–2020 ASW Sales, EBIT, and Retail Stores Growth.

Note: *Since 2013, HWL's annual report has not consolidated the *Marionnaud's* performance under the retail division. Based on the adjustments recorded in the HWL's 2012 and 2013 Annual Reports for the retail division, it could be elucidated that *Marionnaud* reported HK$10.1 billion in revenue and a loss of HK$309 million in EBIT in 2012.

Source: Hutchison Whampoa and CK Hutchison Annual Reports.

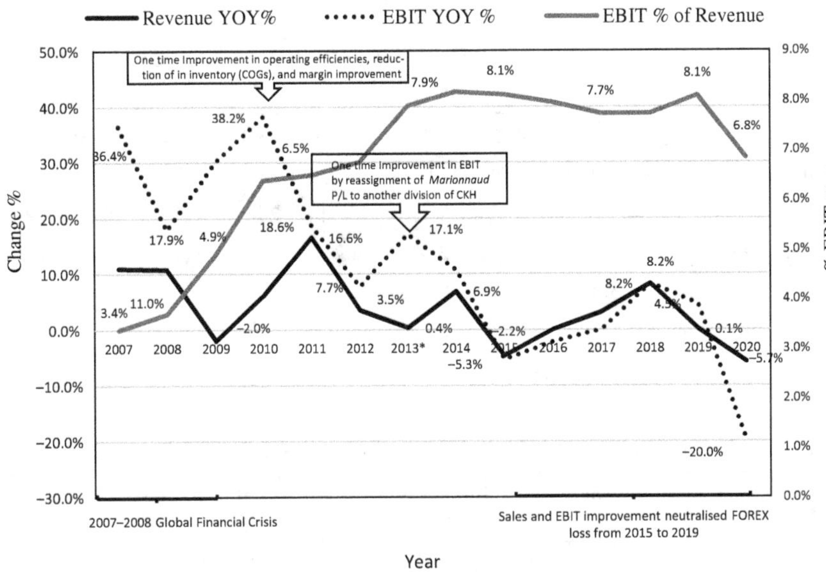

Figure 4. 2007–2020 ASW YOY Sales and EBIT Growth by %.

Note: **Since 2013, HWL and CKH's Annual Reports have not consolidated the *Marionnaud's* performance under the retail division. Based on the adjustments recorded in the HWL's 2012 and 2013 Annual Reports for the retail division, it could be elucidated that *Marionnaud* reported HK$10.1 billion in revenue and a loss of HK$309 million in EBIT in 2012.
Source: Hutchisona Whampoa and CK Hutchison Annual Reports.

fund, became a strategic investor in early 2014. An emphasis on rapid growth became the top priority.

Among the new stores, 42% were from China, 32% from Asia, and 24% from Europe (Table 1). ASW recorded 4% as the revenue CAGR% for the period, with Asia, China, and Europe registering 8.9%, 4.1%, and 1.7%, respectively (Tables 1 and 2).

It was indeed a period of adjustment, and joint ventures were reporting lacklustre performance. ASW in fact exited South Korea in 2017 by selling its 50% equity to its joint venture partner for 11.9 billion won (US$10.4 million). The e-commerce competition and currency depreciation were the two most significant factors in China which adversely affected WTC's profit. ASW compensated for this by opening more new stores in the 3rd and 4th tier cities in the Mainland.

ASW's health and beauty business's consolidated revenue showed a significant drop in 2015 and 2016 due to the weak Euro currency and

Table 1. 2014 and 2020 Health and Beauty Stores Growth by Region.

	Current Year Retail Store Number				YOY Net Addition of Retail Stores			
Year/Region	Asia	China	Europe	Total	Asia	China	Europe	Total
2014	1,940	2,088	6,945	10,923	76	395	404	875
2019	3,367	3,947	8,010	15,314	244	339	203	786
2015–2019 CAGR%	11.7%	13.6%	2.9%	6.7%	NA	NA	NA	NA
2020	3,649	4,115	8,115	15,699	102	168	115	565
2015–2020 CAGR %	13.4%	14.5%	3.2%	7.5%	NA	NA	NA	NA

Source: CK Hutchison Annual Reports.

Table 2. 2014–2020 Retail Health and Beauty Revenue and EBIT Growth by Region.

Year/	Revenue HK$ Million				EBIT HK$ Million			
Region	Asia	China	Europe	Total	Asia	China	Europe	Total
2014	20,843	20,408	78,853	120,104	1,545	3,758	6,284	11,587
2019	31,355	24,951	85,751	141,697	2,505	3,736	4,685	10,953
2015–2019 CAGR %	8.9%	4.1%	1.7%	3.4%	10.2%	0.0%	–6.0%	–1.1%
2020	26,335	19,984	83,722	130,041	1,824	1,952	5,820	9,596
2015–2020 CAGR %	4.8%	–0.4%	1.2%	1.6%	3.4%	–12.4%	–1.5%	–3.7%

Source: CK Hutchison Annual Reports.

China's shop sales slowdown in the face of the rapid rise of e-commerce. The European health and beauty business however showed 11% and 6.5% YOY growth in 2015 and 2016 in local currency terms. From 2014 to 2018, ASW's Health and Beauty and the Other Retail's EBIT margin % were consistent and within the range of 9.2–9.9% (for health and beauty), and varied between 0.9% and 2.9% (for other retail) (Figure 5).

For 2019 and 2020, the Other Retail business had two consecutive good years with EBIT % margin at 3.1% and 4.5%. In 2019, a one-time gain of HK$633 million in the partial disposal of ParkNShop's supermarket business in the Southern province of Guangdong to Yonghui and Tencent was recorded. This was due to the formation of a joint venture, which elevated the EBIT % margin of the Other Retail from 0.9% in 2018 to 3.1%. in 2019. In 2020, the jump in the Other Retail EBIT % margin was due to the closure of many offices and restaurants during the

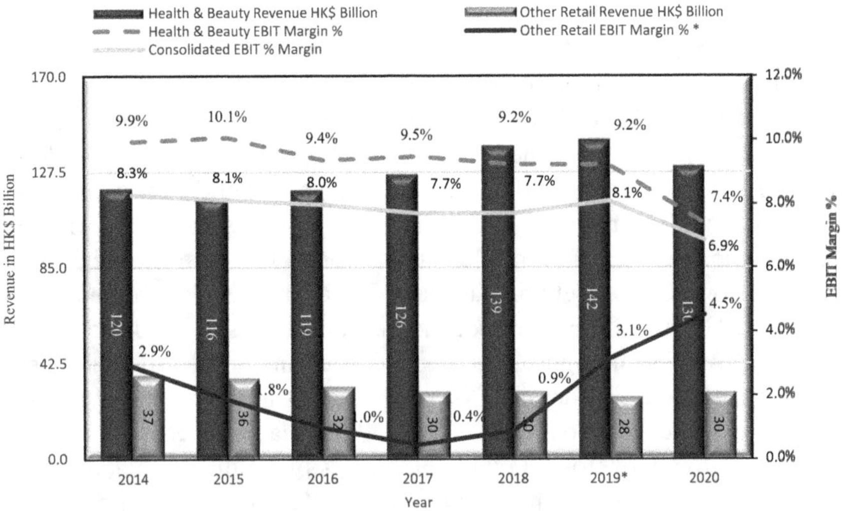

Figure 5. 2014–2020 ASW's Retail Business Performance.

Note: *A one-time gain of HK$633 million in the merger of ParkNShop's supermarket business in the Southern province of Guangdong in China with Yonghui and Tencent in China YOY EBIT % margin of the Other Retail from 0.9% to 3.1% in 2019.

Source: CK Hutchison Annual Reports.

pandemic months in 2020. White collar workers used their homes as offices, which resulted in higher purchases of mobile phones and notebook computers which improved the performance of Fortress electrical and electronics. As restaurants also closed during the lockdown periods, purchases of food for home cooking jumped during the COVID-19 pandemic which benefited PNS supermarket as well as the Retail Wine and beverages manufacturing.

Covid-19 has brought about a disastrous 2020 globally and the CAGR rate for the period of 2015–2020 became somewhat irrelevant. At the same time, behavioural change and exponential growth in e-commerce are set to bring about a more unpredictable market in the years ahead.

The Meteoric Rise and Slow Down of the Mainland Market

The Mainland has always been at the back of ASW's growth plans over the course of its 180-year history. With rapid urbanisation and the rise of disposable income due to China's reform and opening-up policy since

1978, its GDP growth has been phenomenal.[5] In the past four decades from 1982 to 2020, the Mainland's urbanisation rate leapt from 20.9% to 60.6%. Annual per capita household disposal incomes also shot up from RMB1,510 to RMB43,834 or 29 times — a miraculous rise unprecedented in modern history.[6] Investments by ethnic Chinese investors from Hong Kong, Taiwan, Singapore, Malaysia, and Thailand in the light industry as contract manufacturers for global brands in the assembly of mobile phones, sportswear, toys and other items were a key factor. At the same time, the consecutive eight 5-year plans of the Chinese Government from 1981 to 2020 have improved education, public housing, transportation, and infrastructure through public expenditures and accelerated urbanisation, resulting in rising demand for rural workers in urban employment.

ASW opened its first WTC store at the Palace Hotel in Beijing in 1989. The growth of stores in the 1990s was slow in the Mainland until a milestone was reached with the 100th WTC retail store in Guangzhou on January 14, 2005.[7] In the same year, Manning of Dairy Farm International, co-owned by Jardine Matheson, also opened a Guangzhou store. Christian Nothhaft was appointed as the CEO of WTC Stores to drive rapid growth in 2007. Before that, he was the managing director of ASW's Fortress electronic and electrical appliance retail chain of shops in Hong Kong.

From 2007 to 2020, ASW opened 4,000 WTC stores to serve an increasingly affluent urban population living in tier 2 and 3 cities (Figure 4). The meteoric rise of ASW's retail health and beauty business in the Chinese market could be summarised in the five key growth drivers:

- rapid growth in disposable income supports the single child generation's free spending lifestyle;[8]
- brand awareness of ASW as a leading multinational retailer through Mainlanders' shopping visits to Hong Kong and Southeast Asia. Low base rent or turnover rent for retailers with high foot traffic offered by shopping malls in China;[9]
- a full portfolio of high margin house brand personal care products and toiletries, about one third to one-half of the stocked items, enhanced ASW health and beauty business's profitability;[10] and
- young consumers embracing "green, natural, organic and exclusive themes".

The millennials and Gen-Z (also known as "zoomers") have an enormous appetite for new and global brands.[11] Unlike their baby-boomer parents or grandparents who lived frugally in the 1950s to 1970s, the

Mainland's millennials and Gen-Z who live in the urban centres of tier 2 and 3 cities have ample disposable incomes to spend on trendy lifestyles and purchase health and beauty products at will.

For affluent families in tier 1 cities such as Beijing, Shanghai, Guangzhou, Shenzhen, and Hangzhou, Gen-Z youngsters have generous allowances from their parents and grandparents to support their shopping habits once they attend primary school. Gen-Z will also receive imported health supplements from middle-income parents to help them get through the cramming sessions for annual examinations.

In the course of ASW's rapid expansion in the Mainland from 2007 to date, the e-commerce sector began to take off when Alibaba, China's equivalent of Amazon.com, launched Tmall (domestic and international) in addition to Tabao in February 2014.[12] 2016 was the most challenging one for ASW in China, with a 10% decline in comparable sales growth per store despite an increase of 446 stores or YOY store growth of 18%.[13] (Figures 6 and 7). Consumers purchased directly with higher discounts from the official sites of Durex, L'Oreal, Shiseido, and others. The sales decline trend was reversed in 2017 after ASW stepped up its geographical coverage by opening 788 WTC stores, leading to a 31.1% increase in retail outlets within a 2-year period from the end of 2015 to the end of 2017.

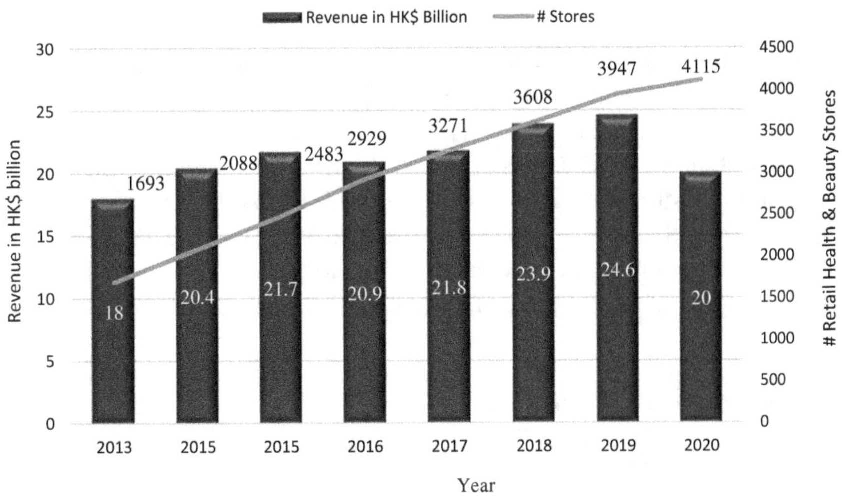

Figure 6. 2013–2020 ASW Health and Beauty Revenue and Store Growth in the Mainland.

Source: CKH Annual Reports.

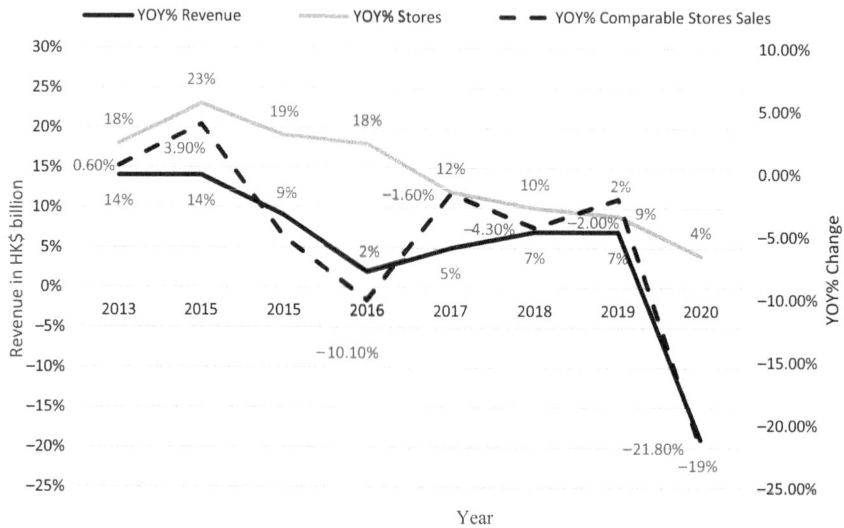

Figure 7. 2013–2020 ASW Health and Beauty YOY% Growth in Annual Revenue (Local Currency), Store Numbers, and Comparable Sales per Store in the Mainland.

Note: A One-time gain of HK$633 million in the merger of ParkNShop's supermarket business in the Southern province of Guangdong in China with Yonghui and Tencent in China elevated the YOY EBIT % margin of the Other Retail from 0.9% to 3.1% in 2019.
Source: CKH Annual Reports.

In the meantime, a change in management took place with Kulvinder Singh Birring succeeding Nothhalf in March 2017. Birring led the local team and relaunched the Watsons brand with a new store concept and exclusive brands. These initiatives paid off after 3 years with a 2% Comparable Store Sales growth in 2019. With COVID-19 lock-downs in many cities in the Mainland, ASW suffered a YOY drop of 19% in sales of local currency, but nevertheless was able to hold the comparable store sales growth at 2% amid the difficulties in 2020.

A Reorganised Business

Before Temasek acquired an indirect shareholding in ASW in 2014, its business portfolio was reorganised with four sub-categories:

- health and beauty with the 7 corporate brands of Drogas (Baltic Countries), Kruidvat (Benelux), Trekpleister (Netherlands), Rossmann

(Central Europe), Savers (UK), Superdrug, (UK), and Watsons (mostly in Asia, China, Turkey, and Russia);
- luxury cosmetics and fragrance excluding the Paris-based Marionnaud, which was transferred to and consolidated under the Finance & Investments and Others Division;
- other Retail including PNS, Fortress, Watson's Wine, Nuance–Watsons Duty Free; and
- manufacturing including beverages and water.

In March 2014, Temasek, one of the holding companies of Singapore's sovereign fund, acquired a 24.95% shareholding in ASW at HK$44 billion. This represented a valuation of ASW at HK$176 billion or 12.4 or 15.0 times of its 2013 EBITDA or EBIT.[14] The financial market viewed Temasek's investment as a short-term one which they would cash out when ASW went to IPO at a higher multiple in the next 3 years.[15] Although ASW's health and beauty business performed well throughout the world from 2015 to 2019, it was adversely impacted by a 15% depreciation of the Eurodollar against the Hong Kong dollar which was pegged with the US dollar.[16] China dealt another blow to ASW with its Renminbi currency depreciating by 10% during this period (see Chapter 14).

The health and beauty business's consolidated revenue showed a significant drop in 2015 to HK$116 billion due to the weak Euro currency and challenges from the rapid rise of e-commerce in China. ASW's UK health and beauty business showed a remarkable turnaround from consolidated losses in 2007 to break even in 2011 and continued to show impressive profitable growth from 2013 onwards, except for the COVID-19 pandemic in 2020, due to the facelift of new stores of Savers and Superdrug and the successful rollout of the customer intimacy strategy[17] (Figure 8).

Defocusing on the Supermarket Category

It is well known in the retail industry that supermarkets generate cash flow but not profit margins. Globally, the giant supermarkets like Walmart, Tesco, and Asda only showed a low single-digit EBITDA margin. The Wellcome supermarket chain, a subsidiary of the Dairy Farm International and a direct competitor of ASW's PNS in Hong Kong, also delivers 1–2% EBITDA margin which is the norm in most markets. The supermarket business's consistently low profitability had raised

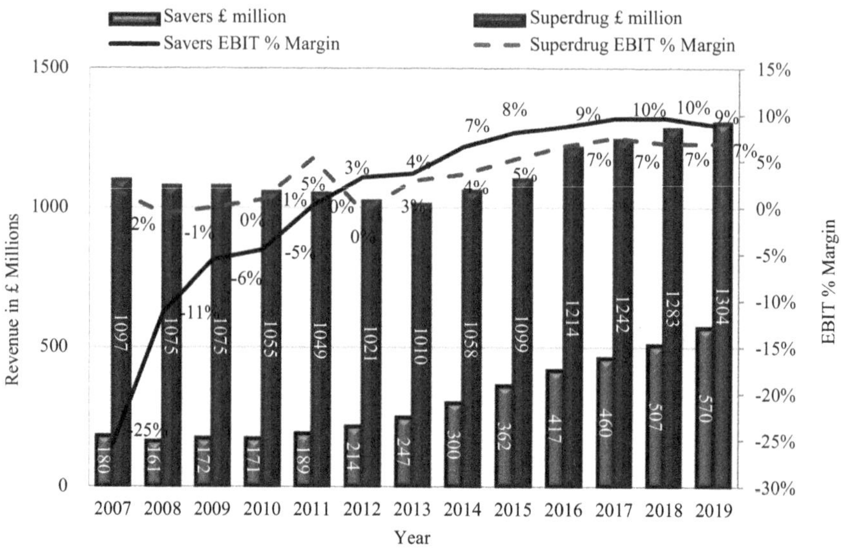

Figure 8. 2007–2019 ASW's UK Health and Beauty Businesses.

Source: HWL and CKH Annual Reports.

eyebrows among the top brass at CKH and ASW who questioned the survivability of PNS.

The Other Retail sub-division with PNS supermarkets as its main business had recorded a decline in EBIT contribution to the ASW group from 5% EBIT in 2015 to 1% in 2017 due to the sale of the airport duty-free operations in 2014. After deduction of financing costs, the Other Retail's profitability would be in the red in most of the 2010s except for the pandemic period of 2020 which recorded an exceptional performance due to social distancing and much more home cooking. With intensifying competition in the Mainland, Hong Kong and Macau and a consistently low 1% EBIT margin, management started to plan for a change in the Mainland of the PNS supermarket business in the mid-2010s.

In October 2018, ASW announced a joint venture with Yonghui, the Mainland's largest supermarket chain, and Tencent, the Mainland tech giant, and created the largest grocery retail business in Guangdong province with a 40:50:10 equity holding. Many see this as a prelude to ASW's eventual exit from the supermarket business on the Mainland.

Internal Transfer of Marionnaud

After 8 years of stagnant growth with continuous losses since it was acquired by ASW in 2005, Marionnaud slipped from # 1 position with 28% market share in France in 2006 to # 2 in 2012 after Sephora (Table 3) (see Chapter 13). Based on the restated value of ASW in the 2013 HWL Annual Report, it could be elucidated that Marionnaud's 2012 business showed HK$10.1 billion in revenues, and HK$54 million or HK$309 million loss in EBITDA or EBIT. Marionnaud contributed 6.8% of ASW's revenue in 2012 (Table 4).

The adjustments without the consolidated results of Marionnaud showed a higher EBITDA at 9.2% and EBIT at 7.4% in 2012, versus 8.56% EBITDA or 6.76% EBIT if Marionnaud were included. It was speculated in the market that in anticipation of ASW going for IPO or

Table 3. 2012 French Luxury Fragrance and Beauty Retailers.

Ranking	Retailer	# Stores in France	2012 Sales in € Million	Remarks
1	Sephora	300	3,613	Subsidiary of LVMH since 1997
2	Marionnaud	560	1,011	Subsidiary of ASW since 2005
3	Nocibe	460	680	Became #2 with 625 stores after acquisition by Douglas in October 2013

Source: Forbes, Reuters etc.

Table 4. Marionnaud Business Performance.

2012 Performance in HK$ Billion	Original incl. Marionnaud	Restated w/o Marionnaud	Difference
Sales in	148.6	138.5	10,107
EBITDA	12.7	12.8	(0.05)
EBIT	10.04	10.4	(0.3)
% EBIT	6.9%	7.4%	(3.1%)
Store Number	10,865	9,742	1,123
Sales per Store in HK$M	13.7	14.2	9

Source: HWL Annual Reports.

divesting itself of part of its business, Marionnaud was reassigned to the Finance & Investment and Others division's portfolio of HWL in 2013.[18]

Exit from South Korea

GS Watsons was formed as a 50:50 joint venture between ASW and GS Retail of South Korea in December 2004 with its first brand store launched in March 2005. After a 12-year partnership, GS Watson had opened 128 stores by the end of 2016, or an average of 10 new stores per annum. This was deemed low by South Korea's market size and potential.

In February 2017, GS Retail acquired the 50 % shareholding owned by ASW at US$10.5 (HK$ 81.9) million with a year of transition and launched its new Lalavla brand in February 2018.[19]

In 2018, the retail health and beauty market in South Korea was estimated at US$4.76 (HK$37.1) billion which was a large market size by Asian standards. The market leader, Olive Young, a CJ Group unit, had over 1,100 retail outlets all over the country at the time.[20] It was generally believed in the market that ASW disposed of its 50% stake to GS Retail due to the Korean partner's seeming focus on and prioritising of its 1,000-strong convenience stores and a low commitment to grow a health and beauty chain in the South Korean market. ASW decided it would be of mutual interest to part ways. Three years after ASW and its Korean partner ended the joint venture, only a total of twelve stores or an average of three per year was opened by GS Retail, reaching a total of 140 stores at the end of 2019. This annual shop opening number was too low to make an impact in the South Korea health and beauty market.

A Successful JV with Dirk Rossmann GmbH

In 2004, ASW became a 40% owner of Dirk Rossmann GmbH (DRG) in Germany. DRG has held the # 2 drug store chain position in Germany for the past 20 years, trailing behind dm-drogerie markt GmbH, ("dm"), but ahead of Mullers Handels GmbH.

Despite the COVID-19 pandemic, which hit Germany and most of Europe hard in 2020, DRG achieved sales growth of 3.5% with €10.35 billion. Of this, 70.8% was derived from the 2,233 stores in Germany out of a total of 4,244 stores in Europe.[21] Poland, which had half of the non-German market stores, was growing much faster during this period (Figure 9). In fact, Germany's revenue share of 70.8% was a decline from 74.4% previously. Overall, DRG managed to deliver about 4% revenue growth p.a. over the past 11 years. To put it in perspective though, its major competitor, dm-drogerie markt, was twice as big with €20.0 billion revenue of which €8.54 billion was derived from 2,000 stores in Germany out of a total of 5,700 drug stores in Europe for 2019.[22]

DRG has proven to be a sound investment and is on a steady growth path with focus on growing in Poland and neighbouring countries. DRG announced in early 2021 that it has committed to invest €200 million in opening 195 new stores, with 75 in Germany.[23]

Retail Sales Amid Politics and Social Unrest in Taiwan and Hong Kong

In Asia, social unrest in the decade upto 2020 has prompted an increase in violent street demonstrations. An unsurprising social phenomenon is that the baby-boomer generation prefers the status quo, whereas the millennials

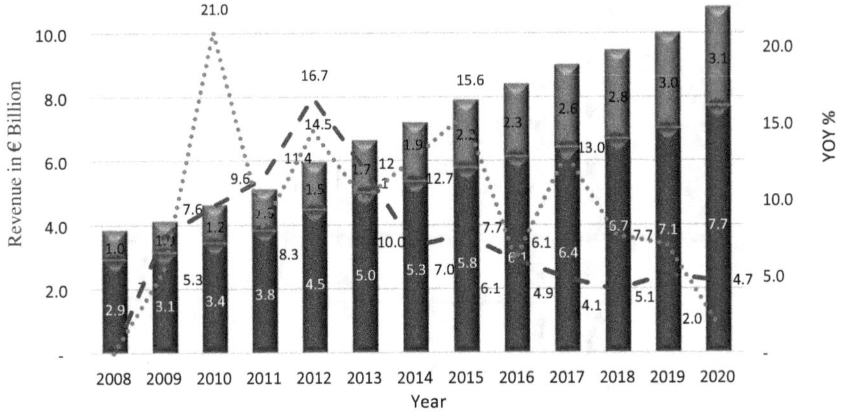

Figure 9. DRG Revenue Growth 2008–2020.

Source: DRG, Miscellaneous.

and Gen-Z opt for radical changes. Social movements in Asia were largely peaceful protests and sit-ins in the 1990s. But in the last decade, they have often led to violent clashes between the demonstrators and police, with radical and often violent and destructive behaviour becoming commonplace. Tourists of course prefer shopping in friendly cities instead of tumultuous streets.

WTC stores are favourable tourist destinations as they offer a wide choice of cosmetics, skincare, health supplements, and personal care consumables. Since around 2010, Mainland tourists have constituted 1/3 to 1/4 of total inbound tourists in many markets across Asia. As they are consumers with the highest per capita expenditure among all tourists, a substantial drop in the number of inbound Mainland tourists would have an immediate and adverse impact on the retail market (Figure 10). In Taiwan, Mainland tourists contributed 4.2 million out of a total of 10.4 million or 40% of all its total inbound tourists in 2015 but had dropped to 2.7 million or 22.9% in 2019 (Figure 11). The Taiwan economy has had to bear the consequences of its politics with the Mainland and a breakthrough is not on the horizon at present.

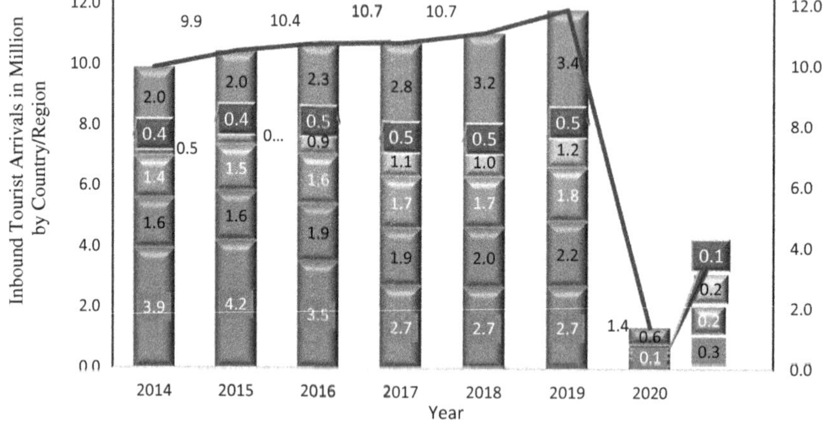

Figure 10. 2014–2020 Top 5 Country/Region Tourist Arrivals in Taiwan.

Source: Taiwan Tourism Bureau.

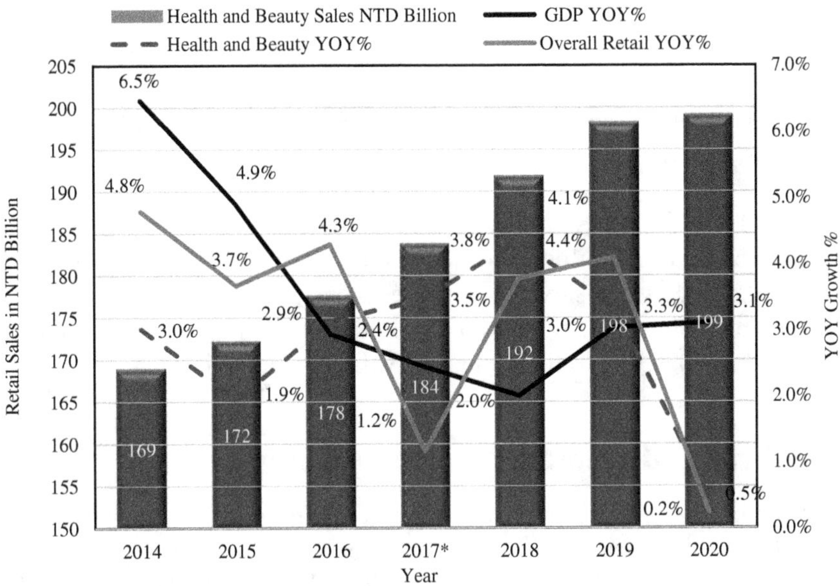

Figure 11. 2014–2020 National and Retail Sales Growth in Taiwan.

Source: Taiwan Statistics Bureau.

Fortunately, ASW has a retail presence across Indonesia, Malaysia, the Philippines, Singapore, and Thailand, so the revenue shortfall in WTC Stores in Taiwan was partially regained from the diversion of Mainland tourists to these ASEAN countries. Furthermore, there were still 2.71 million Mainland tourists visiting Taiwan in 2019. WTC Taiwan in fact stocked more higher- value Chinese traditional medicine, skin care products and health food in its health and beauty stores in order to target both local, Mainland and other Asian tourists. In addition, WTC Taiwan has tried to mitigate the sales shortfall from Mainland tourists by stepping up marketing activities targeting local millennials and Gen-Z, including:

- launching new cosmetic and skincare products with co-brands and own brands with higher sales and margins;
- introducing customer events, e.g., Zumba parties, by expanding the customer base to 5 million paid members, and 1 in 4 Taiwanese had joined the loyalty club membership in 2016;

- buy-one-get-one-free joint marketing activity with McDonalds when a purchase at ASW Taiwan was rewarded with a voucher to redeem the bonus offer for specific food items; and
- opening new-format shops, e.g., Gen-I Store, with connected online–offline experience.

The Health and Beauty sector's YOY revenue growth dropped 1.1% to 3.3% or NTD 1.9 billion in 2019 due to sluggish global tech demand dragging on the island's export-reliant economy, adding to pressures from a protracted Sino-U.S. trade war[24,25] (Figure 11). A dramatic drop was observed in 2020 due to the global COVID-19 pandemic.

"Umbrella Movement" in Hong Kong

Inspired by the Sunflower Movement's occupation of the legislature and the cabinet office building in March and April 2014 in Taiwan, politicians and student leaders in Hong Kong followed suit with the "Umbrella Movement" from September 26 to December 15, 2014.

It commenced with a series of sit-ins and then the occupation of roads and public areas in Admiralty, Wanchai, and Causeway Bay's busy shopping districts. It became violent later on but lost its steam in the second half of 2015. The impact on tourism was severe. Mainland tourists who formed 77% of Hong Kong's inbound tourists dropped by 4.4 million to 42.78 million within 2 years in 2016, but with full recovery to 51.04 million observed in 2018.

After a hiatus of three and a half years, the social unrest revived with more vigour. The June 2019 mass demonstration turnout was initially an attempt to force the withdrawal of the Hong Kong Government's tabled "Fugitive Offenders and Mutual Legal Assistance in Criminal Matters Legislation (Amendment) Bill 2019" or the "Extradition Bill" which was first introduced in February the same year. At the time, a Hong Kong man had confessed to the murder of his girlfriend in Taiwan but applicable local laws were unable to enable his extradition. According to the Hong Kong government, the objective of the Extradition Bill was to allow for criminal suspects who would be sentenced to 7 years or above of imprisonment if convicted to be extradited to the country or region where the crime was committed including Mainland China and Taiwan.

Protests turned ugly and violent clashes were commonplace in many parts of the city at regular intervals over many months. During this

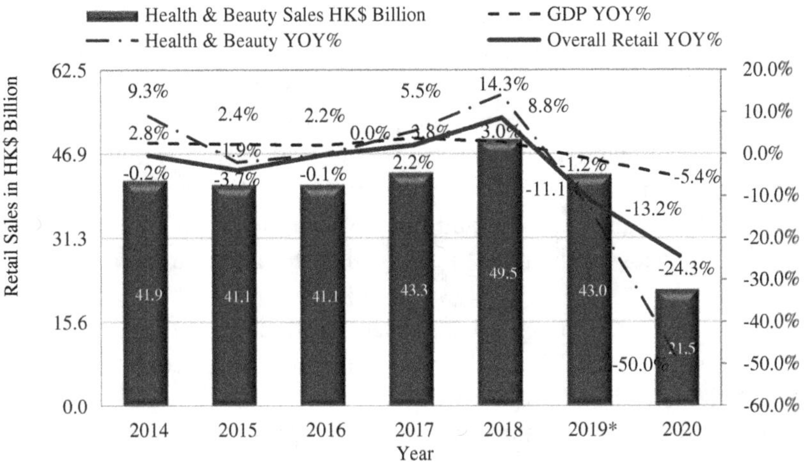

Figure 12. 2014–2020 National and Retail Sales Growth in Hong Kong.

Note: Drop in HK$6.5 Billion Retail Health and Beauty Revenue or YOY 27.3% within the last 7-month of 2019 due to the occurrence of "*Umbrella Movement 2.0*".

Source: Hong Kong Tourism Bureau.

challenging period, the retail business was hit hard once again, with a far more significant drop of 7.2 million high-spending Mainland tourists from 51.0 million in 2018 to 43.8 million in 2019.

Many shops, including dozens of WTC health and beauty stores, closed down for good. Hong Kong's 2019 GDP, overall retail, and health and beauty businesses all recorded a YOY decline of 1.2%, 13.2%, and 11.1%, respectively. Hong Kong had gone into a genuine recession (Figure 12).

Novel Coronavirus Pandemic and Global Recession

The unrest in Hong Kong was bad, but the outbreak of COVID-19 was scary. The coronavirus disease of 2019 (COVID-19) is a highly contagious infectious disease caused by a severe acute respiratory syndrome coronavirus known as SARS-CoV-2. The Chinese Centre for Disease Control and Prevention informed the World Health Organisation (WHO) of its detection in Wuhan, Hubei, China on December 31, 2019.[26,27] By noon, January 23, 2020, 2 days before the lunar Chinese New Year Festival, a total of 581 cases were reported globally, with 571 cases reported in China. Of the 375 reported cases from Hubei province, 95 were severely ill, with 19 deaths reported.[28,29]

Some Western countries, including Sweden, UK, initially alluded to the "herd immunity" theory in the first half of 2020. The wearing of face masks was not practised and its usefulness was largely rejected which led to disastrous results.[30] Since mid-February 2020, when reporting on the COVID-19 pandemic in China became a nightly event, the Organisation of the Petroleum Exporting Countries (OPEC) and the leading stock markets in Asia, Europe, and the US responded with a continuing slide of oil prices and stock indexes due to anticipated economic downturn.

On March 8, 2020, over 100 countries reported laboratory-confirmed cases of COVID-19. By March 23, crude oil and stock prices posted their steepest fall since the 2008 financial crisis at 43%, at roughly between 20.2% to 36.6%. Vítor Constâncio, former vice-president of the European Central Bank, said:

> *The (coronavirus) recession is coming from a demand deficiency and the disturbance on the supply chains. The most affected sectors will be leisure amenities, tourism, travel, transportation, energy, financials. It is possible that banks' risk aversion and lack of market liquidity for bond issuance may affect credit and provoke liquidity squeezes.*[31]

Human and economic losses were phenomenal and disruptions of the global supply chain became a nightmare for all country leaders. With many multinational companies hitherto opting for "just-in-time" deliveries with minimal or nil stockholding, including critical spare parts or ingredients, and with Asia, principally China, playing a key part in the supply chain in the globalisation process over many years, the sudden disruption with closures of factories and transportation at the height of the pandemic was severe all over the world.

Tourism and related industries were all but frozen and recession was seen across the globe. Job losses resulting from business closures in the retail, leisure, hospitality, and service industries were all too common. Lockdowns have hit the retail market sharp and hard but online shopping was a saving grace in this grim period — a behavioural change with lasting impact. The BioNtech/Pfizer COVID-19 vaccines were the first to be approved for emergency release in the US just before Christmas 2020, and vaccination programmes worldwide soon took place, albeit unequally, on a global basis. As at March 5, 2022, 63% or 5.0 billion of the 7.9 billion global population including senior citizens, front-line health care workers, and others have been administered one dose and 4.9 billion or 55% have been fully vaccinated with minimal side effects.

The International Monetary Fund has projected the global economy to grow 5.5% in 2021 and 4.2% in 2022, reflecting expectations of vaccine-powered strengthening activities later in the year and additional policy support in a few large economies.[32]

Victor Li, Chairman of the Board, presented CK Hutchison's 2020 annual report amid the COVID-19 pandemic on March 18, 2021, with the year's outlook of the retail divisions as follows:

> *The Retail division had 16,167 stores across 27 markets at the end of 2020. Despite a 2% increase in store portfolio compared to 2019, the division experienced a material impact on sales starting from February as the pandemic spread globally. As a result, for the full year, Revenue, EBITDA and EBIT of HK$159,619 million, HK$14,397 million and HK$10,933 million decreased by 6%, 15% and 20% respectively. Excluding a one-off dilution gain recognised in the first half of 2019, EBITDA and EBIT decreased by 11% and 16% respectively.*
>
> *As the Group moves into 2021, whilst the market conditions and sentiments continue to be uncertain, health and beauty products remain essential daily consumables. The Retail division will continue with its strategic direction in accelerating its "Online plus Offline" platform strategy to enhance its recovery path.*[33]

As of March 11, 2022, 452 million have been confirmed to be infected by the COVID-19 virus. Over 6.0 million deaths have been reported.[34] It has become the worst pandemic since the Spanish Flu in 1918. The global economy has been hit hard for over a year and is now on the way to recovery, but the road may be longer than many may desire as COVID-19 variants have appeared and are spreading in many parts of the world (see Chapter 14).

The Sustainability of A.S. Watson

The biggest challenge for Lai and his successor in the next few years will be to revitalise the rapidly maturing health and beauty retailing business. The trick is not only to address the online and offline connectivity challenge but to build an agile enterprise by finding the right balance between standardising operations and pursuing sometimes risky operations. Darrell Ridby *et al.* articulated this in their recent *Harvard Business Review*'s publication "A New Approach to Leadership for the Team at the Top":

> *The Principle: If a company wants to continually outpace competitors, it needs more than lots of agile teams. It requires the company's top officers — most, if not all, of the C-suite — to embrace agile principles too.*
>
> *The Team: An agile leadership team must focus on striking the optimal balance between standardizing operations and pursuing innovations.*
>
> *The Challenge: Executives on the team have to play multiple roles: build and run the agile enterprise operating system; oversee business units and functions; serve as mentors and decision makers; and handle the crises of the moment.*[35]

"New Retail" has been rapidly replacing physical retailing in China in the past 5 years and it is expanding fast beyond its borders. This consumer trend has the potential of becoming the real threat to ASW in the years ahead (see Chapter 13).

Endnotes

[1]Directors' Profile, Dominic Lai, HKEXnews: 2001. https://www1.hkexnews.hk/listedco/listconews/sehk/2001/0810/0757/f108.pdf

[2]The European Union began when representatives of the 12-European countries signed the Treaty of the European Union in Maastricht, the Netherlands, on February 7, 1992, which came into effect on November 1, 1993.

[3]The British parliament eventually approved the Brexit agreement's final text on December 30, 2020.

[4]However, the third wave of infections caused by the new Delta variants of COVID-19 emerged in India in May 2021 casting further doubts on when the pandemic will be entirely over. Depreciation of major trading currencies of pound sterling, Chinese yuan, and the Eurodollar hit ASW badly from 2014 to 2019.

[5]China Statistics Year Book, National Bureau of Statistics of China. http://www.stats.gov.cn/tjsj/ndsj/2021/indexeh.htm

[6]Ibid (See note 5).

[7]*Zhang Lisheng, Watsons Opens 100th Mainland Chain Store*, China Daily, January 15, 2005.

[8]The "One-Child Policy" was implemented in 1979 as part of China's birth planning programme to control the size of the rapidly growing population. In January 2016, the national birth planning policy became a universal two-child policy that allowed each couple to have two children.
[9]ASW was perceived as a brand retailer that could attract high foot-traffic, hence a low base rent or a turnover rent was applied by many shopping mall owners and/or operators.
[10]ASW China's retail health and beauty stores had an average of RMB 1 million monthly turnover and a 25% of EBITDA. An initial investment of RMB 1.5 million of store renovation in a new site could be recouped within 15 months.
[11]Mainland consumers become increasingly sophisticated in their choice of global brands; the Watsons house brand has evolved to become a value brand.
[12]Tmall Global is the largest cross-border e-commerce platform in China for online shopping of global brands of consumer products including Coscos from the US, dm-drogerie markt from Germany, etc.
[13]Comparable sales growth represents the percentage change in revenue contributed by stores which, as at the first day of the relevant financial year (a) have been operating for over 12 months and (b) have not undergone major resizing within the previous 12 months.
[14]2014 HWL Annual Report: 8.
[15]Peter Guy, *Did Temasek overpay for its stake in AS Watson?*, Business and Companies, South China Morning Post, April 1, 2014. https://www.scmp.com/business/companies/article/1462305/did-temasek-overpay-its-stake-watson.
[16]Cherowbrier, James, *Euro to U.S. Dollar Annual Average Exchange Rate 1999–2019*, Financial Markets, Statista, January 6, 2020. https://www.statista.com/statistics/412794/euro-to-u-dollar-annual-average-exchange-rate/.
[17]Total UK and Ireland store numbers of both Savers and Superdrug increased by 129 from 1118 to 1247 in the five years.
[18]2013 Hutchison Whampoa Annual Report: 5. Accessed April 15, 2021. https://doc.irasia.com/listco/hk/hutchison/annual/2013/ar2013.pdf.
[19]*GS Retail buys out Watsons Partner*, Inside Retail Asia, February 6, 2017. Accessed April 15, 2021. https://insideretail.asia/2017/02/06/gs-retail-buys-out-watsons-partner/.
[20]*Health and Beauty Stores Prove Lucrative For Retail Conglomerates*, Korea JoongAng Daily, December 5, 2017. http://koreajoongangdaily.joins.com/news/article/article.aspx?aid=3041626.
[21]ROSSMANN is growing significantly in Germany. Business Development 2020, January 14, 2021. https://unternehmen.rossmann.de/presse/pressemeldung/geschaeftsentwicklung-2020.html.
[22]*Positive developments at dm in the 2019/2020 financial year — Sales of EUR 8.5 billion in Germany alone*. Press Release, dm. https://newsroom.dm.de/press-releases/positive-entwicklungen-bei-dm-auch-im-geschaeftsjahr-2019-slash-2020-85-milliarden-euro-umsatz-allein-in-deutschland-3050251.

[23]*Ibid.* (Note 21).
[24]2014–2019, National Economic Growth Rate, National Statistics, Republic of China. https://eng.stat.gov.tw/point.asp?index=1.
[25]2014–2019, Retail Trade, Department of Statistics, Ministry of Economic Affairs, Republic of China. https://eng.stat.gov.tw/point.asp?index=1.
[26]COVID-19 — China, Disease Outbreak News, Emergencies, World Health Organization, January 5, 2020. https://www.who.int/emergencies/disease-outbreak-news/item/2020-DON229.
[27]Situation Report 1, Novocoronavirus (2019-nCOV), World Health Organization, January 21, 2020. https://www.who.int/emergencies/diseases/novelcoronavirus-2019/situation-reports.
[28]Ibid. Situation Report 3, January 23, 2020. (See note 27).
[29]The Chinese government announced the lock-down of Wuhan municipality where 11 million people resided on the same day which soon included most cities of Hubei province This was the so-called Chinese "lockdown" containment policy.
[30]*Herd immunity* refers to a situation where enough people in a population have immunity to an infection to be able to effectively stop that disease.
[31]Victor Constancio, Speech on "Policy Response to COVID-19 and Chance for Recovery", Virtual Round Table, Official Monetary and Financial Institutions Forum, London, April 3, 2020. https://www.omfif.org/events/virtual-roundtable-with-vitor-constancio-former-vice-president-european-central-bank/.
[32]World Economic Update: Policy Support and Vaccines Expected to Lift Activity, International Monetary Fund, January 2021. https://www.imf.org/en/Publications/WEO/Issues/2021/01/26/2021-world-economic-outlook-update.
[33]Victor Li, 2020, Chairman, CK Hutchison Annual Report, March 18, 2021: 11. https://doc.irasia.com/listco/hk/ckh/annual/2020/ar2020.pdf.
[34]WHO Coronavirus (COVID-19) Dashboard, WHO Official Website, March 12, 2022. https://covid19.who.int/.
[35]Darrell K. Darrell, Sarah Elk, and Steve Berez, The Agile C-Suite: A New Approach to Leadership for the Team at the Top, *Harvard Business Review,* May–June 2020, 65–69. Accessed April 16, 2021. https://hbr.org/2020/05/the-agile-c-suite.

Part 2

Best Practice Management and the New Retail Era

Ian Wade — the new *Taipan of ASW* in 1982.

Source: Courtesy of Ian Wade.

Chapter 10

The Three Britons

Who Changed the Destiny of A.S. Watson

"From a Backpacker to a Retail Chemist"

It was the great age of the rise of the British Empire during the reign of Queen Victoria from 1837 to 1901 — and one young Englishman was about to thrive in it for nearly his entire life. In so doing, he took ASW to crowning heights.

His name was John David Humphreys ("JDH", 1837–1897), and he was born in England on September 14, 1837. As a teenager during the mid-1850s, he joined many other young Britons who flocked to the British Empire's new colonies to build their fortunes in the glory of the Victorian Age. Before the Suez Canal opened in 1869, London's sea route to Australia and India was round the Cape of Good Hope on Africa's southern tip. Depending on the weather and the type of vessel, the journey could take 2–4 months to arrive at a faraway destination in British India or via the Malacca Strait to the colonies of Australia or Hong Kong.

JDH set sail from London to Calcutta in the 1850s as what is now called a "backpacker". After spending some years in Calcutta learning commercial skills, he later married Jessie (nee Lambert, also called "Jepie", 1847–1912) in 1864. Calcutta, now called Kolkata, was the capital of British India from 1772 to 1911. They joined the gold rush in Australia soon after the marriage for more adventure. However, the Humphreys stayed in New South Wales a couple of years without much luck, departing for Hong Kong in 1866. Upon arrival, JDH soon found a bookkeeping job at the Hong Kong Dispensary ("the Dispensary") operated by A.S. Watson.

JDH went on to buy the Dispensary together with a partner, Arthur Hunt. After learning the ropes in running a retail and wholesale chemist for 8 years, JDH bought out Hunt, who retired, and became the sole owner and taipan of ASW in 1874. He immediately tapped into the friendship he had built up with his VIP customers at the Dispensary. They were enterprising opium and commodity traders of Armenian, British, Indian, Jewish, and US nationalities in Hong Kong and Shanghai. JDH invited them to join in his new manufacturing project to produce soda water, opium substitutes, and family medicine.

In 1875, JDH had enough funding from investors to acquire a manufacturing site located at 1–3 Stanley Street, Central (now Hing Wai Building), which was a five-minute walk from the retail chemist shop. He also imported modern distillation equipment from the UK for bottling soda water instead of relying on imported soda water from Europe.

In the 1870s, the imported soda water, locally called "Holland Water", became a favourite bubbly drink instead of "English tea" among the expatriate community during the hot and humid summer months. The wealthy Chinese soon picked up the non-alcoholic bubbly drink as a chic beverage over the "Iron Buddha or Ooiloong Tea" in their festivities and celebrations. As an importer and wholesaler supplying the merchant navy and seeing the vast potential of locally produced soda water, JDH decided to take risks in investing in the production line to bottle the soft drink. In 1876, ASW launched six flavours of the Watson's brand of soda water.

The business objective was to serve both domestic and the burgeoning export markets in the Mainland and Southeast Asia. Other than the channels of distribution to cafes, hotels, and restaurants, ASW's soda water business soon became the champion brand surpassing Schweppes via an extensive network of retail drug stores and pharmacies that also stocked the ASW brand of household medicines.

Another German-owned local chemist in Hong Kong, Koeffer Dispensary, which was previously called the German Dispensary (or earlier as the Medicine Hall Dispensary), followed suit, a distant second competitor. The Koeffer Dispensary also had a branch in Shanghai. It was popular among the German-speaking expatriates in both cities.

With an abundant cash flow generated from ASW's opium substitutes and retail and wholesale pharmacy business, JDH dipped his toes in the real estate business by forming the Richmond Terrace Estate and Building Co. Ltd. ("Richard Estate") in the mid-1870s. The latter initially acquired plots of land in the Mid-Levels, and later on the Peak where only non-Chinese were allowed to reside from 1904 to 1947 except with the consent of the colonial governor.[1] Robert Hotung, an influential merchant of Chinese and Jewish descent, was a board member of Richmond Estate.[2] It later changed its name to Humphreys Estate and Finance Company Limited ("Humphreys Estate") in July 1890 and began to acquire large tracts of land in Kowloon's Tsimshatsui area.[3]

JDH invested heavily in building homes and apartments for expatriate families recently settled in Hong Kong. In return, the colonial Government named a street after JDH. Humphreys Avenue in the Tsimshatsui district of Kowloon has evolved over the past century from a residential area to become one of the most favourite shopping stretches for visitors to Hong Kong since the late 1980s. And, in recognition of ASW's contribution to Hong Kong's industry, the Government further named the road where ASW's new soda water and pharmaceutical plant was built in North Point as Watson Road, in the early 1900s (Figure 1).

Towards the end of the 1890s, the firm had a capital of one million dollars and owned close to one million square feet of real estate. Humphreys's business had become a major landlord and a growing business empire at the turn of the 20th century (Table 1).

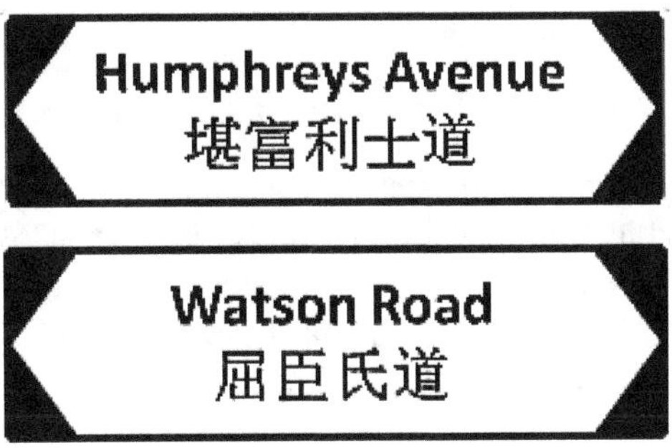

Figure 1. Road Signs of Humphreys Avenue in Tsim Sha Tsui and Watson Road in North Point.

Source: Author's Image Bank.

Table 1. The Commercial Entities of John D. Humphreys.

#	Year	Business Nature	Corporate Name
		Hong Kong and the Mainland	
1	1874	Retail and manufacturing chemist	A.S. Watson Company, operator of Hong Kong Dispensary, Shanghai Dispensary etc.
2	Mid-1870s	Property development in the Mid-Levels and the Peak areas of Hong Kong Island and the Tsimshatsui area of Kowloon	Richmond Terrace Estate & Building Co (Until 1890)
3	1891		Humphreys Estate and Finance Co. Ltd. (to succeed Richmond Terrace Estate & Building)
	1884	Peak Tramway	Hong Kong High-Level Tramways Co. Ltd.
	1886	Publicly listed company	A.S. Watson Company Limited
4	1890s	Family Office	John D. Hutchison and Son Co. Ltd.
		New South Wales, Australia	
5	1890s	Gold mining	New Balmoral Gold Mining Co. Ltd.
6	1890s	Gold mining	Olivers Freehold Miners Ltd.

Source: Hong Kong Government Gazettes, Media Reports, Mis.

He had a brother, Edmund Elias Humphreys, who helped him manage the family office of John D. Hutchison and Son Co. Ltd. in London to source opium substitutes, proprietary medicines and wines and spirits from Europe and the United Kingdom from the 1880s to 1920s.

The English Taipan Who Has Lived a Full Life

JDH was one of the four contesters for an unofficial seat on the Sanitary Board, established in 1883 to supervise and control the Colony's sanitation, and was elected by ratepayers in the special and common jury lists on June 11, 1886. He was re-elected for 1888–1889, 1891–1892, and again for 1893–1894.[4] The editorial of the *Hong Kong Daily Press* commented:

> *Mr Humphreys, who obtained a preponderating majority, is a man of ideas, eminently practical, strong force of character, and thoroughly independent.*[5]

In 1893–1894, JDH was a founding member of the Kowloon College in Nathan Road, Kowloon (subsequently renamed King George V School) which was funded by Sir Robert Hotung — the grandfather of the late Macau gambling tycoon Dr Stanley Ho (1998–2020).

JDH was also on the board of the Diocesan School and Orphanage located on Bonham Road, Hong Kong Island, probably due to his friendship with Dr James Cantile, an appointed member of the Sanitary Board and dean of the Hong Kong College of Medicine for Chinese.[6]

When JDH suffered from a heart illness in 1889, he was cared for by James Cantile who arranged two of his best students including Sun Yat-Sen to provide overnight attendance. This subsequently resulted in JDH's donation to the College which supported Sun Yat-Sen's studies in medicine until his graduation. Dr Sun Yat-sen later became a revoluntionary and organised the October 10 revolution in 1911 and was reckoned as the founding father of the Republic of China.[7]

JDH was also a member of the Masonic Club, a keen racer, and a steward of the Hong Kong Jockey Club. An 1884 trade directory reported:

> *JDH was the owner of no less than ten race horses, nine of which had names beginning with the letter 'V'. Having entered all ten in the 1889 three-day Shanghai Spring Races, his 'Visitant' won a race, vying with entries by such business elites as David Sasson and H.N. Mody.*[8]

Henry Humphreys — A Visionary Retail Chemist

Henry Humphreys ("Humphreys") was born in Hong Kong in 1867, a year after his parents settled down in the Colony. He was 8 years of age when his father became the sole proprietor of ASW after he acquired Arthur Hunt's shares in 1874. With his childhood spent in a family business, he was sent to the UK to study at St. Helen's College in Southsea, Portsmouth, England.

Humphreys subsequently passed the Pharmaceutical Society of Great Britain's major examination with a Certificate of Registration as a Pharmaceutical Chemist in 1888.[9] He returned to Hong Kong in 1889 at the age of 21, joined the family business, and became the pharmacist manager at the Dispensary. Humphreys was one of the three qualified pharmaceutical chemists in the colony at the time.[10] He published an article on "Chinese Cinnamon" in the differentiation of Chinese cinnamon and cassia by visual and chemical identification methods in the October 1890 edition of the *American Journal of Pharmacy.* This was an apparent exercise to establish his position as a qualified pharmacist in the Colony with knowledge of native Chinese herbs.

When Humphreys succeeded his father as the taipan in 1897, he grew the A.S. Watson business to become a multinational drug store chain and manufacturer of opium substitutes, family medicine and beverages with distribution throughout China and the Philippines.

At the turn of the 20th century, the Boxer Rebellion (November 2, 1899–September 7, 1901) was widespread in the capital region of Peking, Manchuria and the treaty ports of Tientsin and Tsingtao. The British Dispensary, co-owned by ASW, was burnt down in Peking in 1901.

In the decade following the Boxer Rebellion, a depleted treasury and a dysfunctional army saw the Qing Empire's final collapse. A string of disasters followed, including the Yangze River's flooding in central and southwest regions in 1908–1909, the pricing collapse of rubber stocks due to speculations by commodity traders at the Shanghai Stock Exchange in 1910, with the Great Manchurian Plague of 1910–1911 in Harbin being the final straw. These fuelled the Nationalist Republican revolution by Dr Sun Yet-Sen, who successfully took over Wuchang in Central China on October 10, 1911. A civil war period between the provincial warlords and the Republican army soon followed.

This led to chaos with millions of refugees fleeing to the southern provinces. The Chinese silver currency depreciated by 50% of its face value, and retail businesses, including those of ASW's wholesale customers, were severely hit. This led to bankruptcies and store closures. As a result, ASW had mounting bad debts with credits and consignment stocks extended to its retail customers in the provinces being written off.

Humphreys sought approval from ASW's shareholders to downsize the operations, with write-off of long overdue debts. He refocused his time building the ASW business in Hong Kong until WWI erupted in Europe in 1914. ASW was able to survive through this period with more pharmacists being employed in the manufacturing of opium substitutes and family medicines.

The ASW's dragon, pagoda and unicorn logo was accepted as a seal of quality for the opium substitues, soda water and worm cakes by its loyal customers in the Mainland, Taiwan, and the Strait Settlements. The trade embargo imposed during WWI to restrict the shipment of strategic commodities, including sugar and medicine, to enemy countries was a big blow as ASW's soda water and household medicines relied on sugar as a key ingredient. Of course, business slowed down in an unprecedented manner in the following decades from 1911 to 1937.

On Family, Social Life, and Retirement

In his personal life, Humphreys married Alice (surname unknown) in Hong Kong when he returned from the UK in 1889 (Figure 2). The couple had three children; John David, Violet Christine, and Dorothy before Alice lamentably died in 1895. Humphreys eventually remarried Eva Humphreys, reportedly a cousin, at St John's Cathedral in Central, Hong Kong Island on April 12, 1898.[11] They had a son, Edmund Cecil, who migrated and settled in Bedford, England. Humphreys followed in his father's footsteps to become an unofficial member of the Sanitary

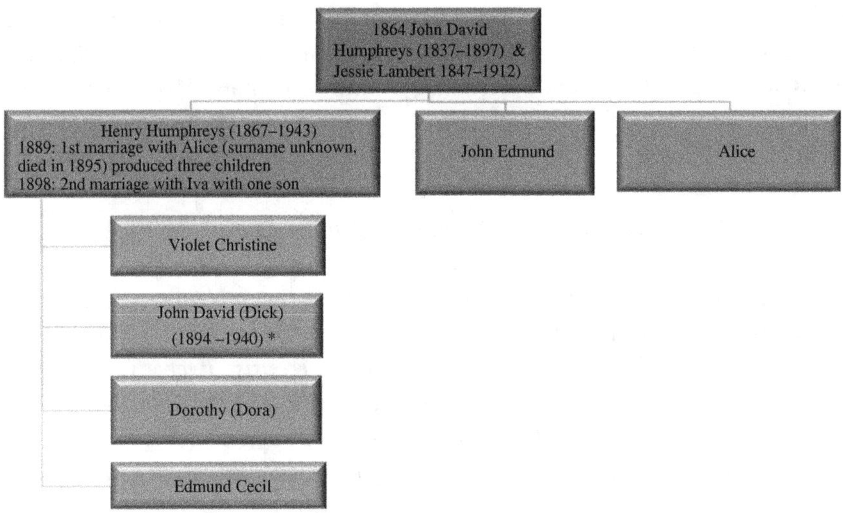

Figure 2. Family Tree of John David Humphreys.

Note: *John David, the eldest son of Henry Humphreys, succeeded as head of the Humphreys family on his father's retirement, managing both John D. Humphreys & Son Co. Ltd., and Humphreys Estate. Unfortunately, he passed away early at the age of 46 in Hong Kong in 1940, a year before the Japanese Occupation in December 1941.[10]

Source: Henry Humphreys (1867–1943), Pharmaceutical Historian, 2018, Volume 48/3.

Board when he was elected uncontested for an allocated seat in 1906. His father had first held the seat as an elected board member some 20 years ago.

In his 3-year tenure at the Sanitary Board, Humphreys was appointed by Governor Matthew Nathan as one of the six-member Public Health and Regulations Ordinance Commission in 1906 to investigate alleged corruption in the Sanitary Department. The findings led to the amendment of the Public Health and Building Ordinance to reform the Sanitary Board in 1908.[12] During WWI, Humphreys joined the Volunteers Corps to keep law and order in Hong Kong when the British military was assigned to fight in Europe. He received the honour of Justice of Peace in 1922 in recognition of his contribution.

For many rich and famous expatriates of his time in colonial Hong Kong, membership of gentlemen's clubs allowed one to meet and exchange gossip.Besides being an avid tennis player, Humphreys was an active participant at the races in Happy Valley, owning several horses like his father. He was also a member and frequent visitor to the Cricket Club in Central, and the Yacht Club in Causeway Bay. Humphreys planned for his retirement in 1918 at the age of 51 when he went to Vancouver Island, British Columbia, Canada, for a vacation. Valerie Green described Grave Hall, Humphreys's retirement home in Vancouver Island:

> *In 1918 they came to the Cowichan Valley and purchased the bungalow from Hirsch to use primarily as a summer cottage. Humphreys soon developed it into a grand, 22 room home with an Oriental flavor. He also added a 21-by-30-foot billiard room and, being an avid gardener, he transformed the grounds into a spectacular oasis. Twelve Chinese gardeners were brought to Canada by Humphreys to work in the estate, and they lived in the bunkhouse behind the greenhouse.*
>
> *In 1939, the Humphreys sold their property and moved to Victoria, where they took up residence at the Empress Hotel. Humphreys became a member of the nearby Union Club.*[13]

Ian Wade — A Metal Dragon Honing His Retail Skills

Among the legends of ASW to take the helm, Ian Francis Wade ("Wade") looms large. Wade was born in Bradford, England in March 1940 to a

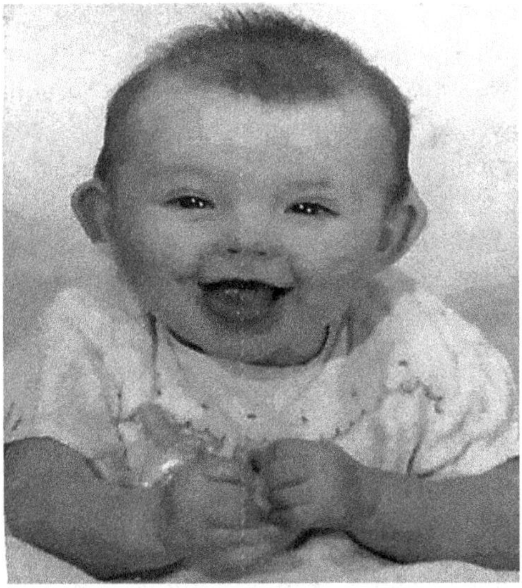

Figure 3. Ian Wade, 1-year-Old.

Source: Courtesy of Ian Wade.

retailer family. In the Chinese zodiac, Wade's birth year is the "metal dragon", and this moniker rang true of him (Figure 3). After all, according to Chinese astrology, a "metal dragon" is a born leader who has great resources and always finds a way to succeed.His late father, Harry, worked at the local Marks & Spencer warehouse before WWII and joined the army as a private. Battling the Nazis, Harry demonstrated bravery and leadership, received many decorations, and achieved the rank of lieutenant colonel.Back in the peace of England after the war, Harry became a general store manager soon after he rejoined Marks & Spencer. He taught Wade discipline, perseverance, planning, and hard work.

Wade attended Crossley-Porter Grammar School in Halifax, and he was good in French and history, with cricket and rugby as his favourite sports. Soon after graduation, he played at the Frickley Colliery Cricket Club, where Freddie Trueman, the renowned cricketer, once played. He initially aspired to becoming a professional cricketer and rugby player at the young age of 16.

After a few years in the cricket world, Wade changed track and entered the retail trade as a trainee at Woolworths' York branch at the age of 19. He worked hard and gained operational experience at different departments of Woolworth Scunthrope, Lincolinshire store. He was a people manager and knew how to motivate sales staff, which helped gain new customers and retain old customers with excellent service. Wade was promoted as a supervisor and later a store manager at the Woolworths Scrunthrope in 1968.[14]

As a young Woolworths store manager at the age of 29, Wade was responsible for store sales and profit. With excellent business turnover, Wade was earning £9,000 a year as a store manager with financial rewards at 10% of the store profit. This was far more than his supervisor, the regional manager who was responsible for several Woolworths retail outlets, would earn per annum. Wade's 21st birthday present in 1961 was a VW "Beetle", a "chic" automobile, from his grandmother who was a grocery owner in the 1930s–1950s (Figure 4).

After 13 years at Woolworths, Wade felt he had reached the ceiling and needed a breath of fresh air. He joined Asda, an upcoming supermarket chain owned by the Associated Dairies of Leeds, as a general store manager in 1972 and continued his fast-track career development. With sharp business acumen and a "can-do attitude", Wade grew with Asda during its fast expansion period in the 1970s and became the youngest board member in 1979 at the age of 38. In the process, he formed his

Figure 4. Ian Wade with His First Automobile, a Beetle, in 1961.

Source: Courtesy of Ian Wade.

strategic vision in high street retailing, honed his business skills, and developed consumer behaviour insights — all crucial attributes in his career later on.

Close Encounter with Colonial Hong Kong

In the autumn of 1981, a global search company contacted Wade for a top business executive position in the retail industry in Hong Kong which was in a fast growth phase. Wade, with the outlook of a shrewd businessman and demeanour of someone who possessed people skills and dared to challenge the "status quo", had good interviews with both John Richardson, the then chief executive officer of HWL and Chairman of ASW, and Li Ka-Shing, the majority owner and chairman of HWL, in November 1981. Wade was offered the job on the spot and began work soon after the Chinese New Year holidays in Hong Kong on Monday, March 15, 1982 — an auspicious day in the Year of the Dog of the Chinese Lunar Year.

ASW was struggling in 1981 with the few PNS supermarkets and WTC retail drug stores. They were either too small or located in expatriate residential areas with little or no foot traffic. Wade joined ASW at the age of 42 as the new taipan, succeeding David Wilson. He oversaw ASW's fragmented business of 20 retail outlets, including 8 supermarkets, five drug stores, three toy shops, four restaurants, a pharmaceutical factory, and a struggling soda water business, employing about 250 people.

Many in Hong Kong's retail industry believed ASW would be closed or sold by HWL within a year or two, but they ignored the fact that it was Li's strategic decision to acquire ASW to generate cash flow to support his other investments.

After 3 months on board, Wade decided that ASW lacked the critical mass in each retail sector to sustain profitability. He identified the key success factors to revitalise ASW's business and started to identify strategic locations populated by the growing middle class. He opened larger PNS and WTC stores stocked with a broader selection of quality Cantonese food products, beauty and health care products, and private-label brands to gain larger volume and higher margins. Within a year, the business began to see some positive signs. However, "heated" negotiations started to flare up between the British and Chinese government representatives on Hong Kong's return to Chinese sovereignty in 1997. The negotiations lasted into the winter of 1984 with a joint declaration issued by both parties guaranteeing that Hong Kong's future would be a capitalist system under a "One Country Two Systems" framework for 50 years after the handover.

During Wade's first 2 years at ASW, business went up quickly but dropped instantly when the "Black Saturday" crash of the Hong Kong currency occurred in October 1983 following unresolved differences between the Chinese and UK governments on the city's future. This crisis became his first close encounter with colonial Hong Kong's dynamic market — one defined by a full set of sensitivities.

A Sportsman at Heart and Active Public Service

Under Wade's leadership, ASW became a more caring corporate citizen. Its charity and The Community Chest of Hong Kong initiatives addressed various social needs from youth education and health programmes to sporting events with far-reaching impacts. ASW launched its charity activities through Watsons Water sponsored sports events as early as the 1985 Macau Grand Prix. It won the Diamond Donor Award of the Community Chest in 1989 in recognition of its fund-raising efforts and the establishment of Watsons Athletic Club to provide local junior athletes with more opportunities to improve their performance and build character through sports. The Hong Kong Social Council first recognised ASW with a "Caring Company" Award in 2002, an honour the company has since kept year after year.

ASW also assisted the Protection of Children's Rights Foundation in Thailand in 2006. In the same year, Superdrug in the UK raised £400,000 to support the Macmillian Cancer Relief's increasing range of services and partnered with the Institute of Cancer Research on a SAFE campaign to increase awareness about skin safety. Wade held a good number of pro bono positions in public office, including the President of the Hong Kong Amateur Athletic Association, the Hong Kong Tennis Association president, a Vice Patron of the Hong Kong Community Chest, and an Advisory Board Member of the Hong Kong Red Cross (Figures 5 and 6). In recognition of his voluntary service to the community in Hong Kong, and his efforts to promote trade between Hong Kong and Italy, he was awarded the Hong Kong Bronze Bauhinia Medal by the Hong Kong Special Administrative Region Government and the Commendatore by the Italian government.

ASW's Journey from Good to Great

Wade succinctly described his experience as the driver of ASW's journey from "Good to Great" over a quarter of a century, and summarised his journey of globalisation with ASW (Table 2).

> *Joining ASW in 1982 had enriched my life and a business career by witnessing the growth of the middle class in the emerging markets of Asia; in particular, China. Under the leadership of Deng Xiao Ping, the Mainland opened up to the outside world.*
>
> *In the quarter-of-a-century I had been with ASW, I have learnt from Li Ka-Shing, whose vision and drive empowered those who served HWL*

Figure 5. 2006 Standard Chartered Marathon Commemorative Plague Presented to Ian Wade, Honorary President of Hong Kong Amateur Athletic Association.

Source: Courtesy of Ian Wade.

Figure 6. Front Row: Ian Wade (2nd Right) with John McEnroe (2nd Left) and Venus Williams (1st Right), at the 2010 Hong Kong Tennis Classic Event.

Source: Courtesy of Ian Wade.

to go all the way without reservation. Each of those who worked in the energy, infrastructure, ports, telecommunications, and financial investment divisions acted in the best interests of the shareholders and as genuine corporate citizens with social responsibilities.

There were turbulent times all along. The currency crisis in September 1983 in Hong Kong, the global stock market crash in October 1987, the events in May and June 1989 in the Mainland, the Asian financial crisis in July 1997, the September 11 terrorist attack in 2001, the SARS epidemic in 2003 etc. With luck and timing, ASW became global #3 in the retail health and beauty sector.

The greatest challenge was the acquisition in France, which took longer to turn around than initially anticipated. Another challenge was not having a separate management of each of the two retail chains of Savers and Superdrug in the UK, soon after acquisition.

Table 2. Ian Wade's Milestones on ASW's Globalisation Journey.

Year	Country/Region	Milestones
1982	Turnaround of a struggling retail business losing HK$40 million to a modern retail trader.	
1983–1984	Hong Kong	Confronted the currency turbulence crisis amid the Sino-British Negotiations
	Shenzhen, PRC	Re-entry into the Mainland since exit in 1949 with PNS in Sekou
1987	Macau & Taiwan	Supported Macau Grand Prix event and direct entry into Taiwan
1988	Singapore	Entered Southeast Asia
1989	Guangzhou	Re-entry into Guangzhou after exit in 1951
1990	Hong Kong	Internal acquisition of Fortress, an electronics retailer
1994	China	Water bottling plant opened in Beijing
1996	Thailand	Succeeded Boots as the leading health and beauty retailer in the Thai market
1997	China	Acquired Shanghai Sparkling Drinking Water
1998	Europe	Launched Watson's Water with a new brand, Powwow, in Europe
	Hong Kong	Watson's Wine cellar opened
	Taiwan	Fortress opened
1999	China	Sold ice cream business in the Mainland and Hong Kong to Wall's of Unilever
2000	UK	Acquired Savers Retail Chain
2001	Switzerland	Acquired Badaracco wine distribution business
2002	Europe	Established a foothold in Europe by acquiring Netherland's Kruidvat Group
2003	Europe	Sold Powwow Water business to Nestle Waters
2004	Eastern Europe & Germany	Acquired 24 Drogas in the Baltics & 40% of Rossmann GmbH in Germany
2005	Estonia	Watsons Your Personal Store opened
	France	Acquired 1300 Marionnaud perfumeries and cosmetics retail stores
	Turkey	Acquired 7 Cosmo Shops
	Russia	Acquired 24 Spektr Stores
	Philippines	1st WTC Store opened with SM as JV partner
	South Korea	1st GS-Watsons Store opened with GS Group as JV partner
	UK	Acquired 110 The Perfume Shop stores

(*Continued*)

Table 2. (*Continued*)

Year	Country/Region	Milestones
2006	Indonesia	1st WPC Store with JV Partner opened in Jakarta
	Solvenia	Opened 1st Store in Zalec
	Ukraine	Acquired 65% equity of DS with 113 stories

Source: HWL Annual Reports, WatsOn and Others.

> *In countries that ASW was not able to acquire or startup due to those countries' national policies, as in the case of Indonesia, the Philippines, South Korea and Thailand, we were able to form joint ventures with local business families or investors. They saw the value of ASW's branding strategy, operations management, and retail expertise which differentiate it hugely from its direct competitors. They were pleased to let ASW be the majority or equal partner driving the rapid growth of the retail health and beauty business so that they could free up their time in other high-yield businesses such as property development.*[15]

Wade also credited the success of ASW to his leadership team, employees, and suppliers during his 25 years leading the business. He was indeed humble, since no one could be lucky consecutively for more than two decades. He expressed his gratitude to and respect for Li Ka-Shing and referred to his empowerment and trust. As the largest contributor at 37% of HWL's 2006 revenue of HK$267 billion (HWL's number 2 revenue contributor was Telecommunications, i.e., 3 Group at HK$50 billion or 19%), ASW had virtually become a corporate "automated teller machine". And cash was king.

Endnotes

[1]While the bubonic plaque ended in 1930, the Peak District Reservation Ordinance, which only allowed non-Chinese to reside in the Peak area, started in 1904 and ended in 1947.

[2]Robert Hotung (1862–1956), the first Eurasian who held British citizenship was made an exception of to live on the Peak in late 1800s. Hotung's father, Charles Henry Maurice Bosman (1839–1892) was a Dutch national of Jewish ancestry and his mother was of Cantonese ancestry. By the age of 35, Hotung was the richest comprador with the Jardine Matheson Holding (JMH). In 1899, Hotong became its board member.

[3]Without an heir to continue the management of Humphreys business in Hong Kong since the 1940s, the Humphreys Estate was acquired by Hong Kong Land Ltd., which is also owned by the Keswick family of Jardine Matheson Holdings, in 1971.

[4]Water, G. and John, J.F., Citizen of Hong Kong, A Biographical Note, *Journal of the Royal Asiatic Society Hong Kong Branch*, 1986, 26: 17. https://hkjo.lib.hku.hk/archive/files/8e5961d522c05baa5acf34c320df96c1.pdf.

[5]The Daily Press (Editorial), *Hong Kong Daily Press*, June 12, 1888, p. 2. https://mmis.hkpl.gov.hk/old-hk-collection.

[6]The Hong Kong College of Medicine for Chinese was founded by the London Missionary Society in 1887. Ho Kai, James Cantlie, Patrick Manson, and G. P. Jordan were the founding members.

[7]In 1949, the Nationalist government of the Republic of China, headed by Generalissimo Chiang Ka-Shek, lost the civil war in the Mainland to the Communists and relocated to the island of Taiwan and set-up an exile government.

[8]The Directory and Chronicle for China, Japan, Corea, IndoChina, Striats Settlements, Malays States, Siam, Netherlands, India, Borneo, the Philippines, etc., Hong Kong Daily Press Office, 1884, p. 235. https://babel.hathitrust.org/cgi/pt?id=nyp.33433082429279&view=1up&seq=657.

[9]Chemists and Druggists Register, Pharmacutical Society of Great Britain, 1919, p. 177. https://archive.org/details/registersofpharm00pharuoft.

[10]The other two pharmaceutical chemists were William Edward Crow, Government Apothecary and Analyst, and Frank Browne, the Government Assistant Apothecary. William Crow was also the secretary of the Sanitary Board of which John David Humphreys was one of the two elected members in 1886 until 1892.

[11]Carl Smith Collection, Hong Kong Public Records Office: 111325. https://www.grs.gov.hk/en/access_our_holdings.html.

[12]Pollock H.E., Report of Public Health and Buildings Commission, *Sessional Papers*, 1907, 10(185): 1. http://sunzi.lib.hku.hk/hkgro/view/s1907/1993.pdf.

[13]Green, V., If More Walls Could Talk: Victoria's Houses from the Past, *Victoria: TouchWood Editions*, 2001, p. 70.

[14]Scunthorpe is a large industrial town with a British Steel plant in North Lincolnshire, England. He bought his first automobile in 1968 when he received his profit entitlements.

[15]Personal interviews of Ian Wade, May 24, 2021.

Chapter 11

Li Ka Shing, *Wangdao*, and From Good to Great

From Rags to Riches

Following the Japanese bombing and invasion of Guangdong province in 1937, waves of terrified refugees fleeing the brutality of war poured into Hong Kong. Young Li Ka-Shing was one of them. During these troubled times, Li was not the only future tycoon to flee to Hong Kong and then endure its surrender to the Japanese on Christmas Day, December 25, 1941.

After WWII, four families among these Guangdong refugees struggled and survived to become top property developers[1] (Figure 1). With personal elbow grease and grit, they harnessed traditional Chinese work ethics and business acumen in an environment of the *laissez-faire* economic policies that the British colonial government had prospered with since the mid-19th century — namely open market concepts from Adam Smith (1723–1790). In so doing, they established formidable business empires that are today run by their second- and third-generation family members (Table 1).

Li is a classic example of this phenomenon. His leadership style is a fusion of Confucian values and Western best practice management. Indeed, his life's work embodies a unique blend of *Wangdao* (literally translated as the Kingly Way) and elements of Western capitalism. In the winter of 1940, Li arrived in Hong Kong from a village in Shantou (or Swatow in the native Chaozhou dialect), Guangdong province at the age of 12. A year earlier, in June 1939, the Japanese imperial army occupied his town so he witnessed their terror first-hand. In Hong Kong, he stayed at his maternal uncle's retail watch shop as an apprentice repairer.

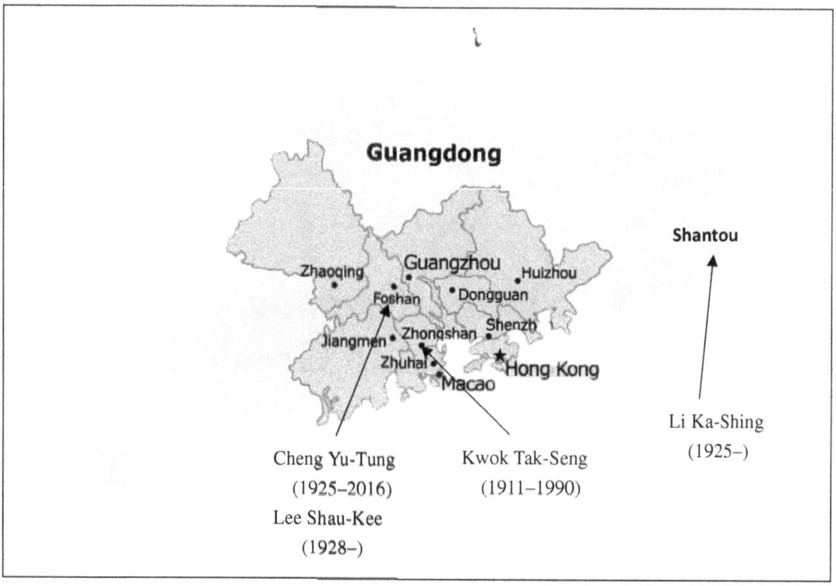

Figure 1. The Big Four Property Developer Families Originating from Guangdong Province.

Source: Author's Image Bank.

Soon after the end of WWII, at the age of 17, Li became a salesman for a watch bracelet factory. The young man would mature as he observed ever more strife-stricken refugees from the Mainland enter Hong Kong as the Civil War raged on between 1946 and 1949. It brought in a ready workforce and Li, at the age of 20 in 1948, became the general manager of a toy company. Two years later, with funding from his relatives, he started his plastic flower factory, Cheung Kong Industrial Co. Ltd. ("CK Industries"), as a contract manufacturer of plastic flowers for the export markets in Europe and the US.[2] By 1955, Li made his first pot of gold and began to invest in the property market.

Education, Life-Long Learning, and Philanthropy

Although Li never received a formal high school education, his late father was a schoolteacher and instilled in him a love of learning. His father tragically died of tuberculosis when Li was just 15. When he

Table 1. 2020 Second Generation of Hong Kong's Richest Families.

Rank	Head of Family Business	Age	Net Worth in US$ Billion	Business Portfolio	Geographical Distribution
1	Lee Ka-Kit & Lee Ka Shing (Sons of Lee Shau Kee)	59 50	30.4	Property	Hong Kong & Mainland
2	Victor Li (Eldest Son of Li Ka-Shing)	57	29.4	Diversified	Global
3	Henry Cheng (Son of Cheng Yu-Tung)	73	20.7	Property	Hong Kong & Mainland
4	Raymond Kwok (Son of Kwok Tak-Seng)	69	13.7	Property	Hong Kong & Mainland

Source: Forbes, Misc.

joined his maternal uncle's watch shop in Hong Kong, he worked 16 hours a day.

Yet Li struggled on with education, diligently studying English and bookkeeping while attending evening classes after the war. This prepared him to manage cash flow for the toy factory when he became the general manager in 1948. Having an inquiring mind, his thirst for all things new was unquenchable. These included skills like the maintenance and repair of delivery vans, details about mould-making for plastic flower pieces, inventory management, warehousing security, and other skills. While his mind remained insatiably curious, his charisma won over legions of allies early on.

Between 1955 and 1958, he was busy building friendships with auditors, bankers, legal professionals, and stockbrokers and at the same time learning from them regulatory matters to enhance the health and sustainability of his business. He also learnt from architects, building surveyors, clerks of works, and structural engineers — coming to understand the common mistakes property developers often made when devising and executing new projects.

His curiosity and quest for knowledge in new technology yielded handsome dividends throughout the years. His companies Cheung Kong and Hutchison increased their stake in and became the largest shareholder of Priceline.com in 2001 at the time when the dot-com bubble burst. A few years later, this investment showed a return of 15 multiples when it was sold in 2006 at a profit of US$154 million (or HK$1.2 billion).[3] The savvy investment history went on. In the early 2010s, Li became interested in biotechnology, leading him to invest in egg substitutes and meatless meat via the Horizon Ventures.[4,5]

Li is not only a man with vision — he strives for the extra mile and beyond.

Professor Wang Gungwu, the current director of the Institute of East Asian Studies at the National University of Singapore, who was also the former vice-chancellor (or president) of the University of Hong Kong (from 1986 to 1995), expressed his personal views on Li Ka-Shing:

> *Mr Li has the strongest memory of any other person I have ever met .... I was once in a meeting with him when he was already in his 70s. I was interrupted by his assistant as he had another urgent business deal. He was able to recall the full names, companies and their relation to the business matters ......*
>
> *Li had a kind heart, but he didn't believe in cash donations alone. Li managed his donations to charities so that the beneficiaries got something out of it more than just money. They had to go and learn something or do something to get his philanthropic assistance. He believed that only diligence would lend to success and breakthrough.*[6]

Li's philanthropic activities are through his private foundation, the Li Ka-Shing Foundation, which is the second largest in the world after the Bill and Melinda Gates Foundation.[7] It might be due to his lack of formal education as a teenager, but Li has spared no effort for charity work in education. He has generously donated a total of HK$30 billion (US$3.9 billion) including the establishment of Shantou University in his hometown.

His work has left indelible impressions beyond business, on the realm of academia.

Confucianism and *Wangdao*

Dr Chen Sun, a renowned Chinese economist and a former president of National Taiwan University (1984–1993), said this in a forum on November 5–6, 2020:

> *The core of Confucianism is benevolence. Benevolence is the practice of compassion and empathy from near to far, from close to distant, and to all mankind, which is why people are human.*[8]

Morality and kindness are values emphasised by a disciple of Confucius named Mencius (372–289 BC), who was a master philosopher of justice and benevolence. In this tradition, Li extends his support and plays his role in society for the well-being of the underprivileged. He inculcates this concept in his chief executives across all companies and supports them to give back to society by participating in charities, hence harnessing a culture of corporate social responsibility. Balancing the two opposites of interests and ethics is the practice of *Wangdao* or modern Confucian business practice.[9]

Among the many wealthy people in Hong Kong, Li is one of the few philanthropists who donate vast sums of money in successive years to support public welfare.[10] He became a devout Buddhist after he married Chong Yuet-ming (1932–1990) and his conduct as a "benevolent well-wisher" has benefited the less fortunate. The most recent example has been the social unrest in Hong Kong in 2019, which adversely affected the city's retail and service industries. With escalating unemployment during the COVID-19 pandemic, Li took the lead to donate HK$1 billion (US$130 million) as an emergency relief fund to support 28,000 retail stores.[11]

Inspired and supported by Li, Wade was one of the early supporters of The Community Chest of Hong Kong and the Inter-School Athletics Competition during his tenure. Since then, ASW's many country subsidiaries have gone on to become good corporate citizens to contribute to local communities. On the practice of delegation, *Wangdao* is about trust and empowerment. Much influenced by his father's Confucian teachings, Li further cultivated them under the warm guidance of his maternal uncle Chuang Ching Un. It was this special uncle's famous saying, "When you employ a man, use him, without doubt", that had a life-long impact on Li's leadership style. This explains why Li values talented individuals, including personnel inherited from companies he acquired. Examples include John Richardson and his successor Simon Murray.[12]

Li also lives up to the Confucian value of "When drinking water, think of its source". Upon the passing of Michael Sandberg at the age of 90 in 2017, the Li Ka-Shing Foundation donated HK$5 million to set up the Lord Sandberg Memorial Scholarship.[13] Lord Sandberg was instrumental in selling the shareholding of HSBC in HWL to Li's Cheung Kong in 1979 and Li became its single largest shareholder and chairman in 1981. The acquisition of HWL allowed Li's business empire to evolve from a local player to a global enterprise within a decade. Speaking of Lord Sandberg, Mr Li said:

> *Lord Sandberg was a true friend of Hong Kong and through his long and illustrious career, including his tenure at HSBC, he was instrumental in making Hong Kong the thriving financial centre it is today. He was always a true advocate for Hong Kong in Britain and created a great many opportunities for many. He was also a dear personal friend, and I will forever treasure fond memories of him. I hope that in a small way this memorial scholarship will help to extend Lord Sandberg's legacy in Hong Kong and in the UK.*[14]

From Local to Global

Three years after Li successfully raised funding for Cheung Kong Industries to become a property development company, he renamed it Cheung Kong Holdings Ltd. ("CKH") in 1958.[15] After 20 years in the property market, CKH became a top property developer, making Li one of the richest men in Hong Kong. In 1979, CKH acquired 22.5% shareholding of Hutchison Whampoa Ltd. ("HWL") from HSBC.[16] Over the next few years, CKH acquired another 8.5% shareholding from the stock market and became the majority owner of HWL in early 1981.

Soon after becoming the chairman of HWL in 1981, Li decided to invest in the business's retail arm ASW with its clear advantage of generating cash flow for the group.[17] In fact, in 1981 Li had in his possession two listed companies, CKH and HWL. Cash flow generated by the service-oriented sectors of retail and communications of HWL further supported infrastructure and port projects in overseas markets.

In December of 1981, Li and John Richardson, then managing director of HWL, appointed Ian Wade to revamp the ASW retail and manufacturing business portfolio. Wade pursued a geographical expansion strategy by focusing on the rising middle class initially in Asia's rapidly emerging markets. He later on entered Europe and the UK through start-ups of new ventures such as Powwow Water and acquisitions of health and beauty retail chains. Wade described ASW's journey to globalisation:

> *When I arrived in Hong Kong in 1982, HWL's top priority was for me to fix the ills of ASW and turn around the money losing business. After absorbing and experimenting in Hong Kong in the first few years, I saw great opportunities in Asia with its growing middle class in Hong Kong, Taiwan, Singapore, and in particular the Mainland with its vast*

> *potential. To learn what it took to become successful in the then socialist economy, a joint venture of the PNS supermarket with the China Merchant Group was opened in Sekou, Shenzhen in 1984. This was followed by a couple of WTCs in Beijing and Guangzhou in 1989. Geographical expansion into Asia took place in 1987, initially with Taiwan and soon into Singapore.*
>
> *The 1997 financial crisis in Thailand and then Southeast Asia and Hong Kong prompted ASW to leapfrog into Europe to spread its risks and not put all its eggs in one single region basket. The success of the Watsons Water business model in Asia helped us to extend the business into the UK in 1998 by establishing the Powwow brand and acquiring the Crystal Spring business. While in the UK, we saw the opportunity in the health and beauty retail business as the largest drug store chain, Boots the Chemists, had only 20–30% of private-label products versus WTC which had more than 50%. Acquisition was the only way forward in Europe.*

In 2000, the IT bubble burst in the US with half of the online businesses going for bankruptcy. Wade received a call from an investment banker enquiring if HWL would be interested in Priceline.com (now called Booking.com), a US online travel business, as it was in distress like the other IT start-ups. He recalled the debate within HWL's leadership team:

> *Although the sentiments in the IT industry in the US were poor in 2000, the technology and people at Priceline were top notch in the industry. Despite the majority of the board of directors of HWL expressing uncertainty about e-commerce which was in its infancy, Li supported my proposition that Priceline's business had a promising future and could take off if one of the two segments of the travel industry, airline or hotel, could be linked up. CKH and HWL soon acquired a combined 30% equity of Priceline and became the single largest shareholder in June 2001.*
>
> *The hotel industry was overwhelmed and offered good discounts of their unsold rooms to Priceline as their anchor partner. After 6 years of growing the business, Priceline's share value leapfrogged to US$ 30 per share when sold bringing a net gain of US$154 million in December 2006. This was the most satisfying part of my business career to turn around a technology company when it was at its bottom only a few years back.*[18]

ASW's Journey from Good to Great

Not many companies with a 180-year history could survive the onslaught of the frequent epidemics, economic and financial crises, social unrests and revolutions, and the two world wars in the 20th century. ASW was one of those few that travelled those roller coaster rides when it was transformed from a near-bankrupt business entity in 1982 to a global pharmacy cum health and beauty retailer by 2006. It continues with its journey of greatness to the present day.

Wade adopted best practice management over the course of his 25 years as the group managing director of ASW. In fact, the management philosophy adopted by Wade closely resembled the discipline described in a best-selling book, *Good to Great — Why Some Companies Make the Leap .... and Others Don't*, authored by Jim Collins in 2001. Wade, Lai, and other ASW leaders performed the seven common characteristics from level 5 leadership to the flywheel with different emphasis.[19] However, retention of the best and the brightest managers have become a recurrent challenge.

In addition, Li's managers including Wade would also practice elements of his business formulas related to cash flow, which remains a strength of ASW, that would resonate across decades. In fact, in an interview with US-based Bloomberg News, on June 30, 2016, Li said:

> *With frequent and sudden waves of global market changes, I am particularly cautious on cash flow. My principle is always to strike a balance between growth and stability.*[20]

Strong cash flow had become the cornerstone in the sustainability of Li's family fortune. His eldest son Victor Li (known locally as *Superman Junior*), became the CK Asset (CKA) and CK Hutchison (CKH) chairman in May 2018.[21] Echoing his father, Superman Junior said in a joint CKA and CKH corporate annual dinner speech on January 11, 2019:

> *Against this challenging backdrop, especially with the property market in Hong Kong showing signs of a downturn, our deliberate strategy of increasing stable recurrent income adopted several years ago has borne fruit. Currently, the Group has a very strong cash flow. As mentioned in the interim results.*[22]

Level 5 Leadership

> *Leaders who are humble but driven to do what's best for the company.*[23]

It is common knowledge that store managers or territory operations directors will have limited progress if they only focus on pursuing annual and monthly financial objectives. So who are level 5 leaders? Would an entry-level associate as an assistant public relations manager progress to become a level 5 executive 20 years down the road, all the while refining his or her personal agility and professional will through commitment and self-learning? (Figure 2).

Take the case of Malina Ngai. Ms. Ngai was the Chief Executive Officer of AS Watson Asia & Europe from October 2019; but she was not a typical leader in the health and beauty sector. She did not spend years at the store front gaining consumer insights through increasing territorial responsibility to assume senior leadership positions. Instead, Ngai was an

Figure 2. The Hierarchy of Five Levels of Leadership.

Source: Good to Great, Collins.

acclaimed track and field star in her high school years and won the first scholarship from the Hong Kong government to study sports administration in Australia in 1988. With knee injuries, Ngai switched to rowing and became a top rower who represented Hong Kong at the Asian Games in Hiroshima in 1993 and won a bronze medal in the rowing contest.

After a brief period of sports administration at the Hong Kong Institute of Sports, Ngai joined ASW as an assistant public relations officer in 2001 and was soon promoted to public relations manager by Wade. The latter recognised her as a competent public relations expert and a contributing member of the management team. She grew with ASW's rapid European expansion programme and became the group corporate communications general manager by demonstrating competency as an effective leader.

When Dominic Lai became Ngai's supervisor in 2006, her contributions were considered and Ngai was promoted as the Director, Operations, Investment, and International Buying soon afterwards. She successfully executed strategies in the standardisation of global operational procedures, central procurement, and international buying, which resulted in an improvement in profitability during the difficult years of the global financial crisis of 2008–2013. In the period 2014–2019, Ngai helped to turnaround the loss of market share in China due to the rapid rise of e-commerce with the formulation of DARE — the Customer Connectivity Strategy across Asia and Europe. She was promoted to chief executive officer (Asia and Europe) in October 2019. Ngai expressed her heartfelt gratitude and shared what she had done in the past 20 years:

> *I always want to make a difference in life and improve (in anything) each day, just like when I was an athlete. As an athlete, I wanted to do the best in the next race and win it. I was never a talented athlete when I first started, and I had to double my efforts competing against other athletes. I still wake up at six o'clock every morning to exercise before going to work. And I set goals every day like I used to when I was a competitor. The discipline helps me find something to improve every day.*[24]

Margaret Lau, a former pharmacist and director of operations who had served ASW since 1986 until her retirement in Hong Kong in 2016, expressed her views on Ngai:

> *Malina was innovative, full of energy and a perfectionist. Ten years ago, the majority of ASW's customer base was the "baby boomer" generation. Malina foresaw the future of WTC would lie with the millennials and Gen-Z and developed a customer connectivity strategy to retain existing customers by means of the VIP membership card to attract these young consumers with new initiatives to enlarge the customer base.*[25]

In the past 20 years, Ngai grew from an entry-level management position to what she is today as a level 5 executive with a steep learning curve. With the attributes of a committed athlete since her school days, Ngai is very much like Wade who would strive for excellence and plan ahead before each contest. It is indeed a rare quality that is not easily replicated across the board. But it became elemental in Li's business arithmetic.

First Who, Then What

Wade was committed to creating a team of A-players who were committed to the team goal without reservations. They would also have to possess the seven characteristics of a great team player to make an effective organisation[26] (Figure 3). He put it succinctly:

> *Get the right people on board and try them out in different positions in the company—each effective team player will possess different skills and strengths to complement each other.*[27]

From 1982 onwards, ASW grew by leaps and bounds from a small base in Hong Kong by the appointment of enterprising managers who had the adventurer's spirit and could deal with uncertainties.

In 1986, Nigel Healy, a British national who came to Hong Kong after working in the grocery trade in Jamaica for a couple of years, was recruited by Wade as the retail operations manager of ParkNShop in Hong Kong. After the June 1989 Tiananmen Square Incident, weak consumer confidence hit Hong Kong's retail business by 30%. Healy was assigned to work in a project team to streamline the retail health and beauty business. One of his jobs was to successfully streamline the retail business to bring about targeted savings. This won him encomiums when the

Figure 3. Seven Characteristics of a Great Team Player.

Source: Good to Great, Collins.

project was completed at the end of December 1990. As a result of this, Healy became the retail operations director in Taiwan soon afterwards.

In 1991, local consumers became furious when Taiwanese media reported the six times price discrepancy of the 125 gram Imperial Leather®, a premium brand of imported bar soap, sold in Hong Kong and Taiwan. With the help of public relations companies, Healy explained that the much higher listed price of Imperial Leather® sold in WTC's Taipei shop was largely due to custom duties and sales tax levied by the Taiwan government. The soap crisis was eventually defused when both WTC and Imperial Leather's distributor in Taiwan agreed to reduce the retail price from NTD 120 to NTD 65, but still much higher than Hong Kong's NTD 21.[28]

Healy was subsequently posted to Singapore and Malaysia and then the Baltic to oversee the start-up of Eastern European country markets in the 2000s. In 2004, Healy was reassigned to the Philippines to head up ASW's joint-venture health and beauty business with the SM group and double-up as the managing director of ASW's Southeast Asia operations until his retirement in 2008.

After years of rapid growth in Taiwan, ASW's health and beauty business was slowing down in the early 2010s. Toby Anderson, managing director of Watsons Health & Beauty Thailand, was relocated to Taiwan as the managing director to revitalise its business in April 2012.[29] With the Gen-X becoming great users of the internet, he saw the opportunities to improve the business by opening up a new distribution channel in e-commerce in Taiwan.

Anderson felt that Taiwan was a market ready to embrace e-commerce as there was an abundance of local talent due to its strengths in the IT industry. Meanwhile, Taiwan would also be ASW's test market for e-commerce in Asia and its success could be readily replicated in other markets, in particular the Mainland which had a similar culture, language, and consumer behaviour.

In February 2016, Anderson was promoted as the CEO of ASW's health and beauty business in Asia, and he continued to take charge of the marketing function of Eastern Europe until he retired in July 2018. Anderson was a key member of ASW's health and beauty leadership team in developing and implementing the DARE strategy. He appointed Irene Lau, a former marketing and brand development director of ASW Singapore between 2008 and –2011 who rejoined ASW in 2013, to take charge of WTC's Taiwan marketing and e-commerce function. Lau successfully built ASW's Taiwan's e-commerce business and fully integrated the online and offline operations, doubling the business in value over a 4-year period under Anderson's supervision.

Lau was subsequently reassigned back to Singapore to head up ASW's local operations in September 2018. She replicated the e-commerce business model in Singapore with online and offline integration in a seamless manner within a year. When the COVID-19 pandemic reached Singapore in the first quarter 2020, ASW was ready to continue its business online when foot traffic was much reduced due to social distancing measures. The business impact on ASW in the Singapore market was kept to a minimum in the first half of 2020, as compared with the neighbouring countries of Malaysia or Thailand. Lau was promoted as the managing director overseeing the 100 Watsons stores in Singapore in July 2020.

Confront the Brutal Facts

> *Accept the reality, be resilient along the journey to greatness and have the discipline to confront the most brutal facts.*[30]

Retail markets in Asia and Europe face frequent, cyclical, and unexpected challenges that negatively impact the market. Li's people understand this. Wade was resilient enough to pull through every crisis during his time from 1982 to –2006, just like Humphreys did in 1909–1932.

When Lai succeeded Wade as the acting group managing director of ASW in 2007, he soon faced the mounting subprime mortgage crisis which originated in the US and spread quickly to Europe, with consumer sentiment falling to the bottom. This hit Marionnaud, a luxury fragrance and cosmetics retailer, badly with many shops bleeding. Lai, as the new helmsman of ASW, found himself in a situation not dissimilar to what Wade was facing in the 1983 Black Saturday nightmare, the 1989 Tiananmen Square Incident and the 1997 Asian financial crises. Closing of the poor performing shops and letting go of good employees were difficult but unavoidable measures.

Marionnaud gradually and slowly recovered and the business began to turn around in 2013. In the same year, Marionnaud's business was transferred to the Finance & Investments and Others division of HWL probably for accounts reporting reasons.

The disastrous year 2020 immediately followed Ngai's becoming the CEO of ASW Asia and Europe in October 2019. ASW reported unprecedented losses due to the COVID-19 pandemic. The leadership took the right decision in keeping stores open and retaining the retail staff. Of course, government pandemic relief subsidies in various countries played a role, too. Ngai reported ASW's UK buinesses in the *Retail Gazette*:

> *With over 18,000 employees and 1550 stores across the three retail brands, the support package is developed based on the principle that no member of staff should be worse off financially because of the crisis. In this challenging time, our top priority is to look after our people and our customers.*[31]

Like in the UK, AS Watson in many markets in Asia and Europe has minimised the closure of retail shops despite a substantial drop in foot traffic and business volume. Confronting the brutal facts and being a responsible employer in times of crisis is indeed a true test of leadership.

The Hedgehog Concept

In the parlance of management planners, theories of success abound — some spin as fast as a hedgehog. "The Hedgehog Concept" with "Big Hairy Audacious Goal" (or BHAG) has been described as causing dynamic transformations in the continuum of "Good to Great", building up fitnessed speed, momentum, and results. It entails making a series of right decisions consistently that are supremely well executed, and accumulate one upon another over a long period (Figure 4).

In 1982, ASW's top priority was to turn around the money-losing retail business to become a profitable cash flow generator within just 3 years. By the end of 1984, when Hong Kong's future was finally settled between the British and Chinese governments, ASW's feet were on solid

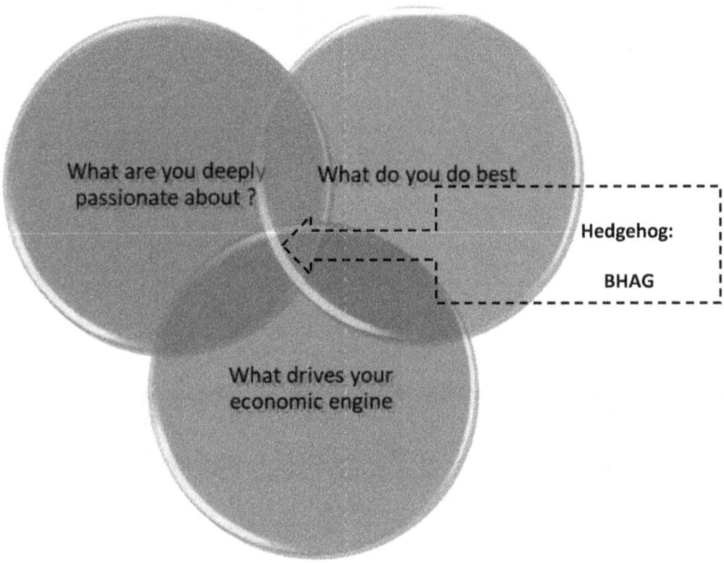

Figure 4. ASW's Hedgehog Concept and BHAG.

Source: Good to Great, Collins.

ground. This meant Wade and his team were busy on the drawing board, back at what they did best — executing with precision.

ASW's ambition was to become a regional company by entering the newly industrialised countries with a growing middle class in Asia. However, the 1997 financial crisis shifted ASW to a higher gear with a campaign code-named the "BHAG" to enter the UK and European continent. The vision was to become a global health and beauty retail empire by 2006 with HK$100 billion revenue, of which WTC would deliver 85% sales of the ASW group.

Indeed, by the end of 2006, ASW had made a quantum leap from 823 retail stores in 1999 to 7,757 retail stores in 2006 with two-thirds acquired in Europe and the UK since 2000. The period of 2007–2020 was mainly one of internal growth and strengthening of the organisation and its core competencies. By the end of 2020, there were 16,167 stores and 138 million loyalty club members. Revenue and EBIT grew from HK$99.1 billion and HK$2.7 billion to HK$159.6 billion and HK$10.9

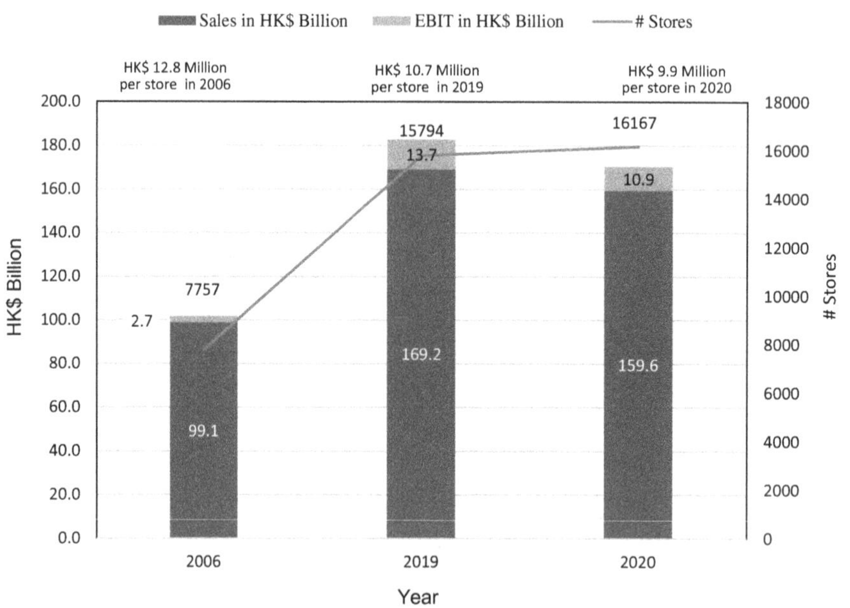

Figure 5. ASW 2016 and 2020 Performance.

Source: CK Hutchison Annual Reports.

billion (Figure 5). A substantial YOY drop in both revenue and EBIT of –6% and –20% was observed in 2020 due to the COVID-19 pandemic.

However, it was an audacious move for ASW to continue to invest in new stores with a 2% new gain of 373 stores primarily in emerging markets.

While sales have increased with the opening of new stores, part of the sales from the global brands have been lost with consumers shopping from the e-commerce platforms of Amazon.com, Grab, TMall Global, and others directly, hence the decline in sales per store over the past decade.

Culture of Discipline

Many successful companies establish a disciplined culture before making the next quantam leap without losing their momentum or position. This is because many managers follow corporate guidelines closely without cutting corners to achieve quick and unsustainable results. Take David Boynton, for example. Boynton had spent time as the retail operations director in WTC Hong Kong when he was transferred to Taiwan as the Head of the Buying and Merchandising Department to develop a portfolio of private label health and beauty products in line with the corporate guidelines in 2001.[32]

Boynton's greatest contribution to ASW's Taiwan venture during his 2 years there was the introduction of standard operating procedures. These laid a strong foundation for ASW's rapid growth of its WTC stores in Taiwan. The standard operating procedures cater to fast-moving consumer products that suit local consumers' tastes and likes yet have the same kind of quality standards as other markets served by ASW.

Dominic Lai was also keen to introduce systems and processes when he became the head of ASW so that measurement of performance would be consistent across the entire organisation while embracing local culture and practices in the interests of serving customers. This strategy of Lai's has remained to date.

Technology Accelerators

Disciplined teams with a common culture have moved ASW forward — but accelerating technology is key to its overall strategy. ASW has always been the first to adopt new technologies to become a relevant retail chemist in the Mainland and Hong Kong. It has gained a position as a market leader from this practice. Although ASW came three decades later than Pfizer (who first marketed its brand of anti-wormer bonbons in the 1850s), the Watson's brand of santonin bonbons became the star product within a short period after it was launched in the late 19th century. ASW retained the market leader position for almost a century in China and the overseas Chinese communities in Southeast Asia with its coloured pagoda-shaped bonbons that contained the herbal ingredient santonin. Watson's Soda Water has been a top seller in most Asian markets over the past 150 years despite Schweppes being the first brand marketed in Hong Kong a couple of decades earlier.

However, since Amazon launched its partnership with Toys "R" Us in the US in 2010, the retail scene has changed dramatically. In 2015–2016, online shopping became a severe threat to the survival of ASW's 3,000 retail stores in the Mainland. Initially, ASW relied on its generous loyal membership programmes to attract its consumers to shop physically at WTC drug stores. But that alone did not prevent its members from shopping at Amazon.com or Strawberry.net. The likes of the powerful Taobao, Tmall Domestic, Tmall Global, and JD.com online shopping platforms have lured away many consumers in China. The situation called for further proactive measures indeed.

Despite being a latecomer to e-commerce, China has definitely caught up. China's e-commerce business was anticipated to reach 37% of all retail business transactions in 2019, with year-on-year growth of 27.3%. For this, in 2018 ASW shifted its focus to pursuing technology as a driver to grow its market share with on-site advice. This is not easily replicable on the e-commerce platform. The pioneering of retail stores as working laboratories for innovations — from DNA testing programmes, click-and-collect solutions, virtual make-up stations, and automated checkouts — have clearly differentiated ASW from its competitors.[33]

It was part of their larger "Flywheel" longevity strategy that goes back nearly 40 years.

The Flywheel

With Wade's arrival in early 1982, ASW embarked on its "Good to Great" journey from a defocused retail and manufacturing business to one which would build on solid ground. The initial years of Wade at ASW were the start-up and building phases. The architect designed the building model and adapted to the time and market's political and economic environment.

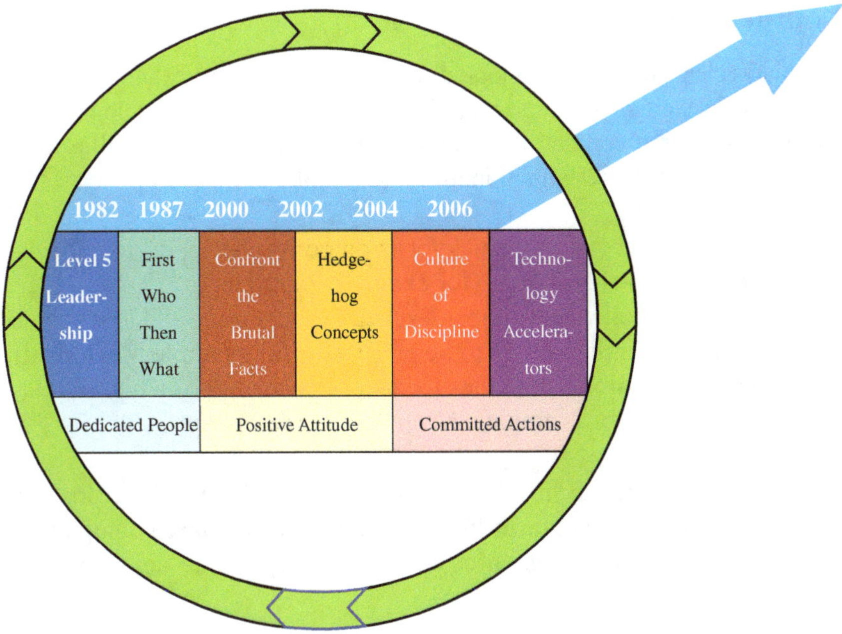

Figure 6. The Flywheel.

Source: The Discipline of Market Leaders.

By the end of 1984, the quality specifications and materials for making three building blocks of Level 5 Leadership, First Who, Then What, and Confront the Brutal Facts, were firmly in place. The momentum continued in the following years of 1985–1999 with three more building blocks — the Hedgehog Concept, Culture of Discipline, and Technology Accelerators.

With the acquisitions of a string of retail drug stores in the UK and continental Europe from 2000 to 2006 and the disposal of the non-core businesses of Powwow water and Mountain Cream ice cream in the 2000's, the flywheel of ASW took-off in 2006 — after a quarter of a century since Wade's arrival in Hong Kong. ASW's journey to greatness continued with Lai succeeding Wade in January 2007 as the acting managing director of ASW with a laser focus on the retail health and beauty sector (Figure 6).

Competitive Strategies

As a market leader, ASW has adopted and adapted what Treacy and Wiersema articulated in their marketing leadership theory in 1995 by developing and executing the three competitive strategies. Treacy and Wiersema illustrated their theory using the restaurant industry's examples[34] (Figure 7).

- Customer Intimacy: Companies focus on convenience, customer relationships, and total solutions (for example Pizza Hut).
- Operational Excellence: Companies focus on low price and low operating cost with a limited menu to be profitable (for example McDonald).
- Product Leadership: Companies focus on a speciality or a high-quality product/service (for example a Michelin-Star restaurant).

ASW's retail health and beauty businesses of WTC, Superdrug, or Kruidvat and its joint ventures like DRG adopt all the three competitive strategies with an emphasis on customer intimacy. Wade developed the

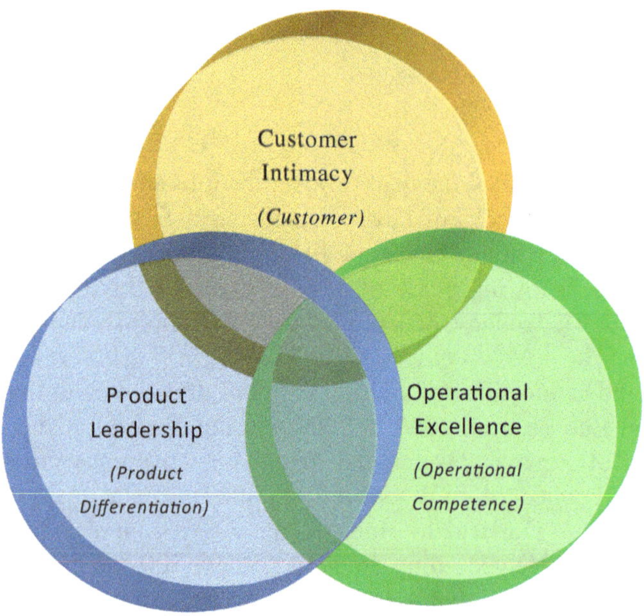

Figure 7. The Three Competitive Strategies.

Source: The Discipline of Market Leaders.

Watson's brand further with a portfolio of private-label products contributing twice the global brands' gross profit margins. A case in point — Holland & Barrett, a health supplements retailer, had a higher net profit margin than ASW for most of the 2010s until 2017.

Indeed, the retail health and beauty market has become increasingly competitive in the past 8 years without any sign of abating. Seen from a different angle though, competition from speciality chain shops such as Holland & Barrett and Sephora in Europe could be a blessing in disguise — it has accelerated ASW's resolve to adopt radical management practices to reverse the downward trends[35,36] (see Chapter 13).

ASW's e-commerce revenue began to jump in the mid-2010s and then lockdowns and social distancing brought on by the COVID-19 pandemic have pushed online shopping to unprecedented levels. This change in consumer behaviour seems irreversible, thus creating new battlefields for businesses for decades to come.

Passing the Baton to "Superman Junior"

Li's *Wangdao* business philosophy can be summarised as benevolence, empowerment, and nurturing of talent. In addition, diversity and innovation are key elements in the make-up of his business empire:

- Diversified investments with a focus on several core industries such as real estate, energy, transportation, retail, telecommunications, and finance;
- Diversity of risks through globalisation to avoid recurrence of sudden financial and economic crises in geopolitics; and
- Innovation and technology (e.g., the development of British and Italian telecommunications markets, with brands of Rabbit, Orange, and 3, investment in Priceline® in early 2000 and the future of plant-based substitutes for meat products such as Impossible Food®).

His business prowess and philosophy have often caught other business leaders by surprise. For example, Li's financial and business savvy in the acquisition of Priceline.com® in the United States surprised many Wall Street and Hong Kong investment bankers and his own executives. Yet, this move harked back to his cash flow lever of operating a plastic flower factory — the one that allowed him to earn his first pot of gold decades ago.

Li's choice of leaders, exemplified by Wade's intrapreneurship skills, their display of best practice management, and the adoption of competitive strategies, have all accounted for ASW's success since it became a fully owned subsidiary of HWL in 1981.[37]

On March 16, 2018, Cheung Kong and Hutchison Group officially announced that Mr. Li Ka-Shing would retire after the annual general meeting on May 10 of the same year. His eldest son, Victor Li ("VL", dubbed by the media as Superman Junior) took over as chairman of the board at both companies.[38] Like father, like son: cash flow has become the cornerstone of the sustainable enrichment of the Li family. VL said:

> *However, liquidity and access to bank and debt capital markets remained robust. Compared to the first half of 2019, the Group's free cash flow in 2020 was higher, resulting in a 1.1% improvement in the Group's net debt to net total capital ratio to 25.1% and a significant reduction in interest financing costs. Improved free cash flow resulted from reducing or deferring expenditure, disciplined working capital management, lower interest and financing costs and lower cash tax costs.*[39]

Endnotes

[1]The four main influential families from Guangdong province who planted their roots in the former colony of Hong Kong are namely; Li Ka-Shing, Lee Shau-Kee, the late Cheng Yu-Tung, and the late Kwok Tak-Seng.

[2]The Chinese words, "Cheung Kong" refer to the great river Yangtze that aggregates countless streams and tributaries. This was the dream of Li Ka-Shing to make CKI as a great Chinese company like the mighty Yangtze.

[3]Li Firms Reap HK$1.2b from Priceline Sale, *South China Morning Post*, December 6, 2006. https://www.scmp.com/article/574330/li-firms-reap-hk12b-priceline-sale.

[4]Paul, D., On a Mission to Dispense with the Egg, *Financial Times*, February 26, 2014. https://www.ft.com/content/14e3bd70-9d39-11e3-83c5-00144feab7de.

[5]Ryan, S., Meatless Meat Revolution Kicks Off in Hong Kong, Where Li Ka-Shing Puts His Money Where His Mouth Is, *South China Morning Post*, May 3, 2019. https://www.scmp.com/business/companies/article/3008774/meatless-meat-revolution-kicks-hong-kong-where-li-ka-shing-puts.

[6]People: A History Memo from Professor Wang Gungwu, on Li Ka-Shing, Lee Kuan Yew and Robert Kuok, Future City Summit, September 8, 2019. Accessed March 15, 2021. https://medium.com/@futurecitysummit/people-a-history-

memo-from-prof-wang-gungwu-on-li-ka-shing-lee-kuan-yew-and-robert-kuok-f3bdcdbae48e.

[7]He founded the Li Ka-Shing Foundation in 1980 and has since donated HK$27 billion (US$3.5 billion) so far to nurture 120 million students and take care of 17 million patients, 80% of whom are in the Greater China region.

[8]Disintegration and Reunion, 18th Global Views Leaders Forum, November 5–6, 2020. Commonwealth Publishing Group, Taipei. https://www.youtube.com/watch?v=O9hjXqpND7M

[9]Wangdao, a term which can be traced back to the era of Confucius (551–479 BCE) regarding virtues of rulers who govern with morality and kindness.

[10]Home, Li Kai Shing Foundation, Corporate Website. https://www.lksf.org/?lang=hk.

[11]Most retailers received a one-time financial subsidy of HK$60,000 (or US$7,700) and many retail stores received HK$30,000 (US$3,000 pounds).

[12]John Richardson, a British born Australian lawyer, who joined HIT as an executive director in 1976 and became the chief executive at the end of 1980. He stayed on until 1984 when Simon Murray, a former French Foreign Legion officer, became his successor when Li acquired the merchant bank which Murray co-founded and managed. After 10 years with HWL, Murray left and started up his own investment company and remains as a non-executive director of CK Hutchison until 2015.

[13]The donation of HK$5million (£500,000) to two designated UK universities was a memorial tribute to Sandberg, a life-long friend of Li for over 50 years. He advised Li to become a global business leader instead of remaining as a wealthy local property tycoon when he acquired HWL in 1978.

[14]Mr. Li Ka-shing establishes a scholarship in memory of Lord Sandberg of Passfield, OBE, CBE, press release, Li Ka-Shing Foundation, September 4, 2017. https://lksf.org/mr-li-ka-shing-establishesa-scholarship-in-memory-oflord-michael-sandberg-of-passfield-obe-cbe/.

[15]CKI changed its name to Cheung Kong (Holding) Co. Ltd. and became a publicly listed company with the Hong Kong Stock Exchange in November 1972.

[16]HSBC provided interim financing through a share swap with HWL's shareholders when the latter faced financial difficulties soon after the 1973 Global Oil Crisis due to over-stretching of its Indonesia investments hit by substantial currency depreciation of the Indonesian rupiah. After the restructuring of HWL in 1975, HSBC was actively seeking investors to take over its shareholding in HWL and CKH was the ideal candidate as Li was keen to pursue the direct investment opportunity.

[17]With an average of 60–90 days payment period upon receipt of goods from suppliers, ASW generates abundant cash flow. In 2018, ASW revenue was HK$168,991 (£16,899) million. A 5% interest p.a. investment would generate an additional HK$8,449 (or approximately £849) million earnings.

[18]Personal interviews of Ian Wade, 24th May 2021.
[19]The 7 common characteristics in the *Good to Great* book are level 5 leadership, first who then what, confront the brutal facts, the hedgehog concept, culture of discipline, and the flywheel.
[20]Lau, A., Hong Kong Billionnaire Li Ka Shing: An In-depth Interview, June 30, 2016.https://www.bloomberg.com/news/videos/2016-06-29/hong-kong-billionaire-li-ka-shing-an-in-depth-interview.
[21]In June 2015, CKH and HWL completed their reorganisation so that each listed company would focus on its core businesses of property and non-property. Prior to that, both companies have duplicated projects in property development. The rationale of reorganisation is to create shareholder value of the many businesses CKH operates globally and the objective is to improve profitability.
[22]Victor Li. Group Annual Dinner, News, CKH Corporate Website. January 11, 2019. https://www.ckah.com/uploaded_files/news/1003_e_content.pdf
[23]Jim, C., *Level 5 Leadership, From Good to Great: Why Some Companies Make the Leap and Others Don't*, Harper Collins, New York, 2001, pp. 17–40.
[24]Chan, K.-W., How Asian Games Medallist Malina Ngai Reached the Top of the Corporate Ladder from the Athletics Track, *South China Morning Post*, July 21, 2018.https://www.scmp.com/sport/hong-kong/article/2156234/how-asian-games-medallist-malina-ngai-reached-top-corporate-ladder.
[25]Margaret Lau, Personal interview, January 19, 2021.
[26]The 7 Characteristics of a Great Team Player, Centre for Management and Organization Effectiveness. https://cmoe.com/blog/characteristics-great-team-player/.
[27]Personal interview of Ian Wade, December 22, 2020.
[28]This public relations exercise caught the attention of the media and the public in Taiwan that Hong Kong's success as Asia's World City was not by accident but dated back to the mid-19th century when the British colonial government of Hong Kong adopted the *laissez faire* economic policy as a duty-free port without sales tax.
[29]Toby Anderson, head of online-business at Sainsbury UK, was recruited by Wade as the country manager of WTC Thailand in December 2005. While there, he also doubled up as the regional marketing director of Asia in October 2008, and his role was later extended to cover Eastern Europe. Toby Anderson joined Mckesson UK responsible for the 1,500-Llyods pharmacies in the UK in September 2018.
[30]Collins, J., *Level 5 Leadership, From Good to Great: Why Some Companies Make the Leap and Others Don't*, Harper Collins, New York, 2001.
[31]Elias Johanson, Coronavirus: Affected Superdrug, Perfume Shop staff to be paid in full, Retail Gazette, March 20, 2020.
https://www.retailgazette.co.uk/blog/2020/03/coronavirus-superdrug-perfume-shop-savers-staff-paid-full-as-watson/.

[32]David Boyton, Who started with Safeway in the UK in 1995, joined WTC as the operations director in Hong Kong in 2000 and eventually became the managing director of WTC Hong Kong and Macau. Boyton joined The Body Shop as chief executive in the UK in December 2017.

[33]A.S. Watson, A Technology Testbed, Inside Retail, Hong Kong, September 18, 2019. Accessed February 13, 2020. https://insideretail.asia/2019/09/18/tech-startup-founder-heads-list-of-top-50-innovative-retail-leaders-in-hong-kong-2019/.

[34]Treacy, M. and Wiersema, F., *The Discipline of Market Leaders*, Adison-Wesley, 1995.

[35]Denning, S., *The Leader's Guide to Radical Management: Reinventing the Workplace for the 21st Century*, John Wiley & Sons Inc. 2010, p. 40.

[36]Radical management is a way to organise the business other than along traditional lines. By adopting principles of delighting clients (customers and employees), client-driven iterations, delivering values to clients in each iteration, interactive communication, etc. market leaders could then continue to grow their business.

[37]Intrapreneurship is better described as an entrepreneur who integrates risk-taking and innovation within a corporate environment.

[38]Prior to the re-organisation of the CK group of companies, both CK Infrastructure and HWL invested in property development projects. Upon completion of the re-organisation in June 2015, CKA and CKH were each responsible for property related and non-property portfolio of businesses, respectively. The rationale for the change is to create shareholder value with the goal to improve profitability.

[39]Victor Li, Chairman's Statement, CKH 2020 Interim Report: 6. https://doc.irasia.com/listco/hk/ckh/interim/2020/intrep.pdf.

Chapter 12

ASW Business Model, Sustainable and Profitable Strategies

The 3C Business Model and Marketing Mix

In 1982, WTC's flagship store located in Melbourne Plaza in the Central District of Hong Kong was serving the prescription needs of private patients attending the high-end medical and surgical clinics in the vicinity, perhaps comparable to medical practices in Harley Street, London. But one should note that the business model of chemists in Hong Kong is far lagging behind most developed markets as the vast majority of private medical practices in Hong Kong also serve as dispensing doctors.

Soon after his arrival in Hong Kong in March 1982, Wade promptly reviewed ASW's fragmented, low margin business portfolio, evaluated the corporate strengths and weaknesses, sought feedback from customers on their needs and wants, and monitored the local market landscape of competitor activities. He saw the opportunity of turning WTC into the "Personal Care Store" — a beauty and health business model which emerged in the UK in the early 1980s.

To improve the low margin issue, a private label product strategy with 2–3 times higher gross profit margins than the global brands which represented more than one-third of its products has become ASW's winning strategy up to this point. On the other hand, ASW's PNS supermarkets in Hong Kong have been facing neck to neck competition with Dairy Farm's Wellcome in terms of product range and pricing, which has limited the scope of profit growth.

In addition to the "Good to Great" and Competitive Strategies, branding and marketing have, since as early as the 19th century, played a key role in strengthening ASW's "first mover" advantage in the field of OTC medicines. This century-old wisdom of branding to minimise risk in pricing competition and sustain business growth has remained valid and ever more important.

We would recall that Humphreys conducted what is known now as a SWOT analysis, and an updated PEST review in his visits to ASW's dispensaries in the Mainland and the Philippines soon after his return from the UK in 1890. He set out his findings to ASW's board of directors and successfully lobbied them to increase the paid-up capital by HK$200,000 (estimated at HK$22 million/US$2.8 million in 2021 value) in cash. The raised funding was to target the mass market instead of the privileged few, by increasing the Watsons brand awareness for the range of its star products through advertising and promotional activities and inventory management. The "marketing mix" and "consumer insights" employed by Humphreys at the end of the 19th century bore a remarkable resemblance to the now commonly practised 4Ps theory and the modern day 4C elements adapted from Kenichi Ohame's 3C Strategic Triangle by Bob Lauterborn in 1991[1,2,3] (Figure 1 and Table 1).

Much earlier on, Alexander Skirving Watson (ASW) had taken over the Dispensary from his uncle and developed the brand as a modern store and medicine shop. ASW's target customers then were the merchant navy whose captains would stock up large quantities of alcoholic drinks, plus family and narcotic medicines for consumption on board. ASW became the preferred chemist since it had a more comprehensive range of products for selection and ASW deliberately introduced the trade name of A S Watson to give it a corporate brand identity (Figure 2).

Later on when JDH became the sole owner in 1874, he launched the Watson's Soda Water brand in 1876 and further extended the distribution network by attracting consumers' attention and those in the supply chain, i.e., chemists, restaurants and cafes, and hotels. The brand of ASW had become a serious player as a retail and manufacturing chemist and the name travelled quickly from Shanghai to Singapore. By the time ASW launched its own brand of opium substitutes and anti-wormer bonbons in the 1880s, retail chemists stocked up these new products without hesitation in the Mainland, the Philippines, and the Straits Settlements.

Business theorists today all recognise the key to early success with branding. For example, Philip Kotler articulated the four levels of brand identity to differentiate a company or product from its competition: to provide characteristics, benefits, value, and individuality.[4] Along the same

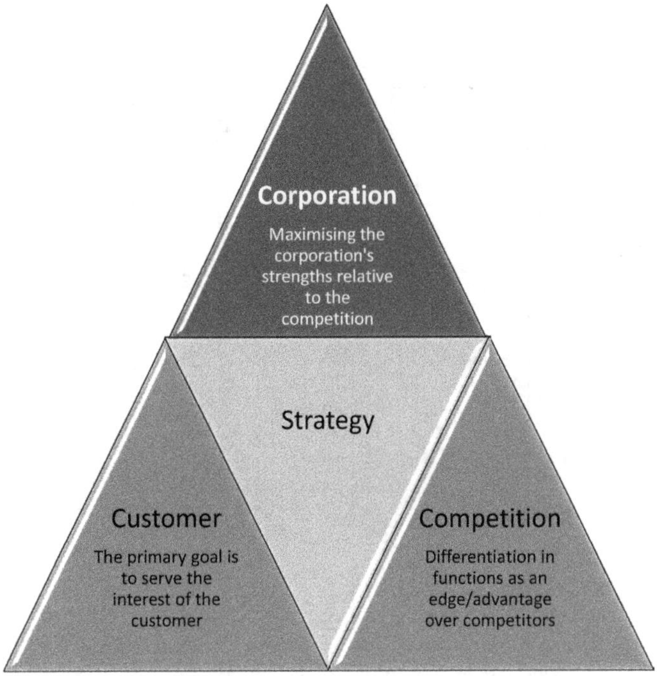

Figure 1. Kenichi Ohame's 3C Strategic Triangle.

Source: The Mind of the Strategist.

lines of Ohmae's business model and Lauderborn's 4Cs marketing mix theory, Dr Andrew C.F. Chan, an academic in marketing management practice, crystallised branding strategy in his "Left-and-Right Thinking Circles" in 1992.[5,6]

The "Left Thinking Circle" is consumer needs, and the "Right Thinking Circle" represents corporate or product strengths. The overlapping area of the two thinking circles is the degree to which the product can satisfy customers. In brand development, it is necessary to consider and target the needs and wants of consumers. Product differentiation will help brand positioning to address consumer needs. (Figure 3) ASW's brand positioning has provided more choice, more quality, and more value.[7] As an established brand in Hong Kong for the past 180 years, local consumers have gained trust in ASW. However, their expectations are also high. This has kept ASW in check at all times: they are on their toes.

Table 1. Marketing Mix and Customer Perspective.

4Ps & 4Cs		Manufacturing			Import and Wholesale		
4P	4C	Beverages	Family Medicines	Opium Substitutes	Liquor	Family Medicines	Beauty Products
		Flavoured Soda Water	Herbal, Bonbons	Opium Substitutes	Wines, Spirits	Seven Seas Fish Oil etc.	Cosmetics, Perfume
Product	Consumer Needs	Chic, Modern	Efficacy	Efficacy, Long Acting	Chic, Modern	Nourishing	Chic, Hygienic
Price	Cost	Affordable			High		
Place	Convenience	Drug Stores (and cafes, restaurants and hotels as additional channels for beverages and liquor)					
Promotion	Communication (Advertising)	Print-Media, Word of Mouth in the 20th C, Radios, TVs etc., in the 20th C, and Digital Media in the 21st C.					

Source: Summary of the 4P and 4C Marketing Management Theories.

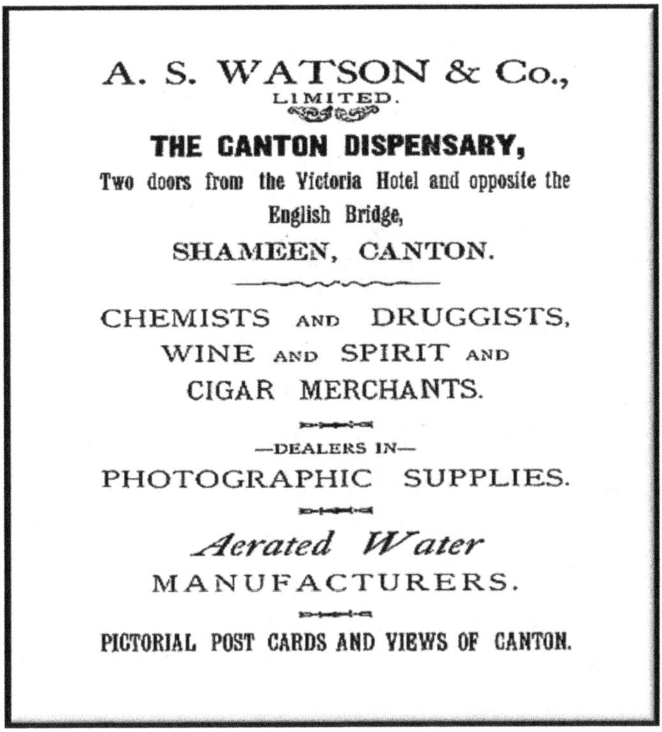

Figure 2. Door Sign of ASW's Branch in *Shameen, Canton* @ 1923.

Source: Courtesy of Shanghai Museum of Medicine.

The 4+2 Formula — The Four Primary Management Practices

Wade and his leadership team developed and implemented ASW's "Growth Strategies" soon after he joined HWL in 1982. This was set in motion to steer its retail and manufacturing division to success.

Harvard Business School professor Nitin Nohria, along with William Joyce and Bruce Roberson, after studying 160 companies that have succeeded, wrote their book *What Really Works*: *The 4+2 Formula for Sustained Business Success*, published in 1992.[8]

A choice pearl of wisdom from this book points out that:

> *"Without exception, companies that outperformed their industry peers excelled at what we call the four primary management practices — strategy,*

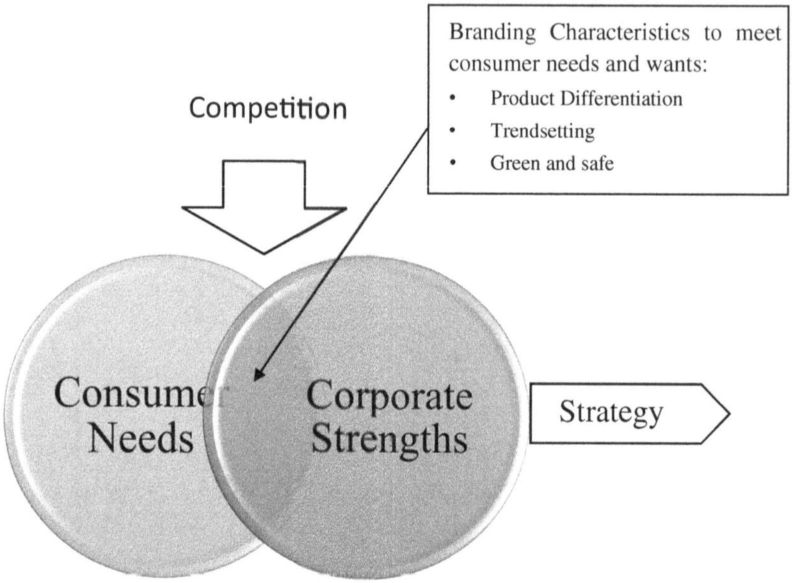

Figure 3. Understanding Hong Kong Corporate Brands.

Source: Author's Interpretation of Dr Andrew CF Chan's "*Left-and-Right Thinking Circles*".

> *execution, culture, and structure. And they supplemented their great skill in those areas with a mastery of any two out of four secondary management practices — talent, innovation, leadership, and mergers and partnerships*".[9]

The decision on which primary or secondary management practices to emphasise on will, of course, depend on the maturity of the industry, the core competencies of the individual company, and short- and long-term views of the board of directors (Figure 4).

Strategy

Geographical expansion by tapping into a ready or fast-growing middle class (initially in the North and Southeast Asia region) was ASW's primary strategy for the supermarket sector from July 1987 to June 1997. With the health and beauty retail business becoming a star in the late 1980s by means of its high-margin private label product portfolio, ASW further developed segmentation strategies according to customers (age,

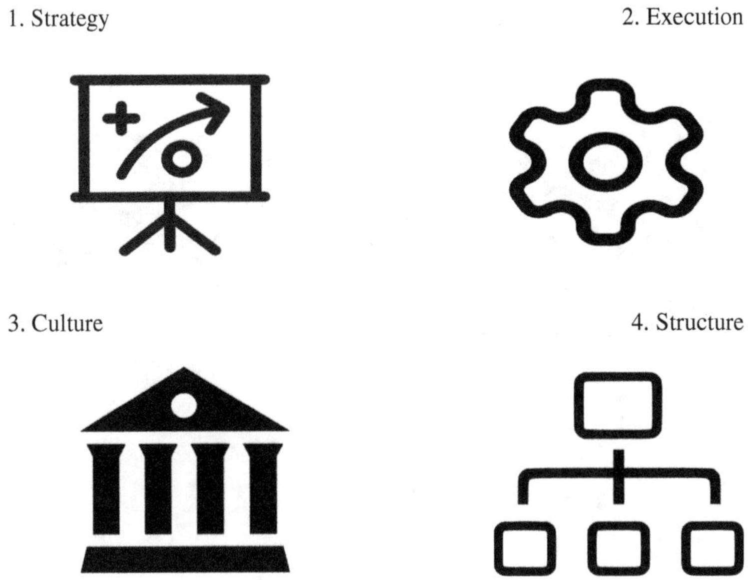

Figure 4. The 4 Primary Management Practices.

Source: What Really Works: The 4+2 Formula for Sustained Business Success.

sex, and other features) and income groups. Once target consumers come to deeply appreciate the value propositions of the marketer, then repeated purchases will follow.

ASW's branding strategy for Watson's The Chemist as a "Personal Care Store" positioned it as an affordable quality brand targeting young, professional females. After it was done initially in Hong Kong, it was then rolled out to retail markets in Taiwan, Singapore, Malaysia, and Thailand in the late 1980s to 1990s. The same applied to consumers in the emerging markets of the Baltic States, China, Russia, Indonesia, and the Philippines, in the 2000s to 2010s. These consumers were willing to pay an affordable premium for a trusted brand, whether it was a global brand or ASW's private label brand.

Entry into the UK by acquiring the Crystal Spring Home and Office Delivery water business in 1998 under the Powwow brand became ASW's springboard to penetrate into Continental Europe. ASW's milestones to becoming the number three global player in the health and beauty sector could be summarised through a string of brand developments, geographical expansions, and acquisitions and mergers from 2000 to 2006 (Figure 5).

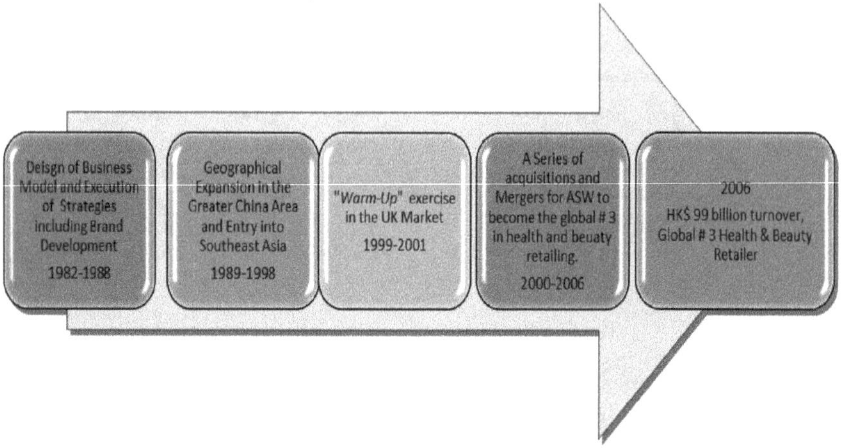

Figure 5. ASW's Milestones in its Global Strategy.

Source: Author's Interpretation.

Execution

However, a bold plan with the "BHAG" required a laser-sharp focus in complex markets.[10] Whether in Asia or Europe, ASW's success hinges on its ability to execute its brand and other business strategies with an athletic, disciplined, no-fuss and quick-on-the-feet approach. This was in addition to an equally important "six-sigma" approach. If the strategy's execution was premature, it would be costly to stock up and mobilise human resources. On the other hand, if the strategy's implementation was slow, competitors might have the "first-mover" advantage.

Based on company failures over previous decades, Arnold van der Maas, a Dutch strategy management expert, has concluded that there are seven reasons why the majority of strategies fail in the implementation phase:[11] One or more weaknesses could be related to incompetent management, a vague strategic vision, inadequate strategy, lacking an implementation plan, inadequate planning and control, and a culture of fear.

It is critical for the steps taken by the team to move in synchrony. A precise articulation of the message is crucial. It allows each team leader to follow and run in the same direction with complete focus. Therefore, a full-time project director's appointment to drive the integration process for a sizeable initiative is a prerequisite. She or he should be the key person to focus on delivering the Gantt chart milestones and getting the project off the ground (Table 2).

Table 2. Gantt Chart in the Acquisition and Sale of the *Kruidvat Group*

Stage	Milestone				Time Frame					Responsible Person
					2001	2002				
	On Track	Attention	Warning	Planning	Q4	Q1	Q2	Q3	Q4	
Decision of the Board of Directors	Reports to supervisor and conduct preliminary feasibility study									AB
	Seeks board decision on Go/No Go					Go if less than 10x EBIT				
	Articulates board decision to *Kruidvat* and seek feedback on valuation if less than 10x EBIT					*Kruidvat* to conduct internal review and revert ASW valuation offer				
Due Diligence	If consensus reached, sign MOU and conduct due diligence					Market, financials, legal and supply chain due diligence				AB/CD
	Reports findings of *Kruidvat* due diligence to the Board	Board supports Go				Project continues				AB
		Board does not Support Go				Project terminates				AB
Negotiation	*Kruidvat* agrees on key points of due diligence					Project continues				AB
										AB

(*Continued*)

Table 2. (*Continued*)

	Time Frame				Time Frame					
					2001	2002				Responsible Person
Stage	On Track	Attention	Warning	Planning	Q4	Q1	Q2	Q3	Q4	
	Kruidvat does not agree on key points of due diligence						Seek consensus on discrepancies and agree on final terms and conditions:			AB
	Based on findings of due diligence, offer to *Kruidvat*									
Transition	Agreement on acquisition and divestment deal of ASW and *Kruidvat* , and apply for EU approval						If agree, continue with transition			AB/CD
							If disagree, project discontinues			
	Transition begins									AB/CD

Source: Author's Improvisation.
Notes: AB and CD are designated project directors from ASW and *Kruidvat*.

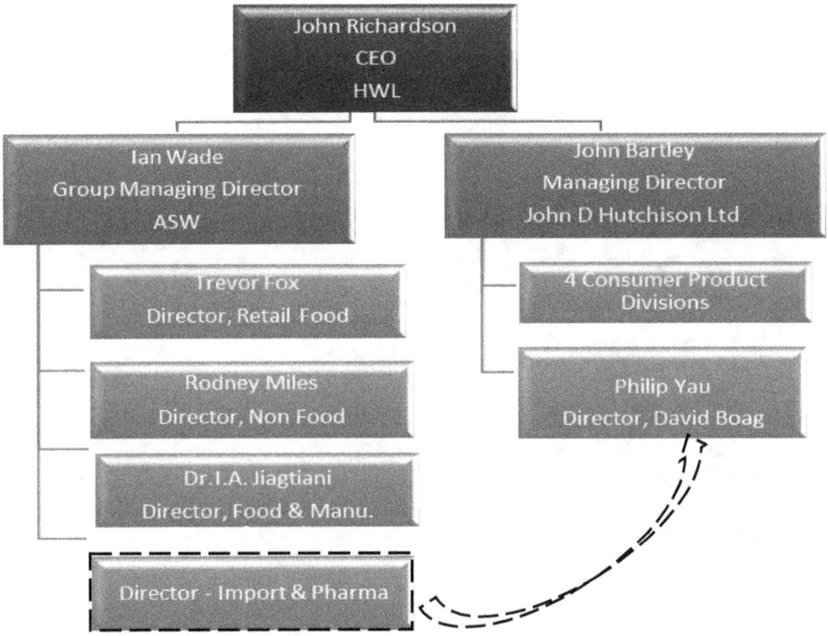

Figure 6. ASW Organisational Structure, September 1, 1982.

Source: Miscellaneous.

Note: The position of Director — Import & Pharmaceutical was made redundant and merged with Director — David Boag at JDH.

Structure

Every store manager dreams of designing a decentralised flat structure to empower country leadership and front-line sales staff to address "floor" issues promptly — without going through the corporate bureaucracy. In this scenario, management time will be better spent on motivating front-line sales staff on-site instead of spending hours reporting or resolving small issues. Over the past 40 years, four significant reorganisations took place at ASW.

- In 1982, when Wade came on board, the non-core import and pharmaceutical agency business was internally transferred to the trading division of John D Hutchison Ltd. (Figure 6).

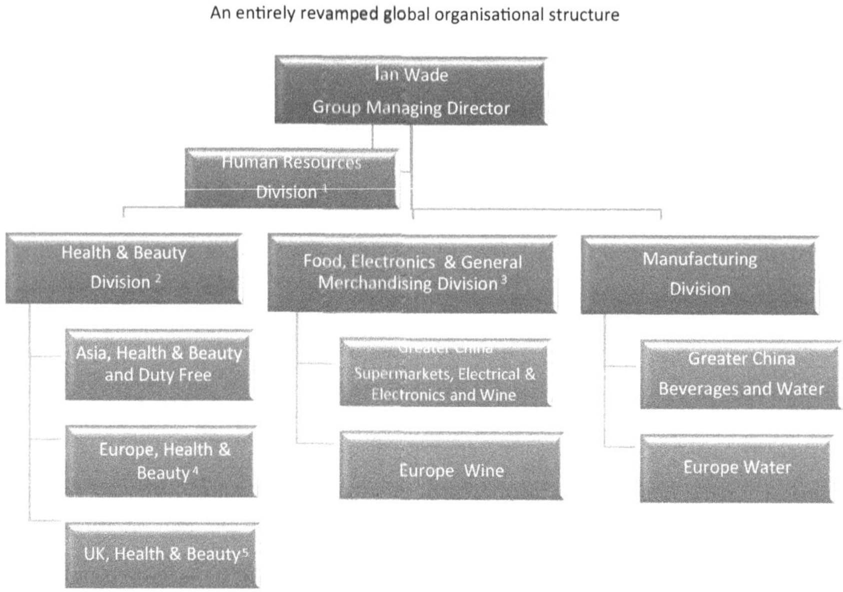

Figure 7. ASW Organisational Structure, January 1, 2003. An entirely revamped global organisational structure.

Source: Miscellaneous.

Notes:

1 Mrs Dora Poon, Director, Human Resources Division who reported to Ian Wade.

2 Wade doubled up as chairman of the Health & Beauty Division with Dick van Hendel as the Vice-Chairman responsible for the European and UK businesses.

3 Ian Ewan, Director and CEO of the Food, Electronics and General Merchandising Division.

4 Dick Siebrand, Director and CEO of Continental Europe who reported to Dick van Hendel.

5 Philip Ingham, Director and CEO of the UK, and who reported to Dick van Hendel.

- In 1989, when Hong Kong's economy was semi-paralysed by the Tiananmen Square Incident episode, a more streamlined organisation with one fewer management layer for operational efficiency and future growth was put in place in 1990.[12]
- In 2003, Wade put the newly acquired businesses in Europe under one roof to reflect the global nature of ASW's business (Figure 7).
- In 2019, Maligna Ngai was promoted as the CEO, Asia and Europe, which set the stage for eventual succession and Mainland supermarket-business divestment.

Prior to 2013, the senior executives of ASW would receive executive training at leading business schools such as Harvard University in the US to embrace the latest research and development in retail and business practice management. Since January 2013, ASW began comprehensive professional training for its middle managers of its retail division in Hong Kong. It then stepped up with an 18-month "Retail Management Professional Diploma" course that was launched with the key staff as the targets. In March 2018, the "Watsons Group Retail Academy" was established to manage all talent development projects. In the past 8 years, ASW's employees have become highly motivated, and job rotation has contributed to a turnover rate lower than its peers. This should also help prepare second level management for changes when faced with crisis situations, the latest being the COVID-19 pandemic.

Culture

Other than the culture of discipline, as described in Chapter 11, ASW's leadership team deftly nurtured a "can-do attitude" among management. This was supplemented with a "think global and act local" culture. It zeroed in on having key stakeholders' interests at heart (consumers, employees, and partners). The first step is to retain the time-honoured corporate brands that local consumers have high awareness of. The brands of Savers, Superdrug, The Perfume Shop, Kruidvat, Marionnaud, and other original brands have all been maintained with the gradual replacement of local brands by the Watsons brand in the smaller Baltic, Russia, Turkey, and Ukraine markets.

While ASW was successful in the UK and the rest of Europe, France has been a "tough cookie" to crack. In the acquisition of Marionnuad, respecting local customary practice was of paramount importance, all the while introducing best practice management to local staff. France is unique in that specific business and labour laws are very much different than in other countries like the Netherlands, Germany, or the UK (Figure 8).

What works best in the Netherlands and the UK might be vastly different in Mediterranean countries and other regions. For example, in Taiwan alone, ASW has 5–6 formats of the WTC stores which cater to different groups of customers for Taiwan's 23 million population, plus its

1. Employee First

2. Customer is *Not* King

3. Hierarchy

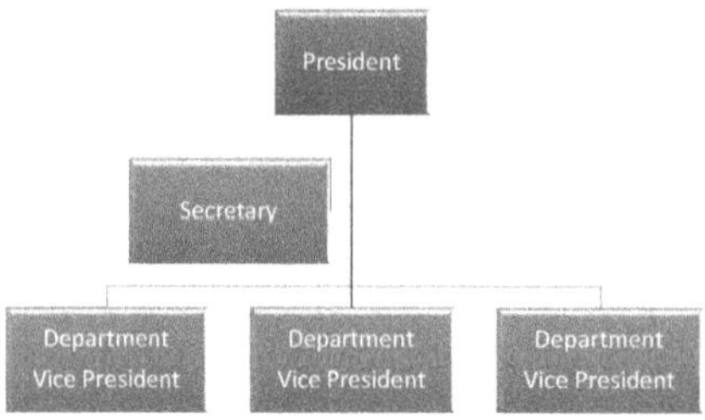

4. Working Hours

Standard Working Hours	
Weekly	35
Daily Maximum	10
Session	4.5

Figure 8. French Business Practice Illustrations.

Source: Author's Image Bank.

growing number of inbound tourists. Even among the Chinese tourists, those from the Mainland and others from Hong Kong/Macau and Singapore have different preferences when shopping for local souvenirs. The challenge for ASW's store in the busy Nanjing East Road shopping area of Taipei City is to decide what to display so as to suit the diverse cultural preferences of shoppers from Japan, South Korea, Malaysia, and Thailand.

The 4+2 Formula — The Four Supplementary Management Practices

The research conducted for the book *What Really Works: The 4+2 Formula for Sustained Business Success* by Noria *et al.*, showed that these sustainable businesses did not need to be outstanding in all management practices.

While industry leaders are required to excel in all four primary management practices (strategy, execution, culture, and structure), they are

Figure 9. Four Supplementary Management Practises.

Source: Author's Illustration.

only required to master two out of four supplementary management practices. These are talent, innovation, leadership, and mergers and partnerships (Figure 9).

Talent

Development of internal talents to create future leaders is an ongoing challenge for ASW. While ASW was able to attract and develop key executives initially, it was sad to lose some in the process. Malina Ngai, CEO, ASW Asia and Europe, Kay Yi, managing director of Watsons Taiwan, and Irene Lau, managing director of Watsons Singapore were all groomed internally by ASW and assumed their present positions. Some senior executives left ASW for greener pastures elsewhere over the past 8 years due to career advancement or family reasons:

For example, Joey Wat, managing director of ASW UK overseeing Savers and Superdrug, left after 11 years in 2014. Wat joined ASW as the Head of Strategy, Europe in 2004 in London.[13] She successfully rebranded Savers as the neighbourhood discounted drug store and Superdrug as the preferred health and beauty store that Gen-Y (or millennials) would shop at for their favourite cosmetics and makeup. Lai promoted Wat as the UK Managing Director of both Savers and Superdrug in 2012. She resigned in mid-2014 with market rumours circulating that she lost the ASW corporate position of Chief Operating Officer to Ngai.[14] Wat subsequently was hired as the president of KFC China in Shanghai in September 2014. She became the Yum China CEO, the parent company of KFC China, overseeing 8,750 restaurants in 1,300 cities and towns in 2019.

Another case: Toby Anderson, head of online business at Sainsbury UK, was recruited by Wade as the country manager of WTC in December 2005. While there, he also doubled up as the regional marketing director of Asia in October 2008, and his role was later extended to cover Eastern Europe. In April 2012, Anderson became the managing director of Taiwan to head up a struggling business until February 2016 when he was promoted to be the CEO of Watsons Asia. Anderson was a key member of ASW's health and beauty leadership team in developing and implementing the DARE strategy. After 12 years with ASW in Asia, Anderson was headhunted by McKesson UK as CEO, overseeing the 1,500-stores-strong Lloyds Chemists Group in the UK in 2018.[15]

Innovation

Innovation to attract customers to experience new products has always been the differentiator between the leader and its followers. Since ASW became the Dispensary's trade name in 1862, successive leaders have thoroughly appreciated its brand value. Although ASW was not the original inventor of opium substitutes, soda water, or anti-wormer bonbons, it was successful in optimising the marketing mix and building the Watson's brand in the late 19th century and for much of the 20th century.[16] Legends of the company resonate with current staff to this day.

Humphreys appreciated Watson's private label products which gave rise to 2–3 times more profit margins than the original brands in the 1890s. Since Wade's arrival in Hong Kong in 1982, he grew the ASW private label product portfolio as a profit engine to sustain the rapid growth of its retail health and beauty business in Asia. In the 21st century and age of accelerated globalisation, ASW continued to leverage Kruidvat,

Savers, Superdrug, and others, to optimise their brand value in the private label products and consolidate its position as the number 1 in Asia and Europe, and the global number 3 after CVS and WBA in terms of financial results.

With retail drugs stores and pharmacy chains losing their recurrent margins in handling film processing in the UK after the replacement of disposable cameras by smartphones, Superdrug was the first retail drug store chain to sell 3G phones at its Basingstoke store in the UK in 2006.[17]

In May 2018, ASW opened up a new shopping concept store CKC18 at the Cheung Kong Centre in Hong Kong to promote a chic lifestyle. It also featured a one-stop-shop for food, beauty and health, video games, digital gadgets, fine wine — essentially, new shopping experiences for customers. In the same year in Thailand, ASW and Shiseido of Japan joined hands and introduced a new line of skincare products for exclusive sales to consumers in its WPS in Bangkok. In January 2020, ASW opened a Tech-Fun store and installed makeup stations in Tuen Mun Town Plaza in Hong Kong. Unfortunately, the COVID-19 pandemic has diluted ASW's promotional efforts in this shining demonstration of innovative ideas in the retail health and beauty market.

Leadership

Leadership is about leaders as role models for their employees. As a leading brand of retail health and beauty stores, ASW's leaders need to inspire, motivate, and empower employees to achieve its corporate vision.

To set the example, Wade was a leader who comfortably mingled and connected with the front-line staff, cashiers, merchandisers, warehouse assistants, security staff, store managers, and customers. He spoke to everyone sending the same message in a clear language without flowery words.

As for Lai, Margate Lau recalled her days with Watsons in Hong Kong and her perceptions of the top leadership:

> *I was promoted as the chief pharmacist in charge of 50 dispensaries in 1999 and had the opportunity to observe the top management's leadership style. Wade focused on growing ASW's geographical footprint and achieved quantum leaps for ASW to be a global player. After Lai assumed his role as the head of ASW, he was also keen to address the frontline staff's recurrent issues.*[18]

Both Wade and Lai share common ground in promoting the corporate vision to all employees, and cultivating team spirit among the management. They communicate with clear, unambiguous messages to all. They motivate employees to work as a team instead of pursuing individual sales goals alone. Notwithstanding the commonality of the two leaders at ASW, leadership style will influence how a business is conducted.

Wade was a seasoned retailer with a track record in the department store, supermarket, and drug store industries. He anticipated changes in customer's purchasing behaviour and their receptiveness to price changes. This would become his instinct, to make bold and prompt decisions. After listening to customers' feedback, Wade would have a good "feel" for whether the product would take off or a market was worth pursuing in the Watson's brand of value products. On the other hand, Lai had a solid financial background and he could extrapolate the slight changes in the profit and loss statements on areas for prompt attention and immediate action.

Acquisitions, Joint Ventures, and Divestments

ASW's history in the acquisitions of the British Dispensary operated by McTavish and Lehmann in Shanghai and the Victoria Dispensary in Hong Kong goes back to the legendary early 20th centuries. These were wild times. Rapid geographical expansion of ASW into the Mainland in the beginning of the 20th century was mainly through a de facto franchising agreement with local drug stores. Divestment of ASW's Shanghai retail business to its regional manager, Dennis Mennie, was a painful but necessary exercise in 1916 to ensure the parent company's survival in Hong Kong during trade restrictions at the height of WWI in Europe.

The Black Saturday crisis in 1983 prompted the HWL board of directors to face the issue of risk control seriously. Then, the Tiananmen Square Incident on June 4, 1989 accelerated the pace of ASW's venturing into Southeast Asia. The Asian financial crisis of 1997 subsequently motivated ASW to enter Europe in 1998 to spread out risks and not put "all eggs into the Asian basket" as Wade once famously characterised it.[19] The latter left a legacy in global expansion which indeed set a very high bar. The momentum from this praxis still guides the company in many ways.

Crossing the River by Feeling the Stones[20]

Since ASW became a wholly owned subsidiary of HWL in 1981, its future has been tied in with Li's "cash is king" financial philosophy and HWL's global investment strategy. In his 25 years with ASW, Wade was able to "cross the river by feeling the stones". He moved along and ahead despite the political and economic crises on the eventful journey.

His successor, Lai, who navigated with steady hands, has faced a different set of rolling challenges during the past 15 years: the sub-prime mortgage crisis, Eurozone crisis, e-commerce advancement, Brexit, and the COVID-19 pandemic. Some events were more dramatic than others. Still, each time ASW emerged stronger than before.

ASW's journey from Good to Great and, in this journey, its implementation of Growth Strategies, Branding, and Marketing, the 4+2 Formula was truly a display of excellence — quite a corporate legacy indeed!

While ASW has ranked third in the global retail health and beauty business since 2002, its profitability ratio is the highest among the top position holders — ahead of both CVS and Walgreen Boots Alliance in 2020 (see the last section, Post COVID-19 Era, in Chapter 14).

Endnotes

[1]Philip Kotler (1931), A world-renowned scholar in marketing management, was instrumental in defining brand identity by utilising the marketing mix or the 4Ps. He was S. C. Johnson & Son Distinguished Professor of International Marketing at the Kellogg School of Management at Northwestern University (1962–2018).
[2]Shapiro, B., Rejuvenating the Marketing Mix, *Harvard Business Review*, Harvard Business School, Boston, September 1985.
[3]Lauterborn, R., New Marketing Litany: Four Ps Passé: C-Words Take Over, *Advertising Age*, 1990, 61(41): 26.
[4]Armstrong, G. and Kotler, P., *Principles of Marketing* (17th Ed.), Pearson, 2018.
[5]Dr. Andrew C.F., Chan, J.P., SBS, was the former Director of EMBA Course (2002–2020) at the Chinese University of Hong Kong and the former Head of Shaw College (2010–2020).
[6]Chan, Andrew C.F., PhD, The Road to Branding, Bowen Public Lecture Series, 50th Anniversary of the Chinese University of Hong Kong. Hong Kong Central Library, July 27, 2013. https://www.cuhk.edu.hk/chinese/features/professor-andrew-chan.html.
[7]Our Own Brands, Our Own Customers, AS Watson Group, Corporate Website. https://www.aswatson.com/our-customers/our-own-brands/#.YADz-ugzbD4.
[8]4+2 = Sustained Business Success, Research & Ideas, July 7, 2002. https://hbswk.hbs.edu/item/42-sustained-business-success.
[9]Nitin, N., William, J., and Bruce, R., What Really Works, *Harvard Business Review*, July 2003. https://hbr.org/2003/07/what-really-works.

[10]A BHAG (Big, Hairy Audacious Goal) is a long-term goal of any company to become a great company in its respective industry or market as articulated by Collin's in his "Good to Great" book.

[11]Arnoud van der Maas, *Why Strategies Fail?* December 8, 2017. https://arnoud-vandermaas.com/why-strategies-fail/.

[12]The 1990 organizational change had a long-term impact with a typical ASW retail store having only 2–3 layers in place under a store manager. The latter is empowered to deal with customer complaints on site in the interest of customer satisfaction. This has been proven to be a key success factor in all served markets; whether it's in Asia, Europe, or the UK.

[13]Joey Wat, A native of Xiamen, Fujian province who arrived in Hong Kong as a teenager, graduated at the University of Hong Kong and joined McKinsey & Company as a management consultant for 10 years before she joined ASW in the UK.

[14]Biography, Joey Wat, Chief Executive Officer, Yum brand. http://ir.yumchina.com/management/joey-wat/.

[15]Mackesson, formerly known as Celesio AG in 2003 and Gehe AG before that, is currently the second largest community pharmacy chain with 1,500 chemists after WBA in the UK. MacKesson UK and its 1,500 Llyod Chemists stores were sold to AURELIUS for £477 million on November 2, 2021.

[16]Schweppes, Pfizer, and E. Merckt of Darmstadt were the inventors of aerated water in the early 1800s, anti-wormer bonbon in the mid-1850s, and opium substitute remedies in the late 19th century, respectively.

[17]Always Innovative at Supedrug®, WatsOn, Quarter 2, 2006, 9. https://www.aswatson.com/wp-content/uploads/2005/09/69-watsON-e.pdf.

[18]Margaret Lau, Personal Interview, January 19, 2020.

[19]*Ibid.* (Note 19): pp. 17–24.

[20]"Cross the river by feeling the stones". These words of wisdom have been passed down for generations and inspired Chinese leaders in the early days of the reform and opening-up in the late 1970s and early 1980s.

Chapter 13

Consumer Trending, E-Commerce, and New Retail

Delighting the Millennials and Gen-Z

The Arrival of New Consumers

Globalisation and the disruptive technologies of 4G, smartphone, and social media have changed the face of retailing and consumerism in the past decade.[1] From 2007 to 2014, ASW's Chinese consumers contributed an average of 24% EBITDA as a percentage of sales, the highest among all countries and regions in Asia and Europe. Although ASW embarked on its digital transformation in 2012, the take-off and lightning change in e-commerce and online shopping by Tmall, JD.com, and other online shopping platforms in China took ASW by surprise.[2,3]

After Temasek became a substantial shareholder of ASW in 2014, the drop in sales in China was an alarm call for ASW. The arrival of new consumers, increasingly millennials and Gen-Z, who ditched physical shopping for online shopping fun, have stormed the retail scene. By 2020, the millennials and Gen-Z were contributing 70% of ASW sales.[4]

At the same time, faced with market threats from speciality shops such as Holland & Barrett and Sephora in the markets served by ASW,[5] a radical management strategy was called for: the DARE Customer Connectivity Strategy, explained in what follows — to keep innovating and delighting its clients and employees as a top priority. Initial results

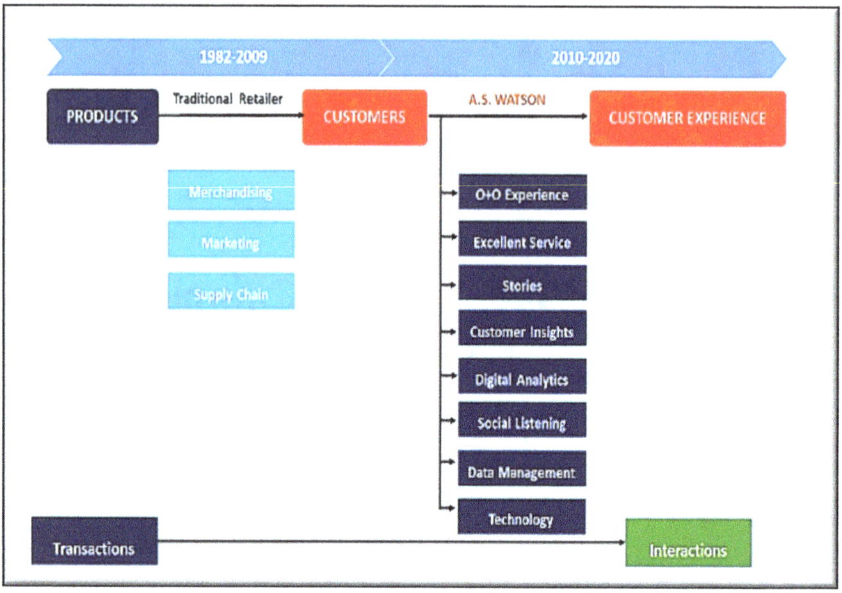

Figure 1. Evolution of ASW's Customer Connectivity Strategy, 1982–2020.

Source: Author's Interpretation.

were positive in 2018, and the momentum continued in Southeast Asia in 2019 until the COVID-19 pandemic arrived in 2020[6,7] (Figure 1).

The Rise of the Global Middle Class

September 2018 marked a tipping point in the world's population; of the 7.6 billion, there were over 3.8 billion people, about 50% of humanity, who were "middle class".[8] At the end of 2020, ASW's 16,167 stores were present across some 24 countries and regions. It has the potential reach of 2.4 billion consumers or 32% of the world's population. This kind of coverage is indeed remarkable.[9]

One should perhaps take a step back here for reflection. When Wade joined ASW in 1982 in Hong Kong, the "four little dragons" of Hong Kong, Singapore, South Korea, and Taiwan were rising. He saw tremendous growth opportunities with the growing middle class in Asia. These retail health and beauty markets ASW had entered into since 1987 outside of

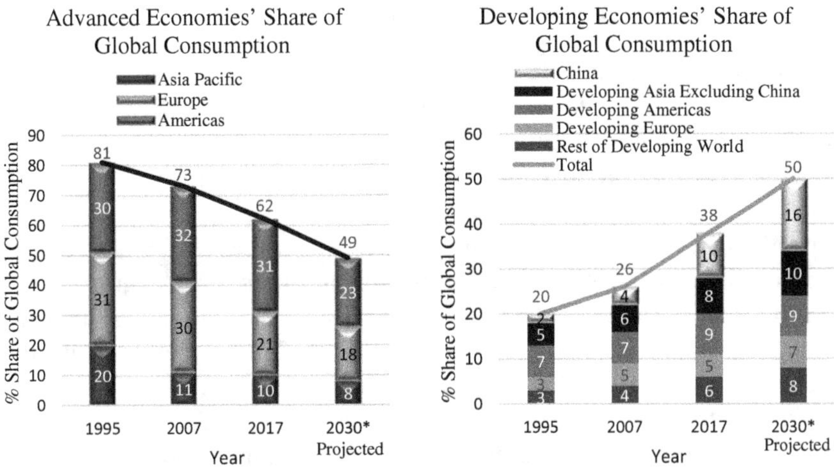

Figure 2. Global Consumption by Developing Markets in 2030.

Source: Mckinsey Global Institute.

Hong Kong have become market leaders and have brought good investment returns. The acquisition of established retail drug stores such as Kruidvat, Savers, and Superdrug in Europe and the UK since the 2000s has strategically extended its reach to another continent.

The COVID-19 pandemic has caused setbacks in middle-class growth in the developing markets, but this is expected to be temporary, and their continued rise will not be deterred. Based on a 2017 study, the developing world's middle class is projected to reach 5.3 billion or 51% of the total by 2030[10] (Figure 2). Also, the global middle class geographical segmentation will be 34% from Asia, including China, 32% from the Americas, 25% from Europe, and 9% from the rest of the world, including Africa. Hence, ASW's future will lie in the rapidly developing markets in Eastern Europe, Asia, and Latin America, particularly the BRICS and MIST countries.[11]

ASW's late entry into Vietnam in 2019, and Dubai, UAE, in 2020, was a catch-up since its last significant entry was into Ukraine in 2006. The markets in Brazil, India, and South Africa have thus far been untouched by ASW. Once the COVID-19 pandemic has subsided, it is expected that other global retail health and beauty groups will be eyeing similar potentials and formulating strategies. It should be interesting to see how they fare in this manoeuvre.

Trends in Consumer Behaviour

Market research companies have taken painstaking efforts to conduct market surveys and hold focus group studies in the past few years to project consumer trends by 2030. The motivational factors in shopping for health and beauty products have become better defined from the market research and studies conducted in recent years. Shopping behaviour depends on a host of factors and not merely on accessibility, awareness, and affordability, which were once the golden rule in FMCG marketing.

In 2012, ASW embarked on its digital journey in building the technology infrastructure and operations in the 2012–2016 period. With the eventual set-up of the long-overdue e-lab in 2015, ASW launched its DARE Customer Connectivity Strategy with a consumer-centric approach to anticipate existing and future customers' changing needs, particularly those of millennials and Gen-Z.

Most retailers including ASW now prioritise their resources towards today's millennials and tomorrow's big spenders of the Gen-Z demographic. Mintel, a global consumer market research company, has defined the seven core drivers of consumer behaviour of modern consumers which will shape the global market in the coming decade[12] (Table 1). Customisation to their varied needs on well-being, surrounding, technology, rights, identity, value, and experiences will separate the winners from losers.

Delighting the Millennials and Gen-Z

Those born in 1980 or later, the millennials and Gen-Z, think, behave, and shop differently from the baby boomers and Gen-X generations. As 70% of ASW's consumers are at or below 35, gaining insights into their behaviour and consumption is of paramount importance to stay relevant in the market. In 2018, ASW conducted its own "2020 Project", which revealed that 70% of its global customers are millennials and Gen-Z. To retain, continue to grow, and serve these "under 35" customers will be the top priority. The same study also revealed the regional spending differences (Figure 3):

- More Asian customers below 35 chose cosmetics, skincare, and health category products than British young people.
- More British customers above 36 purchase health category products than Asian consumers.
- More Asian customers purchase skincare category products.

Table 1. ASW's Response to the seven Core Drivers of Trends in Modern Consumer Behaviour.

#	Core Driver	Individual Interest	Key Motivator	ASW's Winning Strategy	Case Study
1	Well being	Seeking physical and mental wellness	A holistic approach with brands to become well being partners of consumers.	Customised solutions are targeting consumers of different age groups.	ASW conducts exclusive sales of Shiseido's "d program" skincare range in selective markets.
2	Surroun-dings	Feeling connected to the external environment	Communications technology will make it easier for consumers and businesses to share information and knowledge	User-friendly on-site health, personal, and pharmacy services; mobile application software and effective use of social media	"Colour Lab" with *L'Oreal*, and "Virtual Mirror" with make-up and skincare products on trial by customers with on-site help of beauty advisors
3	Technology	Reviewing solutions through technology in the physical and digital worlds.	Sustain growth with repeated purchases by members	Digital Transformation Strategy with DARE and Customer Strategy 2.0	E-lab was set up in 2015 to drive digital growth and e-commerce with analytics, management and marketing as the focus.
4	Rights	Feeling respected, protected, and supported	Consumer demand stronger ethics and greater equality from each other, and brands	Data Privacy Strategy	Scan & Go and self checkout by customers to ensure 100% privacy in consumer shopping

(*Continued*)

Table 1. *(Continued)*

#	Core Driver	Individual Interest	Key Motivator	ASW's Winning Strategy	Case Study
5	Identity	Understanding and expressing one's place in society	Relief from feelings of loneliness and isolation	Development of technology-based solutions to combat loneliness and isolation	Use of robots to relieve anxiety and encourage social interaction
6	Value	Finding tangible, measurable benefits	Affordable, authentic, and unique	"Social Listening" to understand customer insights to develop brands that will meet the expectations and needs of customers	TruNiagen for baby boomers to prevent Alzheimer's Disease
7	Experiences	Seeking and discovering stimulation	Powerful emotional connections to the brands by VIPs	Creating differentiation with online and offline interaction	Perks and privileges for Elite (VIP) members

Source: Mintel.

These are exciting data that are worthy of further analysis of the motivating factors behind such spending patterns.

In a 2019 market research study conducted on 1,200 Gen-Z consumers by The Paul Agency in the UK, it was discovered that their shopping preferences were similar to the baby boomers or millennials in Asia and Europe's urban cities[13,14] (Table 2).

Gen-Z has become the largest expanding consumer group today. The first purchase of a health and beauty product could be by a consumer as young as 12 years old. Hence, brands that have invested in their go-to-market strategy to reach out to this young and upcoming group will move faster and be better positioned as tomorrow's leaders.

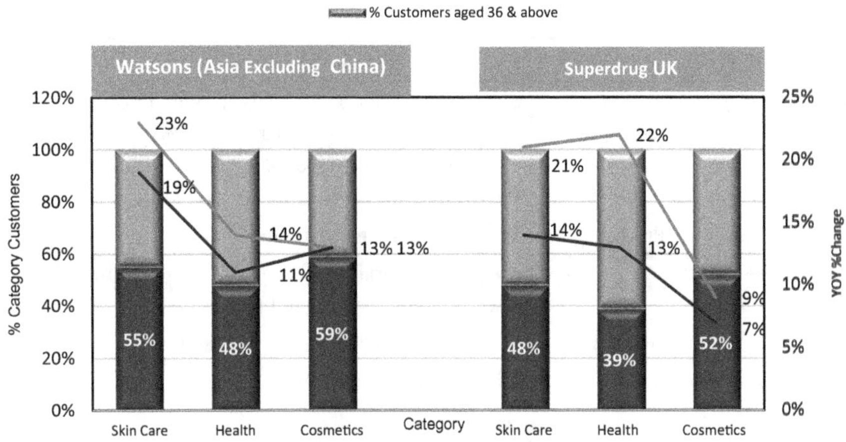

Figure 3. British and Asian (Non-China) Consumers.

Source: ASW 2018 Annual Results Analyst Presentation.

Social Media

Since the launch of Facebook in 2004, social media marketing has become the leading digital media for the past 18 years. In 2007, the launch of Android-based smartphones was followed immediately by Apple's iPhone. Smartphones have now become the most important business-to-consumer (B2C) medium of communication, especially for advertising and promotional media, which have replaced the traditional media of radio, TV, or newspapers. It has also become the main communication channel between family members, friends, and colleagues.

TikTok, the international version of Douyin, launched a video sharing social network service in the United States in August 2018.[15] Nowadays, most consumers will check their popular social media sites (such as Douyin, Instagram, Facebook, Renren, Tiktok, Twitter, Weibo, WeChat, WhatsApp, Youku, and Youtube) or click on the link in Line, Signal, or WhatsApp in developed markets, or Weibo, WeChat in China. Chat groups are set up to collect or disseminate information to their partners, employees, family members, or friends.

Table 2. 2019 Shopping Preferences of Generation Z in the UK.

Health and Beauty Products		Gen-Z and Those Under 25
Consumers	First Age to Purchase	60% at age 14, but could be as early as 12 or even younger in Gen-Z, compared to 39% of millennials and 25% of those aged 50+ Gen-Z is now the largest age group globally
	First Product	45% of those bought make-up
Nature and Feeling	Nature	58% prefer natural ingredients, 51% prefer cruelty-free, 42% prefer recycled packaging
	Good Feeling	71% prefer to always feel good than always look good
Technology	Voice	32% have used voice search for a health and beauty product
	Augmented or Visual Reality	32% have already used AR apps and 72% will continue to use AR or VR
Infor-mation and Influence	Own Initiative	33% of those aged 25 and under are those most likely to investigate their health and beauty product options
	Product Rating and Reviews	Ratings and reviews influence 83%
	Social Media	52% discover new looks and trends on Instagram. YouTube is the second-largest source of influence, and Tiktok is the fastest-growing among Gen-Z in its 15-second video-sharing social media service
	Influencers	33% are most likely influenced by key opinion leaders and key opinion consumers and 14% by celebrities and then by friends and family members
Mode of Shopping	Online	Millennials (aged 25–39) are the most likely to both research and buy online
	Offline (Physical)	48% prefer to shop in a high street chemist like Boots or Superdrug, but 10% will also visit a specialist retailer like Holland & Barret or The Body Shop
Shopping Experience		Retailtainment is the real draw for their physical high street shopping experience

Source: The Paul Agency.

As of April 2021, there are 7.86 billion people globally, of whom 55.1% or 4.33 billion of the world's population are active on the internet. Among them, 99% social media users use mobile phones and 77% of mobile phone users also use social media. It is anticipated that by 2030,

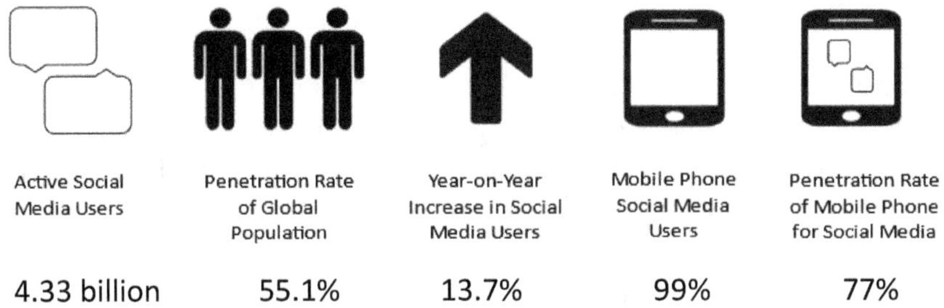

Figure 4. April 2021 Global Social Media Users.

Source: Datareportal.

most of the global population will adopt social media as the primary source of communication and e-retail as the main mode of shopping (Figure 4).[16]

Holland & Barrett (H&B) — Speciality Health and Wellness Stores

ASW has been monitoring its competitors, particularly the health and beauty speciality stores with a strong brand image and an extensive private label portfolio, for some time. The goal is to improve its retail coverage further since they have higher gross margins and EBIT.

One such shop on ASW's radar was H&B — a nutrition retail chain in the UK and a business division of the Long Island, New York State-based Nature's Bounty (now The Bountiful Company) — the global number 1 in vitamins, minerals, and health supplements (VMHS) until it was acquired by L1 Retail, the retail investment arm of LetterOne, on June 26, 2017. For its fiscal year ending September 2019, total sales increased by 2.6% to £715.6 million of which £477.9 million was from the UK. Peter Aldis, the former CEO of H&B who had been with the speciality retailer for 20 years before he retired in March 2019, was a well-known figure in the VMHS industry.[17] He was an innovative and business-focused executive with a record of eight and a half years of consecutive growth despite a weak retail market in 2000, 2009, and 2013. His achievements included:

- Formulating and executing a geographical expansion strategy by entering Europe Franchising H&B's VMHS retail business in Asia, including China and India, the two most complex markets, and forming a master franchise agreement with a "shop-in-shop" concept with ASW for its 200 WTC outlets in Hong Kong.

- Developing and launching a range of natural health supplements and skincare products under the Dr Organic brand, which lured shares away from the long-established The Body Shop.

When Nature's Bounty and its private equity holding company, Carlyle Group, decided to sell H&B, rumours circulating in the market at the time were that ASW was one of several bidders. H&B was eventually sold to L1 Retail, a company owned by Mikhail Friedman, the Russian Israeli oil billionaire, for £1.77 billion (US$2.3 billion) in 2017. H&B's and Superdrug's 2013–2019 financial results could give some hints to each retail chain's performance (Figures 5 and 6).[18]

From 2013 to 2018, the number of physical stores and franchise outlets of H&B in the UK increased from 664 and 72 to 767 and 97, respectively. However, its profit margin deteriorated from 19% to

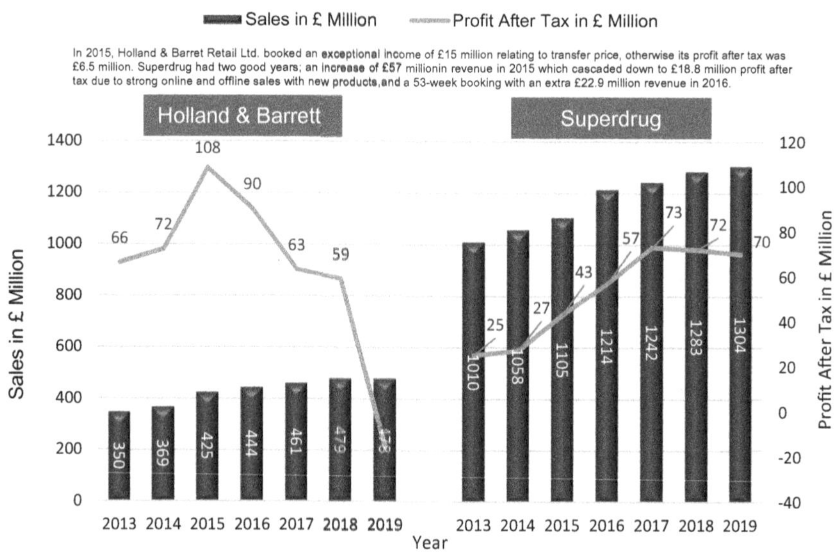

Figure 5. UK Business of Holland & Barrett and Superdrug, 2013–2019.

Source: Holland & Barrett and Superdrug Annual Reports.

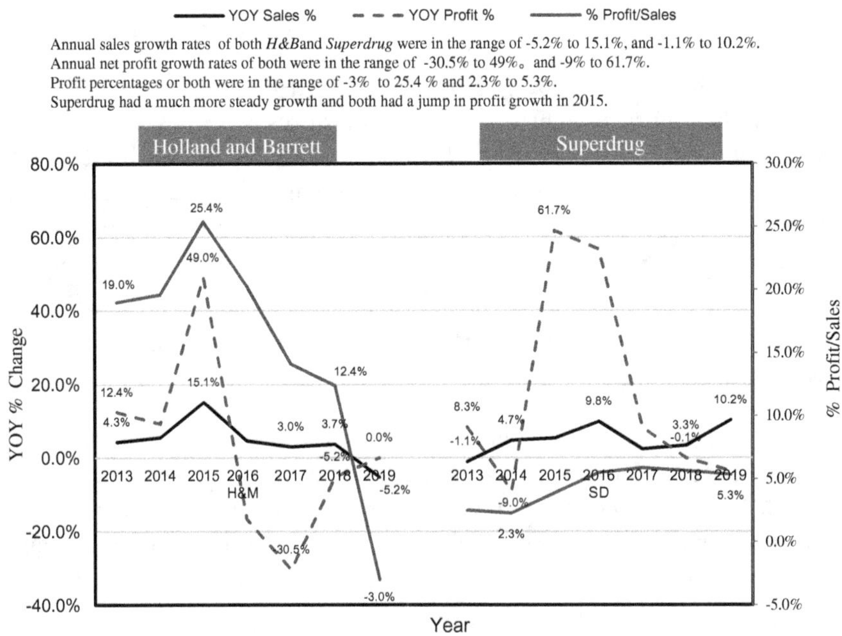

Figure 6. UK Business of Holland & Barret and Superdrug, 2013–2019.

Source: Holland & Barrett Retail and Superdrug Annual Reports.

12.4%. The continuing drop in profit of H&B since 2016 was most likely due to its lack of investment in e-commerce, with a large number of consumers switching to online purchases for greater discounts from global health supplement brands such as Centrum® and and others.

H&B had to offer more significant discounts to retain the customer base and volume of purchase. To increase sales and market penetration to counteract aggressive online shopping, H&B formed a strategic partnership with Tesco, the UK's leading supermarket chain, to market its range of health supplements to shoppers who do their daily or weekly round of stocking-up from Tesco's larger supermarkets.[19]

The lack of investment by Nature's Bounty in H&B's online business was perhaps due to the reluctance of its then owner, the Carlyle Group, which was planning to dispose of Nature's Bounty's business after having held it for more than 6 years since 2010.

On the other hand, one of ASW's UK brands, Superdrug, increased its retail stores from 700 to 806 during the same period 2013–2019. Its profit margins doubled from 2.5% to 5.6% due to upfront investment in digital connectivity, refurbishment of all its retail stores with new beauty and health themes, and marketing of unique and exclusive brands. Its 200 pharmacy stores also offer the latest medical technology in home test kits for DNA and HIV. Since 2010, COVID-19 antigen test has also been sold in the Superdrug stores.

Sephora — Speciality Perfume and Decorative Cosmetic Stores

Another speciality store watched by ASW's was Sephora. Founded in 1969 and based in Paris, Sephora has been owned by the luxury conglomerate LVMH since 1997. It was ranked as one of the top 3 global speciality cosmetics beauty retailers along with Ulta Beauty in the US and Marionnaud France in 2020. Its 2019 revenue was estimated at HK$37 billion (US$4.8 billion), with about 25% from e-commerce.[20]

The success of Sephora is largely based on its omnichannel strategy in the US. Like ASW, Sephora has a large portfolio of 400 private label and exclusive brands of cosmetic products with two to three times the profit margins of the global brands. From 2006, Sephora established a strategic partnership with J.C. Penny and grew to 660 "shop-in-shops" in its 850 department stores across the US in addition to Sephora's 500 stores by the end of 2020.[21]

In 2020, Sephora further expanded its channel of distribution in Kohl's large department stores and planned to add 200 by 2021 and 850 by 2023 out of 1,100 "shop-in-shops".[22] It has successfully covered its customer base by targeting the baby boomers and Gen-X with established brands such as Lancome via the strategic partnership with J.C. Penny stores while also offering younger brands such as Drunken Elephant targeting the millennials and Gen-Z at Kohl's department stores.

Sephora entered the emerging markets of China and India in 2005 and 2016. In India, Sephora operates under a franchise agreement with a local fashion house, Arvind, and had 28–30% of the US$1.2 billion domestic market in 2019.[23]

After years of digital marketing investment, Sephora has become a model of its kind in customer loyalty initiatives, with 80% of consumers having as their first preference to shop at Sephora.[24] Their loyalty initiatives included:

- **Virtual Artist:** This beauty application software launched by Sephora on February 2, 2016 was its augmented reality offer that scanned the faces, lips, and eyes of beauty conscious consumers who could play on lip colours, eye shadows, and false eyelashes and decide which products to order all on a mobile phone;
- **Beauty Insider:** Sephora launched a social media platform in 2017, where users could seek advice from those with prior Sephora product experience. They can connect in a live chat and at the same time browse product pages;
- **Store Companion:** A geofence technology, a location-based mobile application, was launched in January 2018. Sephora customers will be alerted when in the vicinity of a Sephora store and texted with new products or offers;
- **Digital Makeover Guides:** A customer service initiative launched in March 2018 to optimise the customer's personal beauty service experience by capturing the product, application, and look preferences from their makeover. A record of the customer's in-store beauty makeover experience is sent to them via email for easy purchase; and
- **Skincare Advisor on Google Home:** A voice-powered advice service launched in June 2018 that enabled customers to find the nearest Sephora stores, seek skincare advice, and determine their skincare products.

ASW's Omnichannel

In the past 5 years, in particular during the COVID-19 pandemic period in 2020 and 2021, e-commerce has been enjoying an exponential growth. The millennials and Gen-Z in developed markets have become a prime source of consumers and they are increasing their online purchases of health and beauty products. Additionally, cross-border online shopping is becoming a new channel for overseas shopping instead of the occasional purchases when travelling abroad.

With its global presence, ASW is well placed to leverage its unique position to offer its loyalty club members cross-border online shopping with global and private label multi-brands such as Drogas, Kruidvat, Rossmann, Savers, and Superdrug. It will be ASW's unique advantage if Superdrug's loyalty club members in the UK could source a Korean brand of mascara available in Watsons Thailand without having to switch to other e-commerce platforms of Amazon, e-Bay, or Strawberry.net. ASW's strength in online shopping lies in its seamless connection on its digital platform across its diverse national brands in the health and beauty segment.

In January 2021, ASW partnered with Grab, a Singapore based e-commerce food and grocery platform and express delivery company, to deliver online orders within 2 hours in the ASEAN countries, including Singapore, Indonesia, the Philippines, and Thailand. This online and offline connectivity for ASW's products allows its loyalty club members to order via the Watsons App or Grab's members to place orders for ASW's offers via the GrabMart application software.[25]

Global retail health and beauty players such as ASW, Sephora, and WBA have been developing their omnichannel business model to retain their existing customer base and acquire new customers. Amazon.com, a US-based global e-commerce giant, acquired Whole Foods' 400 retail grocery stores in June 2017 to consolidate its position as a leading fresh food retailer. This trend of acquisition and alliance is in fact seen around the globe. As recent as in August 2021, Amazon announced its plan to open large retail locations to sell clothing, household items, electronics, and other items akin to department stores initially in the states of Ohio and California.[26]

In addition, in China, a new trend is emerging with the big e-commerce players expanding to offline especially in the food sector to raise profile and capture the die-hard traditional consumers, e.g., the increasingly popular Hema food stores owned by Alibaba. However, with substantial investments involved, the omnichannel approach is likely to benefit only the large retail chains rather than the stand-alone corner shops.

Although the Asian and European markets are different from the US where many department stores are located in community shopping malls, it is believed that there is still room for Watsons or its other national brands such as Superdrug or The Perfume Shop to make alliances with department stores or supermarkets. One should not overlook the fact that Sephora, the speciality store chain, has excelled in its omnichannel strategy in the US in the past 16 years with the "shop-in-shop" concept.

New Retail

Jack Ma, the founder of Alibaba.com, the most talked about e-commerce platform in Asia and China, is a controversial entrepreneur. In 2016, at Alibaba's corporate annual meeting in Hangzhou, Ma articulated his vision of "New Retail" beyond merging online and offline sales platforms.

In 2021, e-commerce sales in China were estimated at US$2.78 trillion, surpassing the combined total of Europe and the United States. Asia Pacific with China included contributed 60.8%.[27] During the COVID-19 pandemic in 2021, overall global retail sales increased 7.2% due to a rebound of a previous year's drop of 2.8%, but online sales were estimated at US$4.91 trillion, a YOY growth of 16.8% (Figure 7).

In 2021, e-commerce became an established retailing channel in major cities and townships in China, which covered 65% of its 1.4 billion population. The potential to reach out to the remaining 35% or 498 million rural population is tremendous. Currently, consumers in the rural villages, often called "left-behind" grannies, shop in the small village provision stores for daily necessities.[28] The more expensive health supplements are supplied by direct sales representatives from Amway, Infinity, and others who visit them weekly or monthly to introduce new products or replenish their stock. Amid this backdrop, the growth potential is phenomenal.

Going forward, e-commerce will continue but at a slower pace due to an anticipated gradual return to normality with the roll-out of COVID-19 vaccines, which it is hoped will bring the virus under control at least in the developed economies with the creation of herd immunity (Figure 7). It is anticipated that the vast majority the population in these markets will have received vaccination by early 2022. However, with the recent spread of the new Omicron variant (first detected in South Africa) on different continents, the situation is somewhat fluid.

The Five Stages of "New Retail"

Dr Winter Nie, professor in leadership and change management, and her colleagues at IMD, Lausanne, Switzerland, conducted a 4-year research

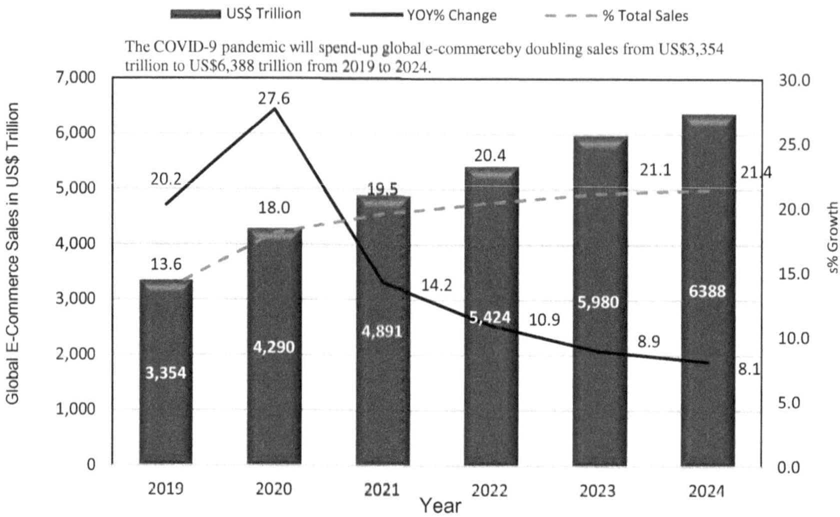

Figure 7. Retail Ecommerce Sales Worldwide, 2019–2024.

Source: eMarketerer, January 14, 2021.

study on the "New Retail" phenomenon in China from 2007 to 2020. They found that New Retail has become a business model adopted by many domestic Chinese companies and is highly likely to spread into other markets. The five stages of New Retail have recently been reported by Nie *et al.*, summarised as follows (Figure 8):[29,30]

- **Stage 1: Lifestyle e-commerce.** Based on the idea that people want experiences and services — from ordering dinner to finding performances or concerts to attend — at the click of their mouse, to purchase tickets online at home or in their office;
- **Stage 2: Online Merge Offline ("OMO") retail.** The seamless integration of online and offline commerce. It started with ordering fresh fruit, vegetables, and seafood (the so-called perishable items) from supermarkets, but has since migrated to other segments;
- **Stage 3: Social e-commerce.** Huge discounts in bulk purchase when a social group has consolidated orders and purchases online. This platform fulfils the basic needs of the low-income rural residents who pull their purchases together and order online;
- **Stage 4: Livestream Retail.** Influential celebrities (otherwise known as KOLs) selling FMCGs on an e-commerce platform have become so

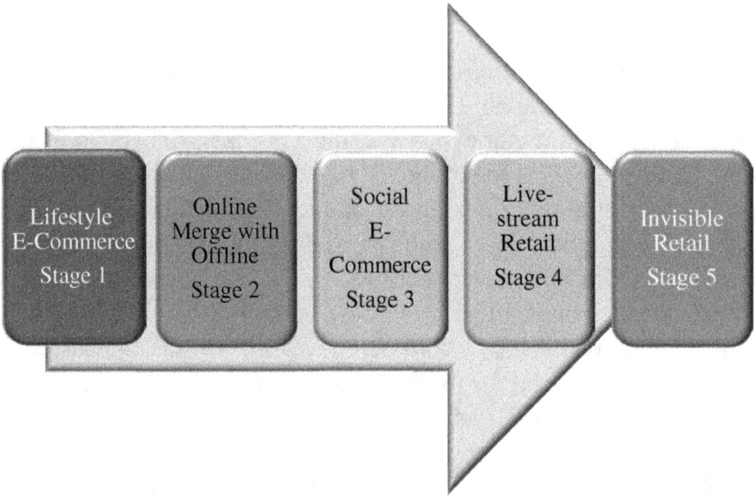

Figure 8. The 5 Stages of New Retail.

Source: Courtesy of Dr Winter Nie *et al*. The Future of Global Retail: Learning from China's Retail Revolution.

ubiquitous in China that when consumers struggle to make selections, personalities or influencers have stepped in to make recommendations for them; and

- **Stage 5: Invisible Retail.** A sophisticated form of indirect advertising has emerged and is analogous to the "Level 5 of Maslow's Needs of Hierarchy", where it stirs our desire and meets our self-fulfilment needs. Personalities or influencers portray green living to inspire their viewers to follow suit. The products or services are separately advertised in a different channel instead.

Likewise, KOLs in the cosmetic trade have become increasingly important in the United States, too. Sephora has taken a lead in the retailing of influencer brands with stocks sold out within 6 weeks of the latest Raft Beauty brand being launched in November 2020.[31] This phenomenon in the rapid dissemination of information and trade practice from one region to the next without any language or cultural barrier is most likely a result of the globalisation of the internet, and the commonly available social media apps such as Instagram, Snapchat, and TikTok favoured by the Gen-Z and millennials.

Beyond Social E-Commerce in China

Since half of the population in China are low-income consumers who would find products available on the popular e-commerce platforms such as TMall and JD.com rather expensive, their needs have been looked after with the emergence of "Pinduoduo". The latter has changed online shopping altogether in the world's largest market. Through social group buying, the online purchase price could drop by 50% or more if the required quantity is met within a preset deadline.

These social groups, most of whom reside in the rural villages, have now become part of the e-commerce world. In the meantime, the Pinduoduo model is gaining followers in urban centres of tier one cities such as Beijing, Shanghai, and Shenzhen; to some shoppers, the whole shopping process is just more fun and entertaining.

Pinduoduo has become China's largest agricultural and grocer e-commerce platform with a 31% rise to 823.8 million annual buyers in the 12-month period ended March 2021, surpassing Alibaba's 811 million and JD.com's 499.8 million active buyers.[32]

In the meantime, the internet celebrities or the KOL phenomenon in New Retail have spread worldwide, influencing consumers' choices and at the same time providing income alternatives for many real or aspiring KOLs.

Live stream retailing in stage 4 of the "New Retail" phenomenon has taken a toll on Carrefour in China. Carrefour, the one-time retail king from France, saw its sales figure in China at RMB 31 billion (US$4.6 billion) generated by 233 hypermarkets and 30,000 employees being closely trailed by one KOL in 2019. The live-streaming star "Big Sister Weiya" and her 500 employees with 30 million fans created 30 billion yuan (US$4.4 billion) in sales without a physical store. This New Retail model as championed by Big Sister Weiya may be unwelcome "noise" to the supermarkets of Walmart and Sam's Club but music to all the millennials and Gen-Z budding celebrities who dream of being the next Big Sister Weiya.

Invisible Retail — stage 5 in New Retail — is epitomised by internet celebrity "Li Ziqi". At the beginning of 2021, her domestic fans exceeded 80 million, ranking first in China. In February of the same year, the YouTube channel, which was not officially operational in China, alone had 14.1 million Li Ziqi fans, breaking the Guinness World Record by accumulating that number of fans in such a short period of time. When urban consumers watch Li Ziqi introducing rural ingredients or condiments in the video, such an inspiring lifestyle will surely make an impression on the viewers. This content-based video is certainly more subtle and enjoyable to watch. At the same time, Li Ziqi sold the products separately on another e-commerce platform.

ASW'S Radical Management — DARE Customer Connectivity Strategy

Retail business has evolved beyond recognition in the last decade due to social media's explosive growth and the rapid emergence of speciality stores such as Holland & Barrett, Sephora, and The Body Shop in the global market. In response, ASW initiated its digital transformation exercise in 2012 to address the opportunities and threats of online shopping. After a decade of learning the ropes in the fast-changing retail world, Lai and his team adopted a radical management practice and launched the DARE strategy in 2018:

- *Different* with unique product offerings co-developed with leading cosmetic companies relevant to customers' needs;
- *Anywhere* within the vicinity of the consumer or a WeChat or WhatsApp distance away;
- A caring *Relationship* manager with its customer service advisors actively serving the needs of ASW members with new products and services without intruding on their privacy; and
- Enthusiastically offering its customers, notably the Elite or VIP members, a unique *Experience.*

In 2019, e-commerce business has accounted for an important share of the total health and beauty retail sales of ASW (17% globally, compared with 37% in China). In 2020, the COVID-19 pandemic accelerated online shopping habits. In the first half of the year, ASW increased its e-commerce business by 90% year-on-year, mainly from its 138 million loyalty club members. By 2021, the company has reached the third stage of social e-commerce in New Retail. Going forward, its ability to make better use of KOLs and to tune up the lifestyle aspects, i.e., the 4th and 5th stages of New Retail, will significantly impact its future growth.

Different — A Blue Ocean Strategy for Air Pollution

ASW's "Derma Care Project", a version of the "Blue Ocean Strategy", was triggered by Bangkok's worst air pollution.[33] It occurred between January 1 and February 21, 2018, straddling the widely celebrated Valentine's Day by Gen-Z in Bangkok, Thailand.[34] Within 4 months from-project conception to product launching, ASW and the Shiseido Group, a Japanese global cosmetic company well known for its formula for Asian women, co-developed the "d program" for a range of skincare products exclusively for sales in ASW's retail drug stores.

Bangkok was chosen as the test market for Asia for relieving the harmful skin effects due to pollution. The "d program" launch in Thailand in the summer of 2018 was an instant success with a quick sell out. Riding on the common theme of air pollution, ASW maintained the momentum with a new line of "Urban Damage Care" dermatological products in the Mainland and Taiwan in the second quarter of 2019.[35]

"Anywhere" Everywhere

Taiwan has been ASW's success story since it entered the market in 1987. WTC's stores are virtually everywhere in the high streets and neighbourhoods of all its major cities in the four corners of this beautiful island. Each store has a professional team comprising a pharmacist, beauty advisor, and customer relationship representatives to provide beauty, health, and personal care support to the millennial and Gen-Z consumers.

By the end of 2020, there were 580 WTC stores and 5,500,000 loyalty club members and holders of the "I Card" among a 23-million population.[36] The launch of an official Watsons LINE account for I Card members in its updated mobile application has reinforced the "Anywhere, Everywhere" perception.[37] Its "Click and Order" online business allows customers to pick up their personal care product deliveries in a Watsons neighbourhood store within 2 hours between 10 am and 9 pm. This unique service also leads customers to purchase additional items when picking up their deliveries. It should be noted that local independent pharmacies that serve as contracted National Health Insurance prescription centres are not ASW's direct competitors.

"Relationship" Management

ASW first launched the PNS loyalty club membership in 2007 in Hong Kong as part of its customer retention strategy with price discounts and redemption points for household utensils. WTC and its European counterparts soon introduced their country's loyalty club membership programmes.

In the first half of 2019, ASW conducted an online Asia Cross-Border Shopping Survey with following findings:

- most frequent travellers were Singaporeans and Hongkongers with 2.7 times and 2.2 times more trips, respectively, than an average Asian,
- most popular travel destinations in Asia were Mainland China, Thailand, and Malaysia;
- most popular cross-border shopping destinations were Hong Kong for Mainlanders, Singapore for Indonesians, and Malaysia for Singaporeans;
- most popular cross-border shopping items were skincare and cosmetics for tourists from the Mainland, Thailand, Indonesia, and personal care products for those from Hong Kong, Singapore, and Malaysia.

Based on the survey results, ASW developed the "Watsons One Pass" programme with initial roll-out for the eight million ASW members living in the Greater Bay Area in the second quarter of 2019.[38] It was expanded to other Asian markets, including Singapore, Malaysia, Thailand, Taiwan, and Indonesia, with the rest joining in 2020.[39,40]

By the end of 2020, ASW had 138 million loyal customers worldwide. Among them, 100 million were paid members in Asia, including China and 8 million in Europe.[41] Of these, 4% are Elite ® membership holders who generate 25% of member sales and eight times more spending than an average member. Fostering a close relationship with these VIP members has become the top priority of ASW's strategy to retain and increase repeated purchases.[42]

Unique "*Experience*"

As early as 2010, Superdrug's "Virtual Mirror" was under trial in two stores to offer consumers a unique experience in choosing cosmetics. After being photographed by an in-built camera, customers can pick up a product from the stand, and scan the product. Then the computer will "apply" the product to the image.[43]

Superdrug was not the first to offer an online doctor service to meet consumers' health needs. However, it covers a broader range of services, including home test kits for DNA, HIV, sexual health, and travel medicine. A customer can receive a prescription of Sildenafil Teva ® 50 mg tablet for as low as £15.00.[44]

In Asia, WTC stores launched a mobile application software, "ColourMe", in 2019 using ModiFace's AR technology to try L'Oreal Paris and Mabelline's make-up products, including lipsticks, mascara, eyeshadow, brow colouring, and foundation.[45] Consumers could order the same products online after viewing their look creations for home delivery or pick-up from a nearby WTC Store.

The central theme to ASW's DARE — Customer Connectivity Strategy — is to delight customers, in particular the millennials and Gen-Z, by its six core strategies.

ASW's China Specific DARE Strategy

China is the single largest market of ASW's health and beauty business with 4,115 or 26% of its 15,699 retail stores, HK$20 billion (US$3 billion) or 16% of its HK$130 billion (US$20 billion) revenue, and HK$1.95 billion (US$0.3 billion) or 20% of its HK$9.59 billion (US$1.5 billion) EBIT in 2020.

Despite an increase of 19% in new stores in 2015, ASW's YOY sales growth declined 9%, and comparable store sales growth also dropped 5.1%. ASW stepped up its investment and focused on Gen-Z. By 2019, ASW had reversed the downward sales trend in the Mainland and started to grow again to retain its 65 million members by implementing the radical management practice with China's DARE — Customer Connectivity Strategy[46] (Table 3).

According to a 4,300-consumer study conducted by Mckinsey in 2019, consumer-facing companies face challenges if they are slow to address the expectations of increasingly sophisticated Chinese consumers.[47] To enlarge its customer base in China, ASW will have to reach out to the rural customers who make up close to 40% of the population, to fully embrace social e-commerce, and create a formula to expand social

Table 3. 2019 ASW China *DARE — Customer Connectivity Strategy.*

#	Strategy	Tactic	Initiative in Delighting Customers
1	Retain and Grow Millennials	Elite Card VIP Membership	Targeted at the 10% highest-spending members Complimentary make-up and skincare services Exclusive invitations to meet celebrity KOLs Accommodation and culinary offers at 5-star hotels
2	Acquire Gen-Z	Engaging, digit-enabled online/offline shopping experiences for Gen-Z	An AR technology, "StyleMe 2.0", offers different mix-and-match *chic* looks on the mobile with a personal make-up session by a professional in-store make-up artist Another Watsons app, "Scan & Go" allows customers to scan a QR code with their mobile phone rather than wait at a cashier to pay
3	Expand Menu	Launch of own or exclusive global brands.	Chinese and US social media brands of "Judydoll", "wet n wild", Korean beauty salon brands "CLIV and BRTC" and own brand of "d program" were introduced
4	Individuals	Customised service by Beauty Consultants to their customers	The Enterprise WeChat platform provides the consumer and Watsons beauty consultant a "One-to-One Beauty Consultation Service" which can also help to order online with a speedy "Click & Collect" or "1-Hour Flash Delivery" service. Coupled with AI-enabled technology, the store staff can recommend suggestions according to individual tastes and likes
5	Easy Shopping	"Cloud Stores" Service	Enables customers to shop digitally from their local store and across the entire Watsons China network at ease and with speed
6	3rd Tier Cities	High Growth Areas	ASW's new 2,000 sq.ft., 3,800th store in China was located in a tier 3 city, Kunming, Yunnan province in November 2019. It serves as a new flagship store for local shoppers, in particular Gen-Z, as well as tourists from neighbouring countries of Laos, Myanmar, and Vietnam

Source: CKH Annual Reports, *WatsOn*, *Financial Times*.

group purchases. If the "Blue Ocean Strategy" is successful, ASW could seek to replicate the same in the developing markets of Indonesia, Turkey, and Vietnam.

Endnotes

[1]Disruptive technologies such as Mobile internet, the Internet of Things, Cloud Technology, and Advanced Robotics are transformative technologies having massive economic impact.

[2]"Customer Connectivity: Strengthening Bonds that Span the Online and Offline Worlds", WatsOn 105, Quarter 4, 2018. pp.1-7. https://www.aswatson.com/wp-content/uploads/2021/06/Watson-105_Eng.pdf.

[3]Chairman Statement, Retail, 2016 CKH Annual Report, March 22, 2017, p. 11. https://doc.irasia.com/listco/hk/ckh/annual/2016/ar2016.pdf.

[4]Baby Boomers are those born after WWII or between 1946 and 1964. Generation X, the age group born before the 1980s but after the Baby Boomers; Generation Y, or Millennials, are those born between 1981 and 1996; and Generation Z, those born between 1997–2012 (*Source*: Pew Research).

[5]Makers of the original brands also sold their products with steep discounts on the e-commerce platforms such as Amazon.com, JD.com, Starwberry.net, T-Mall etc. at greater value and volume.

[6]ASW is losing customers with an aging brand (in the Mainland). Shrinking sales per shop 4 years in a row. https://finance.ifeng.com/c/7lVjfzcpfhy.

[7]Hong Kong, the Mainland, and the UK performed less satisfactorily due to a slowing economy, social unrests, and also Brexit.

[8]The "middle class" classification based on household expenditure developed by Homi Kharas *et al.*, of the Brookings Institution has been used by many researchers as those households with spending of US$10-110 per day per person in 2011 purchasing power parity, or PPP.

[9]Malina Ngai, CKH Interim Results Analyst Presentation — ASW Digital Transformation. https://www.youtube.com/watch?v=g2ldtV6-VDw.

[10]Homi, K., *The Unprecedented Expansion of the Global Middle Class: An Update*, Brookings Institution, Global Economy & Development working paper number 100, February 2017.

[11]The terms BRIC was coined by Jim O'Neil, global economist at Goldman Sachs, in 2001. South Africa was included later on with a new term BRICS as it is widely called nowadays. O'Neil further added the term MIST including the next tier of countries of Mexico, Indonesia, South Korea, and Turkey.

[12]Crabbe, M., Global Consumer Trends 2030, November 5, 2019, Mintel. Accessed January 31, 2022. https://www.mintel.com/global-consumer-trends-2030.

[13]The urban cities in Asia and Europe under-study were Amsterdam, Bangkok, Frankfurt, Hong Kong, Paris, Shanghai, Singapore, or Taipei.

[14]Claire Chance, *Is Your Business Ready for Gen Z?* The Pull Agency, February 27, 2020.

[15]It was estimated 80% of these users were 16–34 year old.

[16]Global Social Media Stats. https://datareportal.com/social-media-users.

[17]Aldis was instrumental in driving the retailer's growth from a few hundred stores to over 1,300 stores including the 50 GNC Shops held under a master franchise agreement since 2003. He shared a similar background to Ian Wade as a former Adas store manager for many years before he joined H&B.

[18]Holland & Barret's fiscal year ending is September 30, which is in line with NBTY, its US holding company. Superdrug's fiscal year ending is December 31, which is in line with CKH, its Hong Kong holding company, year-end closing date.

[19]Gwynn, S. *Tesco Opens Holland & Barrett Concessions After Ditching Nutricentre*, Campaign, July 26, 2016. https://www.campaignlive.com/article/tesco-opens-holland-barrett-concessions-ditching-nutricentre/1403571.

[20]Sephora stocks about 300 brands including its house brand, in 34 countries including China, and the US. It has stayed ahead of customer trends by creating a seamless customer online and offline experience, which is the talk of the town among both consumers and industry veterans. LVMH does not break out Sephora's performance but was consolidated under the Selective Retailing division.

[21]JCPenney and Sephora Reaffirm Partnership, Sephora inside JCPenney Partnership to Continue; Both Companies Focused on Delivering Exciting Beauty Experience to Customers, *Business Wire*, May 7, 2020. https://www.businesswire.com/news/home/20200507006215/en/JCPenney-and-Sephora-Reaffirm-Partnership.

[22]Kohl's and Sephora Announce Major Long-Term Strategic Partnership Bringing Transformative Prestige Beauty Experience to Millions of Consumers, December 1, 2020. https://corporate.kohls.com/news/archive-/2020/december/kohl-s-and-sephora-announce-major-long-term-strategic-partnershi.

[23]Vinay, U., French beauty retailer Sephora aims to have 50 stores in India by 2022, *Business Standard.* November 23, 2019. https://www.business-standard.com/article/companies/french-beauty-retailer-sephora-aims-to-have-50-stores-in-india-by-2022-119112300508_1.html.

[24]5 Ways Sephora Creates a Seamless Customer Experience, National Retail Federation Smart Brief, July 25, 2018. https://nrf.com/blog/5-ways-sephora-creates-seamless-customer-experience.

[25]AS Watson Group and Grab Announce Regional O+O Health Partnership. Latest News, AS Watson Corporate Website, January 19, 2021. https://www.aswatson.com/a-s-watson-group-and-grab-announce-regional-oo-health-and-beauty-partnership/.

[26]Herrera, S. *et al.*, Amazon Plans to Open Large Retail Locations Akin to Department Stores, WJS News Exclusive, *The Wall Street Journal*, August 19, 2021. https://www.wsj.com/articles/amazon-retail-department-stores-11629330842.

[27]Andrew, L., Global E-Commerce 2019, eMarketer, June 27, 2019. https://www.emarketer.com/content/global-ecommerce-2019.

[28]"Left-behind" grannies are those farmers who look after their grand children when their children work as factory hands in larger cities and townships and return home once a year during the lunar New Year holidays.

[29]Winter, N. and Mark, G., For a Glimpse of the Future of Retail, Look at What is Happening in China, Research & Knowledge, IMD, April 2021. https://www.imd.org/research-knowledge/videos/for-a-glimpse-of-the-future-of-retail-look-at-what-s-happening-in-china/.

[30]The global consumer brands of FMCGs such as L'Oreal, Nestle, Starbucks, etc. are monitoring the development of "New Retail" in China, and if this phenomenon will spill-over into other large economies and the BRICS and MIST markets in the coming decade.

[31]Sara, S.F., Sephora Expands its Influencer Brands with Jesse Hunt's Raft Beauty, Gloss Pop. June 8, 2021. https://www.glossy.co/beauty/sephora-expands-its-influencer-brands-with-jess-hunts-refy-beauty/.

[32]Xue, Y., Pinduoduo's Active Buyers Inch Ahead of Rivals as e-Commerce Giant's Quarterly Revenue More Than Triples, Big Tech, South China Morning Post, May 26, 2021. https://www.scmp.com/tech/big-tech/article/3134939/pinduoduo-sees-quarterly-revenue-jump-gamified-e-commerce-strategy.

[33]Chan Kim, W. and Renée, M., Professors at INSEAD, articulated in their book *Blue Ocean Strategy* in 2004 a marketing theory in the simultaneous pursuit of differentiation and low cost to open up a new market space and create new demand.

[34]Green Peace Appeals to the PM to Tackle Air Pollution "Crisis", *Bangkok Post*, February 22, 2018. Accessed March 1, 2020. https://www.bangkokpost.com/thailand/general/1412290/city-smog-worsens-to-danger-level.

[35]D for d program, WatsOn Magazine, Edition No. 108, May 29, 2019: 7. https://www.aswatson.com/wp-content/uploads/2021/06/WatsON108_Eng.pdf.

[36]Watsons loyalty club membership programme was launched in Taiwan in July 2008.

[37]LINE is the most popular messenger app in Taiwan.

[38]The Guangdong–Hong Kong–Macao Greater Bay Area (Greater Bay Area) comprises the two Special Administrative Regions of Hong Kong and Macao, and the nine municipalities of Guangzhou, Shenzhen, Zhuhai, Foshan, Huizhou, Dongguan, Zhongshan, Jiangmen, and Zhaoqing in Guangdong Province. The total area is around 56,000 km^2. At end 2018, the total population is over 71 million, the GDP is US$1,642.5 billion, and GDP per capita is US$23,342.

[39]Watsons One Pass — A Passport to Region-wide Privileges, *WatsOn*, October 2, 2019, 108: 1–6. https://www.aswatson.com/wp-content/uploads/2021/06/WatsON108_Eng.pdf.

[40]After Asia, the programme was extended to European loyalty club members of Kruidvat, Rossmann, Superdrug, Trekpleister, etc.

[41]Annual membership fee is at a token fee of HK$20–30 (£2–3 or €2–3).

[42]14,000 consumers from the seven markets of China, Hong Kong, Taiwan, Malaysia, Singapore, Thailand, and Indonesia participated in the Survey.
[43]Superdrug debuts virtual mirror, Cosmetics Business, August 20, 2010. https://www.cosmeticsbusiness.com/news/article_page/title/56243.
[44]Sildenfil is the generic drug name of the original brand of Viagra, a drug to treat male erectile dysfunction.
[45]Michael, A., AS Watson and L'Oreal Launch Virtual Makeup Try-on Service, *Insider Retail*, March 12, 2019. https://insideretail.asia/2019/03/12/as-watson-and-loreal-launch-virtual-makeup-try-on-service/.
[46]CKHH Interim Results Analyst Presentation — ASW Digital Transformation, https://www.youtube.com/watch?v=Zm33n_3Nsk4.
[47]Lambert, B. *et al.*, *China Digital Consumer Trends 2019*, McKinesy, September 2019. Accessed March 1, 2020. https://www.mckinsey.com/featured-insights/china/china-digital-consumer-trends-in-2019.

Chapter 14

Temasek, India, and the Post-COVID-19 Era

Life-long Friendship of Li Ka Shing and the Late Lee Kuan Yew

One of China's greatest assets in Southeast Asia is its long-term cultural links with the centuries-old Chinese diaspora. Take Lee Kuan Yew (1923–2015), the late prime minister and minister mentor of Singapore, for example. Lee was a fourth-generation Singaporean of Chinese ethnicity. Although he and Li Ka-Shing shared the same surname in the Chinese language, it is pronounced differently in the Chinese dialects of Hakka and Swatow.[1] After graduation from high school in 1942, Lee became an officer with the Singapore Administration Service News Department under the Japanese occupation. At the end of WWII, he went to the UK, for studying law at Cambridge University and ultimately training as a barrister in London.

Upon Lee's return to Singapore in 1950, he entered politics and was elected as the first prime minister of Singapore at 35 under the new constitution in 1958. Lee visited Hong Kong in May 1954 as a tourist and was deeply impressed with the "customer first" attitude of Shanghainese tailors in the colony with same-day delivery service of make-to-measure suits.[2] This shopping experience left an indelible mark in his memory — that Hong Kong's entrepreneurs have a "can do" spirit that a typical Singaporean businessman lacked then.

The encounter between Lee and Li dates back to August 9, 1984 when Li was a member of a group of Hong Kong investors personally invited by Lee to attend the National Day celebrations in Singapore. The invitation aimed to attract Hong Kong investors to set up a second home in Singapore as an insurance policy when Hong Kong reverted to Chinese sovereignty in 1997.

Li had an excellent impression of Singapore under Lee's helmsmanship. He decided to become a substantial investor in the Suntec Investment Private Ltd. (Suntec) in October 1985 when Singapore as the Lion City suffered its worst economic recession.[3] This initial investment subsequently led to ASW's entry into Singapore by building a WTC store network across the city-state in 1988.

In the same year, Suntec acquired a site owned by the Urban Redevelopment Authority of Singapore. The latter eventually became Singapore's largest office, shopping, and convention centre when completed in July 1997.[4]

In September 1994, the Pacific Century Group, owned by Richard Li, the second son of Superman Li, acquired control of a publicly listed company in Singapore. It was subsequently renamed Pacific Century Regional Developments Limited, focusing on Singapore and Southeast Asia.[5] In 2000, Singapore Telecommunications, then headed by Lee's younger son Lee Hsien Yang, competed with Richard Li's Pacific Century Group to acquire Hong Kong Telecom but lost the bid.[6]

This kept Lee and Li at a distance until the ice break occurred in September 2002 when Li made a S$19.5 million donation as an endowment supporting a library and scholarships to the Singapore Management University (SMU).[7] This gesture of goodwill to Singapore was followed by an even bigger donation of S$100 million as an endowment fund through the Li Ka-Shing Foundation to the National University of Singapore (NUS) in 2007.

The NUS strategic initiative rekindled the friendship between Lee and Li, which lasted for the rest of their lives. At a private wake attended by Li, together with his sons Victor Li and Richard Li, held on March 23, 2015, Li said in a condolence letter to Lee's elder son, Singapore Prime Minister Lee Hsien Loong:

> *I will remember Lee Kuan Yew always as a dear friend, and it is in this capacity I mourn his loss the greatest.*[8]

Temasek — Singapore's Sovereign Wealth Fund

Temasek and GIC were the two state investment companies and sovereign wealth funds made up of fixed income and cash, equities and alternatives, including real estate and private equities, when founded. Temasek was formed in June 1974 to manage assets owned by the Government of Singapore.[9] GIC was created later in 1984 with the sole purpose of administering Singapore's foreign reserve.

Since its inception in 1974, Temasek has pursued a prudent approach as a sovereign wealth manager, which enabled it to largely escape the 1997 Asian financial crisis.[10] After the SARS epidemic in late 2003, the market was flooded with assets well below their value. Temasek was actively expanding into other Asian markets and bought into Indonesia's Bank Danamon (2003), Standard Chartered Bank (2006), and Thailand's telecommunication leader — Intouch (2006).[11] These acquisitions in Southeast Asia were made from 2003 to 2006 by Temasek. The Fund was of the genuine belief that these industries would grow in value in parallel with the rise of a flourishing middle class in the emerging markets of Asia.

Temasek became aggressive in 2007, with multi-billion-dollar stakes invested in the then Merrill Lynch (now owned by the Bank of America), Barclays Bank, and others. Despite early signs of serious troubles shown in the global banking sector in early 2007, Temasek continued to build up a portfolio in financial services, which was 40% of its S$185 billion (US$124 billion) assets at the end of March 2008.[12] Following the subprime meltdown in the US in December 2007, Temasek suffered heavy losses, with Merrill Lynch alone resulting in a loss of 69% of its value at US$4 billion out of a US$5.8 billion investment within a year.

After Bank of America took over the troubled Merrill Lynch in January 2009, Temasek disposed of its 3.8% stake and lost another US$1.3 billion.[13]

Ever since Ho Ching became CEO of Temasek in 2004, there has been a notable investment emphasis on regional leaders in particular industries such as banking, biotechnology, consumer and real estate, e-commerce, telecommunication, and transportation.[14] Temasek was one of the early strategic investors in Gilead, a highly successful US pharmaceutical company specialising in anti-viral therapy, including HIV, which generated a high ROI over 5.5 years from 2013 onwards.

Since the set-back in the subprime crisis, Temasek has taken a more balanced investment approach, with one-third in fixed income and cash, one-third in equities, and slightly less than one-third in alternatives. This includes consumer and real estate at 14% where ASW belongs (Figure 1). Furthermore, the geographical distribution of Temasek's 2021 portfolio of assets is 64% in Asia, including China (27%), Singapore (24%), the rest of Asia (13%), with the remaining 36% is in the rest of the world including

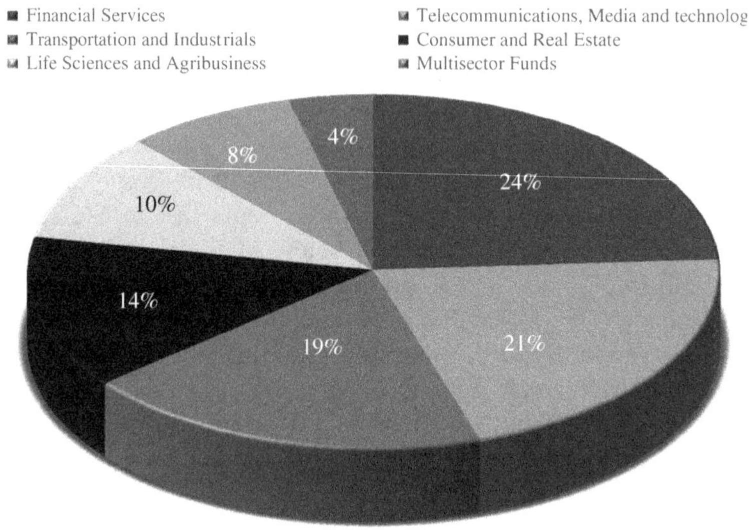

Figure 1. Temasek's Portfolio by Underlying Assets (as of 31 March 2021).

Source: Temasek Investor Presentation 2021.

the US (17%), Europe, Middle East, and Africa (12%), Australia and New Zealand (4%) and others (3%). (Figure 2).[15] And, ASW, being a leader in the health and beauty retail industry in Asia and Europe, fits the bill.

When HWL scrapped the sale option for its supermarket chain PNS in 2013, presumably due to unsatisfactory valuation, the Bank of America Merrill Lynch, HSBC, and Goldman Sachs were soon afterwards appointed to conduct a strategic review of its retail business portfolio. The three investment banks valued ASW at US$23 billion in late 2013.[16] A formal announcement was reported in the press on February 28, 2014 that ASW would go for dual listing in Hong Kong and London at the end of 2014.[17]

Temasek — A Strategic Investor or an Opportunist?

Then on March 24, 2014, Temasek acquired a 24.95 per cent indirect equity interest in AS Watson Group at US$5.7 billion (S$7.3 billion), comprising eight subsidiaries and JVs and 13 retail brands including the PNS supermarket chain (Table 1). At the time, Mr Chia Song Hwee, head of the investment group in Temasek, said in a statement:

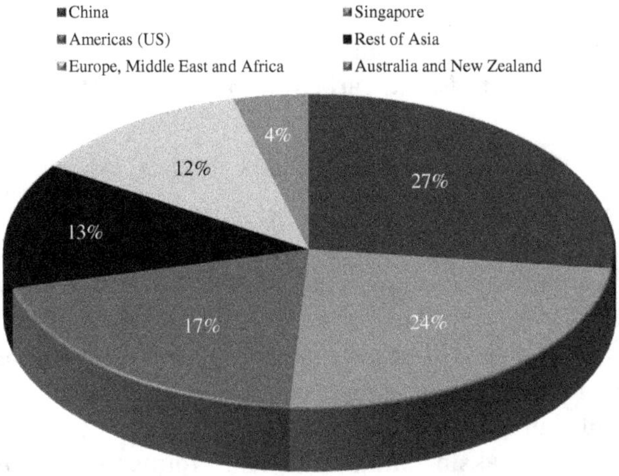

Figure 2. Temasek's Portfolio by Geographical Distribution % (as of 31 March 2021).

Source: Temasek Investor Presentation 2021.

Table 1. 2014 ASW's Portfolio of Subsidiaries and Joint-Ventures.

Subsidiary, JV etc.[22]	Place of Incorporation[23]	% Percentage of Equity[24] 2013 (%)	2014 (%)
AS Watson (Europe) Retail Holdings B.V.	Netherlands	100	75
AS Watson Retail (HK) Ltd.	Hong Kong	100	75
Dirk Rossmann Gmbh	Germany	40	30
Guangzhou Watson's Personal Care Stores Ltd.	China	95	71
PNS (HK) Ltd.	Hong Kong	100	75
Rossmann Supermarkety Polska Sp. Z.o.o.	Poland	70	53
Superdrug Stores plc	U.K.	100	75
Wuhan Watson's Personal Care Stores Co. Ltd.	China	100	75

Source: CKH and HWL Annual Reports.

> *The consumer retail sector is a good proxy to growing middle-income populations and transforming economies. This is very much part of our investment themes as we shape Temasek's portfolio for the long term. We continue to believe in the growth opportunities and long-term prospects of Asia, particularly China, and a recovering Europe.*[18]

For Temasek, perhaps one of the key considerations in acquiring a substantial stake in ASW was an understanding that it will go for IPO, as reflected in a statement issued earlier on March 21, 2014:

> *HWL and Temasek have agreed to work together towards listing AS Watson at a suitable time.*[19]

There is a pattern to follow regarding the duration of investments by Temasek. For Singapore state-owned or strategic assets of national interests such as Singapore Airlines, SingTel, and SMRT, a "permanent" holding of such investments is anticipated. Temasek bought a near 100% ownership of Intouch, a Thai telecommunication company, from its friendly owner, Thaksin Shinawatra, the former prime minister of Thailand who was ousted in a coup d'etat a month after the deal. Temasek then gradually reduced its holding to 10% over 13 years. Whether the change of political leadership in Thailand entered into play was anyone's guess.

As for ASW, the IPO did not materialise within the first 3 years of Temasek's buy-in in 2014. Instead, in October 2018, part of PNS China's shareholding was sold to Yonghui and Tencent, resulting in a 50:40:10 joint-venture. This partial disposal of PNS China contributed to a one-off gain of HK$157.9 million for Temasek's 24.95% shareholding (Table 2). Soon after that, rumours were circulating in the market that Temasek was going to part with 10% in ASW's indirect shareholding of 24.95% for US$3 billion (HK$23.4 billion).[20]

The social unrest that resurfaced in Hong Kong in June 2019 caused unprecedented disruptions in the retail business, which in turn adversely affected the valuation of ASW. It was reported in the press in September 2019 that Temasek decided to hold its 10% stake in ASW due to poor market response.[21] Then, in 2020, the world entered the pandemic phase with the onslaught of COVID-19, bringing with it a global recession that was similar in scale to the Great Depression in the 1930s and the sub-prime mortgage crisis over a decade earlier. Nevertheless, recovery is on the horizon, as shown by recent economic data, albeit at unequal paces around the world. It seems more likely than not that the waiting game is on for a while for any M and A manoeuvre that Temasek may have in mind.

Table 2. 2014–2019 ASW Business Performance.

Value in HK$ billion		2014	2015	2016	2017	2018	2019	2020
Revenue	ASW	157.4	151.9	151.5	156.2	169.0	169.2	159.6
	% YOY Change	6%	–3%	3%	8%	3%	4%	–6%
EBIT	ASW	8.3	8.1	8.0	7.7	7.7	13.	10.9
	% YOY Change	11%	–5%	–2%	3%	8%	5%	–20%
	% ASW/HWL	23.5%	20%	19%	18%	18%	19.2%	20%
Profit After Tax[25]	HWL	33.2	42.3	42.1	43.5	46.8	47.8	37.2
	ASW	9.7	8.5	7.9	7.8	8.4	9.1	7.4
	Temasek's 24.95% shareholding — Current Year	2.4	2.1	2.0	2.0	2.1	2.3	1.9
	Temasek's 24.95% shareholding — Cumulative	2.4	4.5	6.5	8.5	10.6	12.9	14.8

Source: CKH and HWL Annual Reports.

India's Market Potential

ASW is keenly watching the Indian subcontinent. It has been comparing India and China markets with their commonality of massive consumers. For example, when China's per capita GDP reached US$2,099 in 2006, ASW already had opened 200 WTC personal care stores — a reasonable size in standby to take off. After investing in the Mainland for over a decade, China's per capita GDP climbed to US$8,148 in 2016, and by then, ASW had opened 2,929 Watsons stores delivering HK$20.9 billion (US$2.6 billion) turnover.

By comparison, India's 2020 per capita GDP was US$1,901 (a temporary YOY drop of US$203 due to the COVID-19 pandemic) and there is ample room for further expansion of its middle class. The Indian retail market is expected to have a trajectory growth as witnessed in China in the past 15 years (Figure 3). With a population of 1.38 billion in 2020, the second-largest globally, its market potential for ASW in the next decade is too big to ignore.

Currently, foreign investors are not allowed to own 51% or above in India's retail business. This restriction does not apply if the foreign retailer only sells its private label products. L'Oreal, for example, has gained market entry by making use of this exception. Other companies have used

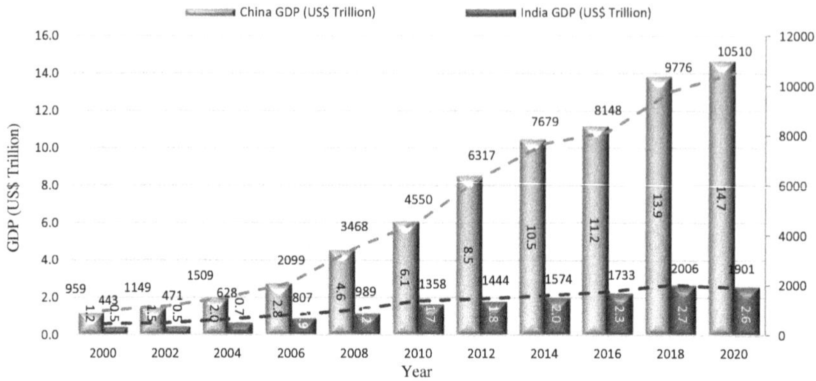

Figure 3. 2000–2020 Growth of China and India GDP and Per Capital GDP (USD Trillion).

Source: The World Bank.

Note: *2019 India per capita GDP was US$2,104 or equivalent to China's 2006 per capita GDP of US$2,099.

other means to enter India. Arvind, an Indian retailer, serves as a master franchisee of Sephora Retail and has carried both Sephora's private label and other global brands of perfume and cosmetics since 2015. Meanwhile, US-based global supermarket chain Walmart entered India as early as 2007. It has built 21 large warehouses in the first 10 years for a B2B and logistics business and has been supplying to millions of India's "mom and pop" general trade stores or "kiranas".

Successive US governments have lobbied Indian policymakers to liberalise the service sector, but to no avail. Then Walmart changed direction to online supermarket business there.[26] In May 2018, it acquired a 77% stake in India's largest e-commerce company, Flipkart. The market believed Walmart's decision was based on its valuation of India's e-commerce market at US$38 billion in 2017, accounting for approximately 3% of the retail market. The rapid increase in middle class families and the millennial and Gen-Z are fuelling forecasts that India's e-commerce market is likely to reach US$200 billion by 2027. With mounting resistance from its domestic agricultural, retail, and service industries, the Modi government withdrew from trade negotiations with 15 Asian and Australian/New Zealand partners in the Regional Comprehensive Economic Partnership (RCEP) in November 2019.

It was perhaps considered too great a political risk to take by the Modi leadership. The withdrawal decision effectively turns away potential overseas investors.

The COVID-19 pandemic has reinforced the importance of kiranas in the hyperlocal communities and their unique advantages in the Indian market. Walmart's majority owned Flipkart is partnering with kiranas to make last-leg deliveries, providing credits, and training them in the use of online ordering and shipping technology.

According to two separate Indian media reports in 2007 and 2013, ASW was not ready to enter the Indian retail market then.[27,28] One reason may be that Hutchison Telecommunications International (HTIL), another business division owned by CKH, has not been able to resolve its longstanding tax dispute with the Income Tax Department (ITD) of India since 2007. The Supreme Court of India ruled in January 2012 that HITL was not liable for profit tax from the sale of its Indian mobile phone business to Vodafone Group Plc back in 2007. Yet, ITD has continued to demand over INR 32,320 crores (US$4.3 billion) from HITL in taxes, interest, and penalty on the alleged gains of HITL back in 2007.[29] HTIL's longstanding tax dispute with the ITD looks likely to drag on for some time yet.

The lifting of trade restrictions or India changing its decision to rejoin RCEP is not expected any time soon, as long as the interests of millions of kirana owners and their election votes remain relevant. This is a great barrier irrespective of which political party comes into power in the next election in 2024. Two possible scenarios are ventured as follows for pondering:

- modern trade will eventually prevail as urban consumers demand choice and value for money, but it may take a decade or longer. Until then, Walmart's super-wholesaler business model may be the only option; and
- competition among the super-wholesalers will be fierce and will end up in a cut-throat price war, with the kiranas owners being the only beneficiaries. At that same time, Walmart is well-positioned to retain its "first mover" advantage in its online and offline connectivity.

In any event, the Indian market is too big a potential to ignore.

As for ASW, since it already has exclusives sales participation which contributed 36% or more of its retail revenue, it is well positioned to operate a 100% foreign-owned retail health and beauty chain stocked exclusively with the Watsons brand consumables in India which is allowed as opposed to a chain store selling branded products supplied by global FMCG manufacturers. As in China, live steaming e-commerce — stage 4 of New Retail — is also fast becoming a channel of distribution of FMCG in India. The Bollywood style of song and dance in India's new trade platform of livestreaming e-commerce will definitely boost retail consumption. This is the China story and there is every reason to believe that the success is replicable in India.

Post-COVID-19 Era

Currently, 70% of ASW's consumers in Asia and Europe's developed markets are millennials and Gen-Z who tend to purchase more beauty products than personal care products. By 2019, e-commerce sales have made up a substantial share of ASW's total revenue (Global 17% versus China's 37%). With the onslaught of the COVID-19 pandemic, the year of 2020 has seen an explosive growth in online business and thrown into ever more uncertainty the long-term survival of independent retailers.

For a long time now, the smaller drug store chains have not competed as well. They do not have the economy of scale to justify investments in advertising and promotion to compete with leading health and beauty retailers such as Boots, Sephora, and Superdrug. The big retailers have their own or exclusive brands enhanced by in-house product research and development capabilities. Through their websites, the integrated mobile application, and the "order and collect" service, consumers enjoy the convenience of ordering a wide range of products for prompt and inexpensive next day delivery. Boots, UK's largest health and beauty retailer completed the closure of 200 stores in 2021 to cut costs as announced by its parent, Walgreen Boots Alliance, in June 2019.[30] This is indeed a reflection of the challenging operating environment.

In the past two decades, the world has experienced intermittent waves of global crises, the latest being the COVID-19 pandemic. At present, there is a silver-lining emerging with massive vaccination underway in developed countries, and a weaker Omicron variant with less severe symptoms in the infected subjects. Many western countries including the United Kingdom have announced an end to all remaining Covid restrictions in England, including the legal requirement to self-isolate commencing in the last week of February 2022.[31]

ASW's business model also faces constant global challenges from competitors, initially supermarkets, and more recently speciality stores; in particular, Holland and Barrett and Sephora, on product portfolio, pricing, as well as omnichannel penetration. Such challenges have been present since 2000 when Savers Health and Beauty Stores were acquired. In such an operating environment, ASW has to consolidate its position as a leader in the health and beauty sector with an expanded range of own or exclusive labels in cosmetics, skin care products, and health supplements.

These hold the potential to enrich its current range of personal care products and enhance profit margins. In the period of 2015–2020, supermarkets such as Walmart, Cosco, and Kroger recorded their % EBIT/Sales in the range of 1.8% to 5%. For retail health and beauty industry leaders of CVS and WBA, the EBIT/Sales % was in the range of 0.9% to 6.2%, with the developed markets as their primary focus. ASW has managed to compare more favourably with its % EBIT/Sales in the range of 6.8% to 9.6%. (Figures 4 and 5). This indicates that the developed markets may already be too mature and crowded to warrant further explorations by ASW.

If the public listing of ASW was to materialise and its venue for listing was on the Singapore Stock Exchange, there would be a more natural logic for Temasek to become a long-term investor in this Singapore publicly listed company. And it would not have to consider exiting every 3–5 years. With its new "Singapore" status, a more independent outlook, and a much watered-down perceived association with CKH, which still has an unsettled major tax dispute with the Indian tax authorities, ASW may be better positioned to access the Indian market. It could partner with a local departmental store chain (as in the case of Sephora) or go independent with the Watsons brand selling its private label products (as in the case of L'Oreal). It would not be at all surprising if ASW had indeed already sought third-party professional opinion on business and corporate approaches in such directions.

Apart from being an option as a listing venue, some if not all of the headquarters functions for meaningful tax concession could also be considered as benefits of locating in Singapore. Tax savings, if granted, could be ploughed back into new business initiatives without affecting dividend

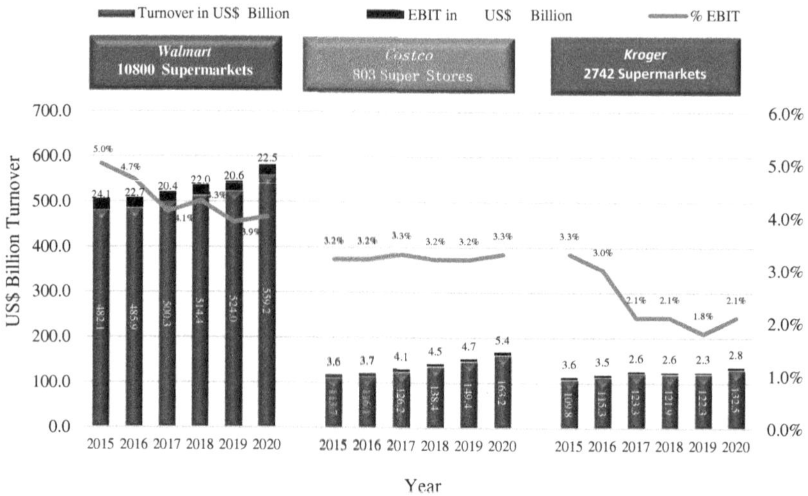

Figure 4. 2015–2020 Performance of Top 3 Global Supermarket Groups.

Source: Annual Reports of Walmart, Costco, and Kroger.

Notes: **Walmart* and *Kroger's* year end of fiscal year is end of January and Cosco's year-end is end of September.

**All three are US based, and 80% of turnover of *Walmart* and *Cosco* came from the US and *Kroger's* turnover came from the US.

***Listed number of retail outlets as per 2020 Annual Report.

payments. The city-state is after all already the regional home to many global companies. This is undoubtedly a complex issue and not merely financial but is food for thought.

The sudden emergence of COVID-19 in December 2019 has had unprecedented consequences in the global retail industry. Like most companies, ASW could not escape unscathed. Its performance in 2020 was the worst since 2007. Nevertheless, with increased inoculations and gradual easing of lockdowns and social distancing in some countries, recovery is starting to be seen among retailers. ASW's performance in the 1st half of 2021 showed 12% and 66% YOY increase in revenue and EBIT or 5% and 54% in local currencies.[32] There is no reason to believe that ASW will not emerge from the gloom this time.

The silver lining does not come from post-COVID recovery alone. Notwithstanding on-going market challenges, growth engines discussed earlier are recapped and should be seized upon:

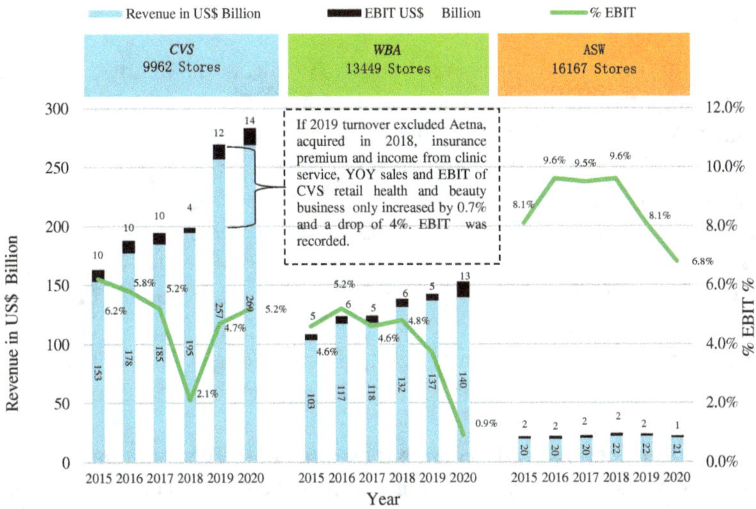

Figure 5. 2015–2020 Performance of Top 3 Global Health and Beauty Retailers.

Source: Annual Reports of CVS, WBA and HWL/CKH.

Notes: **CVS* and *ASW*'s end of fiscal year is end of December and WBA is end of August.

***CVS* and *WBA* are US based with @ 25% and 18%, respectively in prescription sales and the rest from health and beauty segment.

***ASW is based in Hong Kong with @ 3% in prescription sales with @ 30% to 50% sales of high margin private label fast-moving consuming products such as toiletries and beauty care products.

- the insatiable material demands of the millennials and Gen-Zs;
- the power of livestream e-commerce to fuel spending appetite in the New Retail era;
- the growing middle class in large emerging markets of China, Indonesia, Russia, Vietnam, India, and Brazil;
- the ability to differentiate as the time proven master-key to success.

After all, ASW has faced plagues, revolutions, wars, and several financial crises for nearly two centuries. The company has the knowledge of history and wherewithal to increase cash flow, invest, expand, or exit as needed. It has had a world-class pool of executive lessons to guide it further. It truly is one of the legends of Hong Kong, China, and Asia business. And for that, it deserves a hearty salute — because the odds are a company with such prowess will be able to chart, navigate, and lead the next course of its own destiny, whatever the odds.

A new frontier is now awaiting in the great journey.

Endnotes

[1]Both Hakka and Swatow dialects are common dialects spoken by people living in Guangdong province and the Chinese diaspora in Southeast Asia.

[2]Lee Kuan Yew, Li Ka-Shing Lecture by Lee Kuan Yew, University of Hong Kong, National Archives of Singapore, December 14, 1992, p. 5. https://www.nas.gov.sg/archivesonline/data/pdfdoc/lky19921214.pdf.

[3]Tim, B. *et al.* (Ed.), *Critical Reflections on Cities of Southeast Asia*, Times Academic Press, Singapore, 2002, pp. 171–176.

[4]Paul W. Bearmish (Ed.), *Co-operative Strategies: Asian Pacific Perspectives*, The New Lexington Press, 1997: 40.

[5]Pacific Century Group Holdings Ltd., Hong Kong General Chamber of Commerce. http://www.chamber.org.hk/en/membership/directory_detail.aspx?id=HKP0338.

[6]The loss of the Hong Kong Telecom bid by Singapore Telecommunications was due to the government policy that that majority ownership of companies of public interests such as telephone, subway, radio, and television stations, etc. would belong to local residents.

[7]*Entrepreneur and Philanthropist Li Ka-Shing, Donates Record S$19.5 Million to Singapore Management University*, Press Release, SMU. September 9, 2002. https://ink.library.smu.edu.sg/cgi/viewcontent.cgi?article=1025&context=oh_pressrelease.

[8]Tong, C. *et al.*, Hong Kong's Richest Man Li Ka-Shing Leads Tributes to "Dear Friend", Lee Kuan Yew, *South China Morning Post*, March 23, 2015. https://www.scmp.com/news/hong-kong/article/1745236/cy-leung-pays-tribute-lee-kuan-yew-singaporeans-mourn-former-leaders.

[9]Temasek Holding is incorporated, History SG. http://eresources.nlb.gov.sg/history/events/3237d990-f72e-4cce-b86d-71e33f5f9695.

[10]Temasek, However, was not immune to the burst of the global technology bubble at the beginning of the century which resulted in the appointment of Ho Ching as the executive director of Temasek in 2002.

[11]Temasek Value Since Inception, Portfolio Performance, *Our Financials*, Temasek.

[12]Jordan, R., Singapore in Its Worst Recession for Years. The Effects of the Current Economic Crisis on the City-State's Economy, *Journal of Current Southeast Asia Affairs*, 2009, 28(4): 95–110. https://journals.sub.uni-hamburg.de/giga/jsaa/article/view/172/172.html.

[13]*Ibid.* (Note 12): pp. 102–103.

[14]Ho Ching, an engineer by training, became a business executive later on in her career. Ho first joined Temasek Holdings as a director in January 2002, then became its executive director in May 2002, and was appointed chief executive officer on January 1, 2004. She is married to the current prime minister of Singapore, Lee Hsien Loong.

[15]Temasek, Portfolio. https://www.temasek.com.sg/en/our-investments/our-portfolio.
[16]Thomas, D., UPDATE 1-Beauty parade: Watsons IPO could arm Li Ka-shing to extend China lead, Reuters, October 23, 2013. https://finance.yahoo.com/news/beauty-parade-watsons-ipo-could-205851043.html.
[17]Barreto, E., Update 1-Watson IPO likely for 2014 in HK and 2nd venue — Li Ka-shing, *Reuters*, February 28, 2014. https://www.reuters.com/article/watson-ipo-idUSL3N0LX23520140228.
[18]Kwok, J., Temasek Holdings Buying 25% of A.S. Watson; Deal Worth $7.3 Billion, *The Straits Times*, Singapore, March 24, 2014. https://www.straitstimes.com/business/temasek-holdings-buying-25-of-as-watson-deal-worth-73-billion.
[19]HWL Forms Strategic Alliance with Temasek, A.S. Watson, Corporate Website, Hutchsion Whampoa, March 21, 2014. https://www.ckh.com.hk/en/media/topic/2674/HWL-Temasek-Watsons/.
[20]Temasek Weighting Sale of 10% Stake in Watson for $4; Tencent Interested, Say Sources, *The Strait Times*, March 20, 2019. https://www.straitstimes.com/business/companies-markets/tencent-weighing-us3b-bid-for-part-of-temaseks-25-stake-in-watson.
[21]Temasek Postpones Sale of US$3b A.S. Watson Stake, *The Business Times*, Singapore, September 4, 2019. https://www.businesstimes.com.sg/companies-markets/temasek-postpones-sale-of-us3b-as-watson-stake.
[22]Including associated companies and joint ventures.
[23]Including principal place of operations.
[24]Attributable to the ASW Group prior to and after Temasek's Investments as a Strategic Shareholder as at December 31 of the year.
[25]For simplicity's sake, Interest Expenses and other finance costs incurred in ASW were assumed to be pro rata to the total HWL's charges. ASW's "non-controlling interests in other businesses" were also assumed to be pro rata to the total of HWL charges. Temasek's entitled dividends were assumed to pro rata to the Profit After Tax.
[26]Walmart to Invest in Flipkart Group, India's Innovative e-Commerce Company, Press Release, *Walmart*, May 9, 2020. https://corporate.walmart.com/newsroom/2018/05/09/walmart-to-invest-in-flipkart-group-indias-innovative-ecommerce-company.
[27]Deepshikha, M., A.S. Watson Not to Enter India Until 51% Retail FDI Allowed, *The Economic Times*, Industry, February 24, 2007. https://economictimes.indiatimes.com/industry/services/retail/as-watson-not-to-enter-india-until-51-retail-fdi-allowed/articleshow/1670501.cms?from=.
[28]Raghuvir, B., A.S. Watson Group Eyes India Entry, *Business Standard*, Bangalore, January 20, 2013. https://www.business-standard.com/article/companies/a-s-watson-group-eyes-india-entry-111033000046_1.html.

[29]Income Tax Department Seeks Rs. 32,320 Crore from Hutchison Over Vodafone Deal, *The Economic Times*, August 30, 2017. https://economictimes.indiatimes.com/news/economy/policy/income-tax-department-imposes-rs-7900-crore-penalty-on-vodafone-for-tax-dues/articleshow/60273810.cms.
[30]Boots shuts nearly all 200 pharmacies earmarked for closure. Pharmaceutical Journal, January 18, 2022. https://pharmaceutical-journal.com/article/news/bootsshuts-nearly-all-200-pharmacies-earmarked-for-closure.
[31]What is England's 'Living with Covid' plan and what are the rules in the rest of the UK?, BBC News, February 22, 2022. https://www.bbc.com/news/explainers-52530518
[32] Li, V., *Retail Business, Chairman's Statement*, 2021 Interim Report, August 5, 2021: 6. https://www.ckh.com.hk/upload/attachments/en/pr/e_CKHH_IR_2021_full_20210805.pdf.

Appendices

Appendix 1. Abbreviations and Terminology Used in the Book

Abbreviations/ Terminology	Description/Full Names
Apothecary	A medical/surgical clinic which also dispensed medicine on-site in the 19th century.
B/S	Balanced sheet.
BEP	Breakeven point.
DIV	Dividends.
Canton	Anglicised term for Guangzhou, capital of Kwangtung (now Guangdong) province.
Chemist	Otherwise known as a retail pharmacy, which is still currently used in the UK.
Coolie	A Hindu term, "kuli", an unskilled labourer or porter engaged in heavy lifting work.
COVID-19	In December 2019, SARS-Cov-2, another strain of SARS-CoV, was identified which causes coronavirus disease 2019 (COVID-19) and the pandemic in 2020–2022.
CVS	A US-based health care company and the world's number 1 pharmacy chain.
Dispensary	A retail pharmacy in the former British colonies in India, the Strait Settlements), Australia and New Zealand, and Hong Kong, which performed the functions of an apothecary, and is still currently used.

(*Continued*)

Appendix 1. (*Continued*)

Abbreviations/ Terminology	Description/Full Names
Drug Store	Dutch: Drogiste-rij, German: rogeriemarkt: a term used to describe a retailer selling OTC drugs without a pharmacist in Europe and the UK.
GP %	Gross profit margin percentage.
EBIT	Earning before interest and tax (earning margins or operating income).
% EBIT	Earning margins as a percentage of revenue, sales, or turnover .
EBITDA	Earning before interest, tax, depreciation, and amortisation .
Equity	Equity is measured for accounting purposes by subtracting liabilities from the value of the assets.
FMCGs	Fast moving consumer goods (or perishable goods).
GDP	Gross domestic product — total monetary or market value of all the finished goods and services produced.
Holland and Barrett	A UK-based multinational health and supplements retailer.
IPO	Initial public offering (commonly referred to listing as a public company).
NDER	Net debt to equity ratio.
NPBT	Net profit before tax.
NPAT	Net profit after tax.
PER	Price to earnings ratio (a form of valuation of a business).
P&L Statement	Profit and Loss Statement — Audited on an annual basis, of a limited liability company.
ROI	Return on investment is a profitability metric used to evaluate the performance of an investment.
Income	Income — A company's profit over a 1-year period.
Savers	Savers Health and Beauty Stores were acquired by ASW in 2000.
SARS	The first strain of coronavirus, (SARS-CoV), discovered in late 2002 resulted in the Severe acute respiratory syndrome (SARS) became widespread in Mainland China, Hong Kong and Taiwan in the first half of 2003.
SE	Shareholders equity.
Superdrug Stores	Superdrug Stores PLC was a subsidiary of the Kruidvat Group of the Netherlands before its acquisition by ASW in 2002.

Appendix 1. (*Continued*)

Abbreviations/ Terminology	Description/Full Names
Taipan	A Cantonese term, a powerful foreign business executive or entrepreneur used in Hong Kong and pre-1949 Shangha.
TSR	Total shareholders return.
WBA	Walgreen Boots Alliance, founded in 2014, is the world's #2 pharmacy and wholesale chain. Prior to that Alliance Boots was formed in 2006 by the merger of Boots in the UK and Allaince Unichem, a pan-European pharmaceutical wholesaler.
WTC	Watson's The Chemist is officially used as a trade name since 1970s.
WPCS	"Watsons Your Personal Store" is used as a trade name in lieu of WTC in some Asian and European markets.
YOY	Year on year.

Source: Open Sources.

Appendix 2. Key Executives, Subsidiaries & Partners of AS Watson & CK Hutchison

Last Name and First Name/Initials		Description/Full Names
ASW or Watsons		AS Watson became the owner of "Hong Kong Dispensary" in 1860 and changed its business from an apothecary to a retail and wholesale chemist supplying drugs and sundries to the expatriate community and the merchant navy.
CK Assets Holding Ltd.		CK Assets Holding Ltd., name changed from Cheung Kong Property Holdings Ltd. in 2015.
CK Hutchison Holding Ltd.		CK Hutchison Holding Ltd., name changed from Cheung Kong Holdings Ltd,. which Hutchison Whampoa Holdings Ltd. was part of it, in 2015.
Claque	Douglas	1959–1975: Chairman, AS Watson. 1963–1975: Chairman, Hutchison International Ltd.
Clark	Douglas	1933–1941, 1947–1950: Chairman, AS Watson.
Fok	Canning	1994–: Successor of Simon Murray, Managing Director, HWL and CKH
J.D. Hutchison Ltd.		J.D. Hutchison Ltd.
HIL		Hutchison International Ltd.
HWL		Hutchison Whampoa Holding Ltd.
Humphreys	John David	"JDH", 1874–1896, Chairman of AS Watson Ltd., and Humphreys & Son Estate Ltd.
Humphreys	Henry	"Humphreys", eldest son of John David Humphreys, succeeded as Chairman of AS Watson and Humphreys & Son Estate Ltd. (1897–1933).
Lai	Dominic	"Lai", 2007–: Successor of Ian Wade, Group Managing Director of ASW.
Li	Ka-Shing	Li Ka-Shing, nickname "Superman Li", 1981–2018 Chairman, Cheung Kong Holdings Ltd. (name changed to CK Assets Holding Ltd. in 2015), and Hutchison Whampoa Ltd. (name changed to CK Hutchison. Holdings Ltd. in 2015).
Li	Richard	Second son of Li Ka-Shing, and Chairman of PCCW Ltd.
Li	Victor	"Superman Junior", elder son of Li Ka-Shing, and Chairman of CKA, CKH, and ASW since October 2018.
Murray	Simon	1984–1993: Successor of John Richardson.

Appendix 2. (*Continued*)

Last Name and First Name/Initials		Description/Full Names
Richardson	John	1981–1984: CEO, Hutchison Whampoa Ltd., and Chairman of AS Watson.
Rossmann	Dirk	1972–: Founder and Chairman of Dirk Rossmann GmbH (DRG).
Dirk Rossmann GmbH		Dirk Rossmann is the founder, chairman, and CEO of Dirk Rossmann Gmbh. GmbH is the German equivalent of a limited liability company.
Temasek		Temasek is a global investment company headquartered in Singapore in 1974 with government backing.
Wade	Ian	"Wade", 1982–2006: Group Managing Director of AS Watson. Succeeded by Lai in 2007.
Watson	Alexander Skirving	"Alexander Skirving", 1858–1865: Manager of "Hong Kong Dispensary", nephew of Dr Thomas Boswell Watson.
Watson	Thomas Boswell	"Watson", 1856–1859 Senior Partner of "Hong Kong Dispensary", uncle of Alexander Skirving Watson.
Willie	Bill	1975–1980: Chairman of Hutchison International Ltd. (later on called Hutchison Holdings Ltd., and Deputy Chairman of Hutchison Whampoa Holdings Ltd.) and AS Watson Ltd.

Source: AS Watson, CK Hutchison, and Hutchison Whampoa Ltd. Annual Reports.

Appendix 3. 1984–2021 Global and Regional Events Impacting Business Growth of ASW

October 1984	Hong Kong	"Black Saturday" resulted in a drop of 30% in Hong Kong currency vs. US dollar.
October 1987	Taiwan	End of 40-year martial law by the "nationalist" government resulted in the liberalisation of trade and investment.
June 1989	China	Tiananmen Square Incident refers to social unrests in Beijing caused by student protesters and workers which led to crackdown with over-spill effect on Hong Kong. The colonial government initiated a 7-year "Rose Garden" project with heavy investment in infrastructure to restore confidence.
July 1997–June 1999	Asia Pacific Ex-China	Short-sell in Thai currency by the global hedge fund managers on July 2, 1997, resulting in a basket of Asian currencies depreciated from South Korea to Thailand. Asian economies ground to a halt with recovery due to Y2K.
1999–2003	Europe	The collapse of the Berlin Wall and the disintegration of the Soviet Union led to the unification of Germany's eastern and western parts with a higher tax levied to fund the integration costs. Economic chaos in Eastern European countries slowed down the economy and weakened consumer confidence.
January – June 2003	Asia	SARS epidemic resulted in a drop in the retail economy in 1H of 2003.
2007–2008	Global	The collapse of the subprime market due to overleverageing of the US financial industry resulted in liquidity issues, bankruptcies, massive layoffs, and a heavy blow to the retail market.
2013–2014	Hong Kong	"Umbrella Movement" initiated by some local politicians to seek universal suffrage resulted in the blockage of central business districts with disgruntled students and young people. A substantial drop in inbound tourists resulted with a negative impact on retail trade.
Mid-2016–End 2020	UK	Uncertainty of Brexit lowered consumer and business confidence and adversely affected UK leadership in financial services.
Q4 2018–Q4 2019	China	De-coupling of China and the US economy due to protective "America First" policy slowed down the Chinese economy with over-spilling effect on Australia and Asia countries which had substantial exports to China.

Appendix 3. (*Continued*)

Q2–Q4 2019	Hong Kong	Opposition to the "Extradition Bill" by democrats and many others began with peaceful protests but soon erupted into persistent violence. A substantial drop in inbound tourists with retail businesses closed en masse.
Q1–Q2 2020	Global	COVID-19 first surfaced in Wuhan, China which resulted in mandatory quarantine measures taken by local governments with an unprecedented drop in retail trade in Hong Kong and the Mainland. Mandatory quarantine of overseas visitors to limit the spread of COVID-19 infections ground tourism to a halt.
Q3–Q4 2020		COVID-19 vaccination, under emergency release in the US, started in December 2020. The global economy was estimated to have contracted 4.3 per cent in 2020 by the World Bank. In advanced economies, the initial contraction was less severe than anticipated, but a substantial resurgence of COVID19 cases dampens recovery. COVID-19 vaccines began to roll out before Christmas in the US.
Q1–Q4 2021		With massive immunization of COVID-19 in China, Europe the US and a few developed economies in 2021, the global economy was recovering and estimated to grow at 5.6% YOY by the World Bank. The Delta variant emerging in India has given rise to a new wave of infections since May 2021 which has been rapidly replaced by Omicron, a much weaker but highly infectious variant originated in South Africa in late 2021.

Source: Hong Kong Year Book, World Health Organization, etc.

Name Index

Subject Index

B

C

www.ingramcontent.com/pod-product-compliance
Lightning Source LLC
LaVergne TN
LVHW010332220926
848484LV00004BB/883